W9-BIH-579

Praise for

I INVENTED THE MODERN AGE

"No one has told the story of Henry Ford's incredible rise and achievements better than Richard Snow in this book. Snow is unmatched in his ability to write smoothly with telling descriptions that make this biography as engaging as and even easier to read than the best page-turning whodunits."

—**Steve Forbes,** *Forbes*

"[Snow] gets to the meat of a biographer's task—demonstrating how psychology and circumstances blend to create a life. . . . Snow's supple and informative effort reminds us that although we've bought the automobiles and the assembly line, we continue to wrestle with the issues that concerned their creator: the concentration of wealth, the representation of women, the fate of our immigrants, the threat of war."

—**Jane Smiley,** *Harper's Magazine*

"The Detroit that Mr. Snow describes was so rich with the creative chaos of hundreds of would-be auto entrepreneurs, from the Dodge brothers to James Ward Packard, that it reminds us of Silicon Valley in the early days of the personal computer. . . . Mr. Snow has a conversational, highly readable style. . . . [Henry Ford] would die, at 83, with $26.5 million in the bank and a pocketknife in his trousers. He was not really so simple, or so one concludes from . . . Mr. Snow . . . and there is probably no reconciling his greatness and his malignancy. He had both."

—**Roger Lowenstein (author of** *The End of Wall Street* **and** *Buffett: The Making of an American Capitalist***),** *The Wall Street Journal*

"Snow displays excellent storytelling skill as, stiffening by the years, Ford's character develops through anecdotes and events in a lively narrative sequence that will engross readers curious about Ford and the Model T."

—*Booklist*

"Snow delivers a highly readable account of the life and times of Henry Ford. . . . Snow clearly demonstrates how Ford's imagination, perseverance, and single-mindedness enabled him to overcome obstacles to perfect automobile assembly-line production."

—*Library Journal*

"By breaking up the trajectory of this complicated figure's life into neat, digestible segments, Snow . . . delivers a highly readable biographical account of Ford's ascendance to automobile baron. . . . Supplemented with detailed research into Ford's relationships . . . Snow's portrait is of a man equally easy to admire and disdain, but impossible to dismiss."

—*Publishers Weekly*

"Richard Snow's lively biography will make you rethink the man whose legacy sits in your garage."

—*Parade*

"Stylistically, Snow mimics the marvelously folksy, protean temperament of his subject, dwelling on Ford's early mechanical inventions rather than his latter problematic prickliness, and everywhere portraying a compelling character."

—*Kirkus Reviews*

"Richard Snow presents a biography of a brilliant, difficult, and strange man, a technological thriller about the most important machine he made, and a social history of the country it transformed. You live in the world Henry Ford made; here is how it happened. *I Invented the Modern Age* is clear, amusing, stern, and poignant."

—Richard Brookhiser, author of *James Madison*

"*I Invented the Modern Age* is the amazing story of an amazing man, told with wit, insight, style, and zest. Richard Snow makes the invention of the automobile intelligible and fascinating even to car ignoramuses such as myself. His story of Ford the man is simply riveting. This is history as it should always be told."

—Kevin Baker, author of *Strivers Row*

ALSO BY RICHARD SNOW

The Funny Place

Freelon Starbird

The Iron Road: A Portrait of American Railroading

The Burning

Coney Island: A Postcard Journey to the City of Fire

*A Measureless Peril: America in the Fight for the Atlantic,
the Longest Battle of World War II*

I INVENTED THE MODERN AGE

The RISE *of* HENRY FORD

Richard Snow

SCRIBNER

New York   London   Toronto   Sydney   New Delhi

SCRIBNER

A Division of Simon & Schuster, Inc.

1230 Avenue of the Americas

New York, NY 10020

Copyright © 2013 by Richard Snow

All rights reserved, including the right to reproduce this book or portions thereof in any form whatsoever. For information address Scribner Subsidiary Rights Department, 1230 Avenue of the Americas, New York, NY 10020.

First Scribner trade paperback edition May 2014

SCRIBNER and design are registered trademarks of The Gale Group, Inc., used under license by Simon & Schuster, Inc., the publisher of this work.

For information about special discounts for bulk purchases, please contact Simon & Schuster Special Sales at 1-866-506-1949 or business@simonandschuster.com.

The Simon & Schuster Speakers Bureau can bring authors to your live event. For more information or to book an event contact the Simon & Schuster Speakers Bureau at 1-866-248-3049 or visit our website at www.simonspeakers.com.

Designed by Maura Fadden Rosenthal
Cover design by David Ter-Avanesyan
Cover photograph © Getty Images

Manufactured in the United States of America

5   7   9   10   8   6   4

Library of Congress Control Number: 2012037554

ISBN 978-1-4516-4558-3
ISBN 978-1-4516-4559-0 (ebook)

All pictures are from the collections of The Henry Ford, except the photo of Ford with Evangeline Dahlinger, which appeared in *The Secret Life of Henry Ford* by John Côté Dahlinger.

FOR CAROL,

who brightened my explorations of Greenfield Village,
just as she has everything else I've done
for the last quarter century.

ACHIEVEMENT, *n.* The death of endeavor and the birth of disgust.

—Ambrose Bierce, *The Devil's Dictionary*

. . . Yes, Tin, Tin, Tin,
You exasperating puzzle, Hunk o' Tin.
I've abused you and I've flayed you,
But by Henry Ford who made you,
You are better than a Packard, Hunk o' Tin.

—C. C. Battershell, "Dedicated to the Memory
of Car No. 423," a Model T ambulance
destroyed on the Western Front in 1917.
After Rudyard Kipling's "Gunga Din."

CONTENTS

CHAPTER 9

Inventing the Universal Car ... 141

Who wanted it?; Sorensen's locked room; steering wheel on the left—forever; new experts, new engine, new steel, new car; "Without doubt the greatest creation in automobiles ever placed before a people."

CHAPTER 10

The Man Who Owned Every Car in America ... 153

Selden files a patent on all gas-powered automobiles and sues their makers; the court finds for him; most carmakers give in; Ford won't pay "graft money"; a second trial; "One of the greatest things Mr. Ford did..."

CHAPTER 11

The Model T Takes Over ... 171

New York to Seattle on thin ice; learning to drive the Model T; birth of a dealer; the farmer and the car; caring for your Model T; the perils of starting it; "Funny Stories About the Ford"; five thousand accessories; remaking the nation in a decade: "I'll go without food before I'll go without my car."

CHAPTER 12

Terrible Efficiency ... 197

The Crystal Palace; taking the work to the worker; speeding up; the twentieth century's only industrial revolution; the workers hate it.

CONTENTS

------\\\\\\\\\\\\\\\\------

CHAPTER 17

The End of the Line . . . 283

------\\\\\\\\\\\\\\------

Epilogue . . . 323

In 1913 the Ford Motor Company issued this cross-section of its world-changing creation, assuring the recipient that "the better you know your car, the better . . . you will enjoy it."

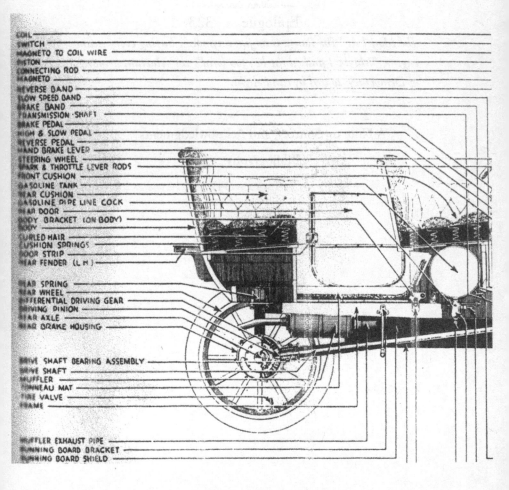

I INVENTED THE
MODERN AGE

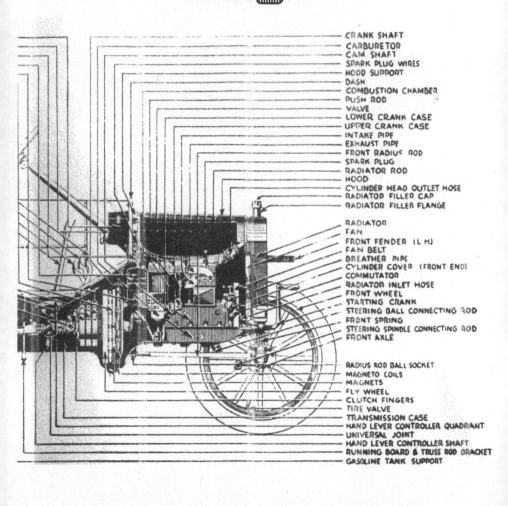

CRANK SHAFT
CARBURETOR
CAM SHAFT
SPARK PLUG WIRES
HOOD SUPPORT
DASH
COMBUSTION CHAMBER
PUSH ROD
VALVE
LOWER CRANK CASE
UPPER CRANK CASE
INTAKE PIPE
EXHAUST PIPE
FRONT RADIUS ROD
SPARK PLUG
RADIATOR ROD
HOOD
CYLINDER HEAD OUTLET HOSE
RADIATOR FILLER CAP
RADIATOR FILLER FLANGE

RADIATOR
FAN
FRONT FENDER (L H)
FAN BELT
BREATHER PIPE
CYLINDER COVER (FRONT END)
COMMUTATOR
RADIATOR INLET HOSE
FRONT WHEEL
STARTING CRANK
STEERING BALL CONNECTING ROD
FRONT SPRING
STEERING SPINDLE CONNECTING ROD
FRONT AXLE

RADIUS ROD BALL SOCKET
MAGNETO COILS
MAGNETS
FLY WHEEL
CLUTCH FINGERS
TIRE VALVE
TRANSMISSION CASE
HAND LEVER CONTROLLER QUADRANT
UNIVERSAL JOINT
HAND LEVER CONTROLLER SHAFT
RUNNING BOARD & TRUSS ROD BRACKET
GASOLINE TANK SUPPORT

CHAPTER 1

A Homecoming

Saving the farm, then saving the entire past; between the steam engine and the Apple; "nobody knew anything about cars"; Fordism.

On a summer day in 1919 a middle-aged man left his Detroit office and drove out to Dearborn, ten miles away, to see the house where he'd been born. It was a farmhouse, long past its best days, and any passersby who noticed him poking around it must briefly have wondered what this visitor was doing there.

He wasn't in any way flamboyant, but he was obviously prosperous, probably wearing one of the neat, quiet gray suits he favored year-round. A little over middle height, he stood so straight that most who met him described him as "tall." He was moderately good-looking, but what might have been an ordinary face had already somehow proved impossible for painters, journalists, and even photographers to capture satisfactorily. Team sports had never interested him although he was athletic and loved to challenge friends to footraces; each time he moved to another vantage point in the farmhouse yard, he did it suddenly and quickly, almost as if he were answering a starting gun. He was not an architect, but he knew how things were put together,

1

and carefully studied the window frames, the chimney, the pitch of the roof. This might be his last chance to see the farmstead, because the house was about to be destroyed.

That was largely his fault. The flow of traffic had grown so heavy in the past decade that the Dearborn city fathers had decided the road bordering the sixty-year-old building needed to be widened. Every second car contributing to that traffic bore the man's name. Henry Ford was making half the automobiles in America.

Few people have the means to defy this sort of progress, but Ford did. He had the farmhouse moved two hundred feet back from the new road. But once the house was safe, it wouldn't let him alone. At first he merely had it restored—some carpentry, fresh paint—but that wasn't enough. He found that he wanted it furnished as it had been in the 1870s, when he was a boy interested in machinery, taking watches apart in his room there.

Now the tenacious perfectionism of the man took over. Representative furniture, typical furniture of the 1860s, wouldn't do. It had to be the same furniture. He'd kept warm in the Michigan winters beside a Starlight Stove in the front parlor. He spent months searching for one, found a near-perfect example—but no, it was a bit too small, it wasn't a Model 25. Then there was the carpeting on the stairs, a faded rusty crimson that he remembered precisely. He had one of the fifty thousand men who worked for him go through antiques shops—local ones, at first, then as far away as Cincinnati—to match it.

The family china: He could remember the stair carpet, but not the plates he had once eaten off. Workers excavated where the dooryard had been, and came up with a ceramic shard large enough to reveal the pattern. Ford had a full dinner service reproduced. Beds, chairs, sofas were found and reupholstered. Ford's agents got the right bureau, and Ford specified exactly what needles and thread should stock one of the drawers. He deviated from utter fidelity with the family organ. It was born with a foot-pump, but Ford had the instrument electrified—nobody could see the difference, after all—and when he stepped back into his youth he would sit at the keyboard for hours, laboriously playing with a finger or two the first songs he'd heard: "Turkey in the Straw," "Flow Gently Sweet Afton."

Upstairs the beds were made with fresh linen; out back stood the stacks of firewood, just as they had in his boyhood; the reservoirs of all the kerosene lamps were full, their wicks trimmed and ready for the match.

Ford had got more things than he'd needed to furnish his farmhouse. He kept the overflow in his office until 1922, when one of his tractor operations moved, leaving behind it an empty building that covered three acres. With this repository available, the carmaker's ambitions expanded beyond the home of his youth to encompass the world of his youth.

Once again his agents went out, this time in their hundreds. They were, said the boss, to bring back "a complete series of every article ever used or made in America from the days of the first settlers down to the present time."

The stream began to flow in: birdcages and settees and patent washboards; carriages, rifles, apple-parers; reapers and binders and the lunch wagon where Ford had grabbed meals when he was working for Detroit Edison back in the nineties. Ford accumulated enough objects, as it turned out, to entirely furnish, from weather vane and lightning rod to mantel clock and furnace, 107 buildings.

At the time, those buildings were living out their lives far from Ford and far from one another. One was a courthouse in Illinois where the young Abraham Lincoln had argued cases; two were Georgia slave cabins, one the brick storefront where Wilbur and Orville Wright sold bicycles while they conducted their momentous experiments.

The homely items Ford had collected still radiated the residual warmth of life from a vanished time, but the signals they sent out were faint, diffuse, cluttered. Put them in a landscape where men and women had used them, though, and their feeble, dissonant notes might become a powerful harmony.

Beyond the airport Ford had just built in Dearborn—it was 1926 now—lay a tract of land where nothing much at all had ever happened. He would, he decided, inject these anonymous acres with history by building on them a monument to the past: a village that would preserve the "American life as lived" of what he called a "saner and sweeter" time.

The man incubating this plan had done more than anyone else alive to annihilate that life; and he found much of its sweet sanity repellent. Everyone today knows his name, but very few could attribute more than one statement to him, which is that history was "bunk." The "bunk" part he perceived in history may have been the sheer mass of it, all those names you had to learn, all those treaties and tariffs and boundary disputes. Ford always liked to see the thing itself. Years later some of his old lieutenants would say he couldn't read a blueprint. He could, and competently, too. But it is perfectly true that he would far rather see the objects encoded in the cool white lines. His sense of what was sound engineering transmitted itself most surely through his fingertips.

So it was with the past. Ford wanted to be able to handle it, to walk inside it and look around. He bought the Illinois courthouse and moved it to Dearborn, to the town he had named Greenfield Village, after his wife's birthplace. He bought the Wright brothers' cycle shop, and moved it there, too—and, to keep it company, the carpentry Queen Anne house the brothers grew up in. He brought Thomas Edison's laboratory from Menlo Park, New Jersey, along with a dozen freight-car loads of Jersey dirt so it could stand amid the snails and fungi it had always known, and the boardinghouse where Edison's hard-pressed staff hadn't slept enough.

The Edison Illuminating Company and its dynamos took up residence near Noah Webster's home. Toward the end of his life Ford moved his farmstead there, and you can walk right into it today and see that perfectly retrieved stair carpeting.

What you won't see in Greenfield village is a bank, or a law office: Ford had no use for bankers and lawyers. Many of them were Jews, he believed, and all were leeches who lived off the blood of creativity. He had no hesitation—for many years, at least—in sharing this information with anyone who would listen. This was Ford at his most independent and least attractive, tirelessly venting the cranky certainties that had seeped into his character even as he became famous.

All was mixed together as he conjured up his village, and it remains a place of contradictions, at least as far as his first expressed purpose goes. Edison and the Wrights had not worked to preserve the agrarian world of Ford's boyhood. And neither had Ford.

As his village took shape, it turned out to be a wistful tribute not only to the sturdy American small farmer and the one-room schoolhouse where his children absorbed virtue along with grammar from their McGuffey's Readers, but also to the forces that swept that world away, the dynamo and the electricity it conjured, the airplane, and of course the machine that Ford began building in 1903 in his Mack Avenue factory, whose gray-painted board front he carefully re-created.

Once, stopping at a house he was planning to move, where he had spent a good deal of time as a boy, Ford made a discovery. "I found some marbles, put a few of them in the palm of my hand, and as I applied pressure, they disintegrated. Life, change, had gone on."

Not in Greenfield Village. As building after building arrived, as the automobile factory rose near the smithy, it became increasingly clear that this town was a concrete representation of Henry Ford's mind, the things he missed, the things he took pride in, his ability to banish the things he disliked.

It was a monument not only to the agrarian youth of the nation, but also to the vehemently nonagrarian youth of Henry Ford.

Greenfield Village is a place unlike any other because its creator's youth was unlike any other. Walking its streets as dusk fell, or going through the enormous museum he built next to it, Ford could retrieve that youth. And such was the strength of his engaging, elusive, infuriating personality that more than sixty years after his death, so can you and I.

He would have wanted that. His willful egotism only grew stronger as he aged, but it never got strong enough to blind him to the fact that the first half of his life was by far the better half.

Those were the years before an improvident libel suit had brought him into a nationally publicized trial in which the prosecution set out to prove his ignorance; before his bigotry boiled over and he was tormented into making insincere public retractions; before he was scared of his workers; before he got at odds with his only son and, in the view of his grandson Henry II, literally badgered him to death.

No, there's none of that in Greenfield Village. Passing by its yards and alleys its founder would have caught spectral glimpses of his mother, dead when he was thirteen, of his first car jittering triumphantly through the vacant streets of two-in-the-morning Detroit, of the Grosse Pointe racetrack in 1901, where the pennant of blue smoke from the engine of Alexander Winton's far more powerful automobile signaled Ford that he was about to win a career-saving victory, and of the day not long after his mother's death when he and his father went into town. Their wagon came upon a steam-powered farm engine heading toward a job. There was nothing unusual about that, but rather than attaching it to draft horses, the owner had thought to attach it to itself. Hissing and smoking right there in the everyday road, the engine was moving toward the enchanted boy under its own power.

———∿∿∿∿∿∿∿———

Every century or so, our republic has been remade by a new technology: 170 years ago it was the railroad; in our time it's the microprocessor. These technologies do more than change our habits; they change the way we think. Henry David Thoreau, hearing the trains passing Walden Pond, wrote, "Have not men improved somewhat in punctuality since the railroad was invented? Do they not talk and think faster in the depot than they did in the stage-office?" And of course anyone over the age of twenty (younger, and it's simply the air you breathe) knows what computers and the Internet are doing to us now.

In between the steam locomotive and the Apple came Henry Ford's Model T. One day toward the end of his life its maker was talking with a local high school boy named John Dahlinger, whose father had helped lay out his village, and they got onto the subject of education. Ford spoke of the virtues of the McGuffey's Reader era, and this sounded pretty fusty to Dahlinger. "But, sir," he protested, "these are different times, this is the modern age and—"

"Young man," Ford snapped, "I invented the modern age."

The claim is as preposterous as it is megalomaniacal. It is also largely true.

———~~~~~~~———

Sometime early in 1908 a knot of workmen stood peering up at the ceiling in a building on Piquette Avenue in Detroit. A few years later, these men would have been drenched in daylight in a new factory so lavishly windowed that it was known as the Crystal Palace. But this was just like any other big factory, and the object of their attention glinted dully above them in the perpetual industrial dusk.

A new kind of engine, swaddled in more rope than the task demanded, was inching its way down toward the chassis of a new kind of car.

The descending engine began to swing heavily in its slings, and, accompanied by impotent shouted instructions, started to revolve, slowly and then faster, until it tore loose and plummeted down through the car body to the factory floor.

A worker named James O'Connor remembered the moment of horrible silence that followed ended when the two men superintending the mounting of the engine got into a heated disagreement about which of them had been responsible for the catastrophe.

"I know more about cars than you will ever know!" one yelled.

His colleague came back predictably with, "I know more about cars than *you* will ever know!"

Henry Ford didn't find this a productive discussion. The slender man in the neat suit stepped forward and gestured them to pipe down. They'd fix the engine and try again. He'd stay around until the job got done. He was annoyed, of course, but not full of fury and blame. There might be time for such indulgences in the years ahead, right now he was building his first Model T and he just wanted to get on with it. The engine went in the next morning.

Decades later, James O'Connor, looking back on the squabble between the men in charge of the job, said, "I often think about them saying, 'I know more about cars than you do.' Nobody knew anything about cars." That was not entirely true—253 American carmakers were in business at the time the engine fell—but it was true enough.

———∿∿∿∿∿∿∿∿———

In 1925 an editor of the *Encyclopedia Britannica*, seeking a contribution on a topic still too recent to have been mentioned in earlier editions, asked Henry Ford to write an article about "mass production."

The essay appeared over Ford's name. It is a lucid, concise, occasionally eloquent statement that, a little more than a decade later, the historian Roger Burlingame described as "a colossal blurb that begins 'In origin, mass production is American and recent; its earliest notable appearance falls within the first decade of the 20th century,' and devotes the remainder of the article and two full pages of half-tone plates [photographs] to the Ford factory."

Burlingame said Ford's "great one-man show" suggested that mass production had "never existed in the world before." What about Eli Whitney, Burlingame asked, who had pioneered the idea of interchangeable parts for rifles back in the 1790s? What about Oliver Evans, whose fully automated flour mill had prefigured Ford's moving assembly line at almost the same time? And Singer, who had deluged the world with his sewing machines a generation before Henry Ford ever thought of an automobile?

Burlingame's ridicule did not touch on the question of the article's authorship, although the man who actually wrote it, Ford's spokesman and explainer William J. Cameron, said he "should be very much surprised to learn" that his boss had even read it.

Here, for example, is a passage from the *Britannica* essay that accurately states a belief Ford held: "The early factory system was uneconomical in all its aspects. Its beginnings brought greater risk and loss of capital than had been known before, lower wages and a more precarious outlook for the workers, and a decrease in quality with no compensating increase in the general supply of goods. More hours, more workers, more machines did not improve conditions; every increase did but enlarge the scale of fallacies built into business. Mere massing of men and tools was not enough; the profit motive, which damaged enterprise, was not enough."

And here is a sample of this essay's putative author writing, just a few years earlier, on the futility of war: "But the people who *profitt* [sic] from war must go. . . . War is created by people who have no country or home except Hadies Hell and live in every country."

Ford wouldn't have cared about Burlingame's criticisms, nor would he have been in the least embarrassed had anyone accused him of putting his name to an article he'd never seen. He would have known he was in the right. He was always sure of that.

Often he was disastrously wrong about things, but he was not wrong about this big one. Mass production, which reshaped America in a decade, and which created our national prosperity in the twentieth century, was Henry Ford's doing.

To a degree, even the phrase itself is. The *Britannica*'s editor asked him to write about "mass production," but it was the "H.F." attached to the article that planted the term in the language forever. Before that, people had called what it described "Fordism."

CHAPTER 2

"My Toys Were All Tools"

The boy who hated farming; McGuffey's "new green world"; steam and clockwork; a house without a mainspring; "the biggest event in those early years"; into Detroit.

his man, who lived to read about the atomic bombs falling on Hiroshima and Nagasaki, was born three weeks after the battle of Gettysburg into a rural America whose routines he disliked as soon as he became aware of them.

The first thing I remember in my life is my Father taking my brother John and myself to see a bird's nest under a large oak log twenty yards east of our Home and my birthplace, John was so young that he could not walk Father carried Him I being two years older could run along with them this must have been the year 1866 in June I remember the nest with the 4 eggs and also the bird and hearing it sing I have remembered the song and in later years found it was a song sparrow.

He would love birds all his long life. Not so the other fauna around him. Unlike most farm boys, he never developed the least fondness for horses, and he detested cows. "The cow must go!" he declared decades later, apparently in complete seriousness. He wrote, "Milk is a mess." Whatever wholesome ingredients it might contain should be counterfeited with soybeans: "We MUST make milk out of something—Heaven can't." As for chickens, he wouldn't even eat one: "Chicken is fit only for hawks."

Not that he disliked rural life itself. He believed it contained inherent virtues—just that they didn't have anything to do with the labor that accompanied them. "I was born on July 30, 1863, on a farm at Dearborn Michigan, and my earliest recollection [after the sparrow, presumably] is that, considering the results, there was too much work on the place. That is the way I still feel about farming."

But despite the considerable task of having to make things grow on it, Henry Ford would always be drawn—sometimes merely wistfully, sometimes with a reformer's zeal—back to the farming world.

Michigan had been a state only for a quarter century when he was born, and much of it was still frontier. Forest stood all about him during his childhood, but his was not the hardscrabble infancy of a cider-barrel cradle in the dooryard of a log cabin.

William Ford, Henry's father, had been born in County Cork to a Protestant family of English ancestry. In 1847, the second year of the potato famine, the twenty-year-old carpenter and his family—his father and mother, John and Thomasina, his brother, and four sisters—followed two of his uncles across the Atlantic to Michigan where, one promoter had written, there was loam "four feet deep and so fat it will grease your fingers."

William Ford ended up in Dearbornville, in Springwells Township, a community eight miles west of Detroit—a site chosen because it was one day's journey by oxcart from the city whose factories and machine shops were already beginning to offer a livelihood that didn't involve hoeing and threshing.

That smoky, young alternative world had no appeal for William

Ford. He worked for a while as a carpenter for the Michigan Central Railroad, but his heart was in farming, and he saved what money he could toward getting some land of his own, in his spare time working the eighty acres that his father, John, had bought and paid off.

In the late 1850s, William Ford did some carpentering for a neighbor, Patrick O'Hern, another County Cork man. He and his wife had adopted an orphaned child, a girl named Mary Litogot. Nobody ever knew where she came from, despite Henry Ford's using all his later resources to find out.

In 1858 William Ford paid six hundred dollars for half of his father's acreage and, thus established, married Mary Litogot in 1861. He was thirty-five; she, twenty-one.

The couple moved into the spacious, comfortable frame house that William had built for the O'Herns, with whom they lived harmoniously for years.

In the first week of 1862 Mary delivered a stillborn son. She was soon pregnant again, but the parents passed an anxious few months until, at seven o'clock on a summer morning, Henry Ford was born, full of the vigorous health that would serve him all his days.

He formed a strong attachment to the home he would re-create down to its sewing drawer. In it he was joined by siblings on a precise biannual schedule: John came in 1865, Margaret in '67, Jane two years later, William Junior two years after Jane, and finally Robert, in 1873.

From the start Henry was interested in machinery. "Even when I was very young I suspected that much [farmwork] might somehow be done in a better way. That is what took me into mechanics—although my mother always said I was a born mechanic."

He was to begin school at the age of seven on the second day of January 1871. Rural America valued education, but the necessity of survival dictated it not interfere with the fall harvest. The first week of the year found the Ford family snowbound, and Henry didn't get to the Scotch Settlement School, two miles distant, until the ninth. It was a one-room schoolhouse, and like so many of the architectural surroundings of Ford's youth is now living out the years in Greenfield Village. The curriculum was supplied by an Ohio schoolmaster named William Holmes McGuffey, who in the 1830s had conceived a series of six books: a primer, a speller, and four readers. For these, he received royalties capped at one thousand dollars. By the early 1840s the series was selling a million copies a year, by 1860, two million. Between the year Henry Ford started school and 1890 Americans bought 60 million.

These readers were attuned to the society into which Henry Ford was born. McGuffey intended them to be universal (or at least national, although by 1890 they were instructing children in Tokyo), but the midwestern critic and social historian Walter Havighurst believed them directed toward the trans-Appalachian West—"a new green world," as he put it, "a world of creeks and woods and meadows, of dogs and horses, sheep and cattle, orchards, pastures and farmyards."

The first page of the first speller featured the most indispensable of frontier tools—"A is for Ax"—and as McGuffey's audiences grew older and learned to read, succeeding volumes offered little morality tales mostly set in rural scenes.

They were often far from comforting. One is headed by a drawing of a farmer carrying a boy whose hair is dripping water past another boy about the same age who is standing, hands in pockets, staring abjectly at the ground.

"Look, look, is this not Frank Brown? What can be the mat-ter with him?

"The poor boy is dead.

"He was on his way to school when a bad boy met him and said:

"'Come Frank, go with me to the pond.'"

Frank protested that he had to get to school, but the bad boy prevailed, and Frank went to the pond and fell in. "He cried 'Help!' 'Help!' A man heard him and ran to the pond. But when he got there, poor Frank was dead.

"What will his pa-rents do when he is ta-ken home dead?"

Not all the stories ended so grimly, and most offered redemption.

Although "the idle boy is always poor and miserable," said the *Third Reader,* "the industrious boy is happy and prosperous."

Virtue was espoused for virtue's sake, but had its practical advantages, too. When in the *Second Reader* George breaks a merchant's window with a snowball, he confesses and feels much better. And possibly better still when "George became the merchant's partner and is now rich."

Good boys, boys who would not be seduced by the splendors of the pond, get rich. The books are full of exhortations to hard work, hustle, and enterprise, coupled with homilies urging religious faith (Christian faith, that is: the *Fourth Reader* explains that "Jewish authors were incapable of the diction and strangers to the morality contained in the Bible") and strict obedience to the stern dictates of conscience. In the advanced readers the mandates were softened somewhat by the addition of increasingly sophisticated selections from Longfellow, Hawthorne, Whittier, and Dickens. The frontier memoirist Hamlin Garland wrote in his popular *A Son of the Middle Border,* "I wish to acknowledge my deep obligation to Professor McGuffey, whoever he may have been, for the dignity and grace of his selections. From the pages of his readers I learned to know and love the poems of Scott, Byron, Southey, Wordsworth . . . I got my first taste of Shakespeare from the selections I read in those books."

No schoolchild could escape the books and the freight of their message in those expansive, pious postwar decades. Henry Ford loved the readers, and took their precepts, with the possible exception of piety, to heart. In time, drawing on the determination William Holmes McGuffey had helped instill in him, he tracked down the whitewashed log cabin in which the schoolmaster had been born and moved it near the schoolhouse where Ford had first read his primers.

He went further than that. For those who couldn't make the pilgrimage to McGuffey's transplanted cabin, he reprinted the run of 1857 primers and readers, and sent them out across the country, saying, "Truth, honesty, fair-dealing, initiative, invention, self-reliance— these were the fundamentals of the McGuffey readers and they are as timeless and dateless now as they were when he assembled his texts."

He made friends with Hamlin Garland. William Richards, a Detroit newspaperman who met Ford in 1917, remembered that the two of them "not only shared a common resentment against theoretical farm lovers who painted rural life in rosy color as if the cows milked themselves and crops were self harvesting, but both were McGuffey alumni. Ford would sit on one side of a desk and Garland on the other and try each other's memory on what McGuffey had put in his books. One would recite a line, the other would follow with a second, and they'd go on until one or the other was stumped—then start afresh on other stanzas."

Ford found things to do in school when he wasn't mourning poor drowned Frank. The boys shared two-seat desks, and he was put next to Edsel Ruddiman, a neighbor who was to become his best friend. Edsel was afforded an early glimpse of two traits that would stay with his seatmate all his life: mechanical aptitude and a fondness for practical jokes. Once, when recess had emptied the classroom, Ford drilled two small holes through the seat of the desk in front of him, and set a needle in one threaded through the second with a near-invisible strand that ran to Ford's desk. Later, during a quiet moment, Ford gave the thread a sharp tug, driving the needle up into his classmate's rump. (Ford would have found this prank equally hilarious when he was in his seventies.)

The boy's mechanical ingenuity took forms more constructive than getting a yelp out of a school friend. When Henry was seven, one of William Ford's hired hands opened the back of his pocket watch and showed him how it worked: the jewel bearings, the tiny cogs, the busy mandibles of the escapement. Ford was fascinated, and spent all the time he could during trips to Detroit peering into watchmakers' windows. He began making tools: screwdrivers filed and hammered out of knitting needles, a pair of tweezers fashioned from one of his mother's corset stays. In 1922 he wrote, "My toys were all tools—they still are!" Of course he put the tools to work. A neighbor remarked that "every clock in the Ford home shuddered when it saw him coming," and his sister Margaret remembered, "When we had mechanical or 'wind-up' toys given to us at Christmas, we always said, 'Don't let Henry have them. He just takes them apart.' He wanted to see what made them go rather than just watching them go."

Once he saw what made them go, he understood it. By the time he was twelve, he could not only take watches apart, but put them back together so that they worked better. At school he dissected them behind the screen of his open geometry book. His teacher must have seen something unusual in Henry Ford, for he fully acquiesced in these explorations, so long as his pupil didn't disturb the class with the rasping of a file.

Ford's interest in machinery ran right across the scale from the balance wheels of watches to the driving wheels of locomotives. On a visit to Detroit, William Ford brought Henry to the yards of one of the ten railroads that were nourishing the young city. In the roundhouse there, an engineer took the delighted boy up on the deck of his locomotive, showed him the levers and gauges in the cab, and explained how the firebox heated the water in the boiler into steam, which, when the throttle was cracked open, made its way to the cylinders and punched the pistons that turned the wheels. Seven decades later Ford still remembered the engineer's name: Tommy Garrett.

The boy left the roundhouse to begin years of steam experiments. For many of these he recruited helpers who were glad to follow his directions. This gift of swiftly being able to establish a cordial, happily received dictatorship would stay with him all through the time of his greatest achievements. As Margaret put it, "He had the ability of getting his brothers and his companions to work for him."

Occasionally his projects had spectacular results. Once he had his schoolmates help him build a fire beneath some sort of vessel resting on a circle of stones: Ford remembered it as a "turbine." As Tommy Garrett had surely told him, steam is powerful stuff. The vessel exploded, setting the school fence ablaze and, the grown Henry Ford jotted in one of the pocket notebooks he always carried with him, "a piece hit Robert Blake in the stomach-abdomen and put him *out!*"

As for the work he was supposed to be doing, he dodged it. A neighbor said of the young Ford, "You know, that little devil was the laziest bugger on the face of the earth. . . . Henry would work along all right until about ten o'clock in the morning, and then he would want to go to the house for a drink of water. He would go and get the drink of water, but he would never come back."

However adroitly the boy avoided its sweaty particulars, he never lost his fondness for the world he lived in: joking with his brothers, teasing his sisters, nut-hunting in the woods, the twelve-by-sixteen-foot shed his father granted him as a workshop, the family singing around the pump-organ, the ruby glow the stove cast on the parlor rug. He later compressed his youth into one of the hastily scribbled telegraphic messages he sometimes liked to send to his past: "Remember sleigh, wood hauling, cold winters, setting sun, sleighbell, long walks, cold weather, boys and girls."

Mary Ford's first child had been born dead, but the next six came into the world without difficulty. In mid-March of 1876, however, when she was thirty-seven, her eighth child died being born, and twelve days later she died, too.

Henry said, expressing it as accurately as he could, "The house was like a watch without a mainspring."

Ford would ever after speak of his mother with the greatest warmth, in time coming to contrast her understanding and generosity of spirit with what he chose to see as his father's attempts to sway him from his car-building destiny. Yet often he makes her sound sterner than he may have intended: "She was of that rarest type of mothers—one who so loved her children that she did not care whether they loved her. What I mean by this is that she would do whatever she considered necessary for our welfare even if she thereby temporarily lost our goodwill."

However sympathetic she might have been toward her eldest son, that sympathy did not extend to his dislike of milking or plowing: "Life will give you many unpleasant things to do; your duty will be hard and disagreeable and painful to you at times, but you must do it."

On candy: "Let your health, not your diet be your guide. Never eat merely for the pleasure of eating."

Surely McGuffey can be heard at his most minatory in this reminiscence: "Fun we had and plenty of it, but she was forever reminding us that life cannot be all fun. 'You must earn the right to play,' she used to say to me."

Years after she died, Ford said, "I thought a great wrong had been done to me." He was just thirteen at the time, after all, but he never did speak of how his father must have been affected by the death, trying to repair that broken mainspring with the help of a few desolated children.

Four months later, in July, William Ford brought his son to what Henry called "the biggest event of those early years."

They were driving into Detroit when, about eight miles outside the city, they met a steam farm engine laboring toward them beneath a sooty turban of coal smoke.

"I remember that engine as though I had seen it only yesterday," Ford wrote, "for it was the first vehicle other than horse-drawn that I had ever seen. It was intended primarily for driving threshing machines and sawmills and was simply a portable engine and boiler mounted on wheels with a water tank and coal cart trailing behind. I had seen plenty of these engines hauled around by horses, but this one had a chain that made a connection between the engine and the rear wheels of the wagon-like frame on which the boiler was mounted. The engine was placed over the boiler and one man standing on the platform behind the boiler shoveled coal, managed the throttle, and did the steering. It had been made by Nichols, Shepard & Company of Battle Creek. I found that out at once. The engine had stopped to let us pass with our horses and I was off the wagon and talking to the engineer before my father, who was driving, knew what I was up to. The engineer was very glad to explain the whole affair. He was proud of it. He showed me how the chain was disconnected from the propelling wheel and a belt put on to drive the machinery. He told me that the engine made two hundred revolutions a minute and that the chain pinion could be shifted to let the wagon stop while the engine was still running."

And here Ford, so much of whose youth and early development is elusive, makes a clear and plausible statement of the moment his life took a course that would intersect with everyone else's.

"This last"—the engine running in neutral while not driving the wagon—"is a feature which, although in different fashion, is incorporated into modern automobiles. It was not important with steam engines, which are easily stopped and started, but it became very important with the gasoline engine. It was that engine which took me into automotive transportation."

Henry Ford followed that traction engine for the rest of his life.

In 1922 he wrote, "I wanted to have something to do with machinery. My father was not entirely in sympathy with my bent for mechanics. He thought I ought to be a farmer. When I left school at seventeen and became an apprentice in the machine shop of the Drydock Engine Works I was all but given up for lost."

This account is a small miracle of compression and omission.

He did leave home, in 1879, but not for the chances and perils of the road. He made the journey to Detroit, and when he got there moved in with his aunt, Mrs. Rebecca Ford Flaherty. From this haven he could look for a job in a city that could scarcely have offered more promise to a young would-be mechanic.

Once a fur-trading outpost, then a lumber town, Detroit had been phenomenally boosted when the Erie Canal opened in 1825, connecting the Eastern Seaboard with what was then the western frontier. The home to 9,000 people on the eve of the Erie's completion, it had a population of 116,000 by the time Ford got there. The mines to the north produced iron and copper; the timber stood everywhere. Cornish ironworkers got word, and came, and soon Detroit was selling cast-iron stoves, and railroad cars, and any boiler or stanchion a Lakes steamer might need. All that metal and lumber fed close to a thousand companies large and small, ranging from coachbuilders to leatherworks, that would within a generation be turning out automobile components. The city's ties with the East were close enough for Detroiters to have begun the nearly century-long custom of having oyster stew on Christmas, the delicacy's main ingredient arriving alive in casks, packed safely on cushions of Atlantic seaweed.

Ford quickly found a job in the Michigan Car Works—the cars were streetcars—and was just as quickly fired, gone after six days. He never said why. Perhaps he realized for the first time how restive having a boss made him. Perhaps, as seems to be the flattering consensus, he showed such speed and skill in diagnosing and fixing ailing machinery that he made the older machinists jealous.

Whatever the cause, he was fired, and his father stepped in. William may have wanted Henry back on the farm, but he was friendly with James Flower, who, with his two brothers, owned one of the best machine shops in the city. He brought his son by and got him a job there. The pay wasn't nearly as good as it had been at the car works: There Henry got $1.10 a day, and at the new job $2.25 for a sixty-hour workweek. But he loved Flower Brothers.

Fred Strauss, a twelve-year-old floor sweeper at the time, explained why: "It was a great old shop. . . . They manufactured everything in the line of brass and iron—globe and gate valves, gongs, steam-whistles, fire hydrants, and valves for water pipes. There was a great variety of work. Some of the castings on the iron bodies of the large gate valves weighed a ton or more."

> They made so many different articles that they had all kinds of machines, large and small lathes and drill presses. Some of the large lathes stood for months without having been used, but they had to have them to take care of the different jobs.
>
> They had more machines than workmen in that shop.

This living museum was in effect Ford's college, and he incessantly explored its exhibits, some busy spewing sparks and bright curls of metal, some shadowy and still, all of them increasingly eloquent to him.

He also acquired a friend at Flower Brothers, Fred Strauss, even though the sweeper was four years his junior. "My job was roustabout in the brass shop," Strauss said long after. "Henry was working on a small milling machine, milling hexagons on brass valves.

"They put Henry in with me and he and I got chummy right away. Henry was to do the same work I did. He didn't sweep the floor. I did that because I was more of a worker than he was. He never was a good worker, but he was a good fellow."

However content he might have been at Flower Brothers, the shop put him in a financial squeeze. He had moved from his aunt's into a boardinghouse on Baker Street to be closer to his work, and room and board came to $3.50. This left him a dollar short every week.

To compensate, he went to Robert Magill, a jeweler on Michigan Avenue whom Ford had spent hours observing bent over his watches. Magill liked Henry—everybody liked Henry—and gave him $3.00 a week: fifty cents for six hours of work a night.

Ford was full of bouncy stamina—an old friend remembered that he seemed to be "made of springs"—and the sixteen-hour days didn't wear on him. But he looked young, even for sixteen, and Magill would smuggle him through a side door of his shop and into a back room lest the customers think their watches had been entrusted to a child.

Ford liked his work at the jeweler's, too, and so, sure enough, Robert Magill's shop is now in Greenfield Village, complete with the display cases, Mrs. Magill's needlepoint, and the side door where Ford used to slip in.

He stayed at Flower Brothers for nine months—just about the span of an academic year—and then decided he'd learned all it had to teach him. He went home to help his family with the harvest, and in the fall of 1880 returned to the city and machinery, this time at the Detroit Dry Dock Engine Works, a larger operation than Flower Brothers.

He stayed friends with Fred Strauss, who said, "Henry always wanted to make things. The first time I ever saw him spend any money (he usually got the other fellow to spend it) he bought a set of castings for $1.25 . . . castings of a little steam engine. . . .

"Henry always had another idea. We never did get that machine finished. He always wanted to have something else."

As it turned out, he needn't have finished that steam engine, because he was about to be given charge of a full-size one. By 1882 one of William Ford's neighbors, John Gleason, had done well enough to buy a portable steam engine. Nowhere near as large as the Nichols & Shepard that had astounded Henry half a dozen years earlier, it was nevertheless a sturdy, capable machine that generated almost the same amount of power. Manufactured by Westinghouse, Number 345 had its engine in front beneath a tractor seat, a vertical boiler in back, and, like the Nichols & Shepard, it could drive itself. "The power was applied to the back wheels by a belt," Ford recalled. "They could make twelve miles an hour on the road even though the self-propelling feature was only an incident of the construction."

Number 345's primary function was not to roll across the landscape, but to plant itself next to a job and thresh clover, grind feed, and saw planks, all of which Ford was about to make it do.

Gleason had hired an operator, but "the man knew little about it," said Ford, ". . . and he found himself in trouble. I have an idea he was afraid of his machine. The little high-speed, quick steaming thing made him nervous, and he did little work with it that first day."

Gleason had heard that William's boy Henry was good with machinery, and early the next morning he showed up at the door of the Ford farmhouse. "I was about as proud as I have ever been when he asked if I might run the engine while it was on his place."

William Ford was hesitant. "He was afraid, I am sure, to let me have anything to do with an engine that had proved too much for a professional engineer. . . . He asked me if I felt certain of my ability and his tone showed that he doubted.

"To tell the truth, I was frightened myself. . . . But I was unwilling to be beaten by an engine and I solemnly assured my father and the farmer that I was sure." William and Gleason talked it over. Henry's younger brothers had grown big enough so that he was not necessary to bring in the harvest, and it was indisputable that he had a bump for machinery. "They finally decided to let me try."

He approached the machine with as much seeming nonchalance as he could muster. He called it a "little engine," but its stack stood a good six feet taller than he did, and it had already scared away a pro. Still, he fed the firebox and adjusted valves and "it was not long before my doubts entirely disappeared, and getting a grip on the engine, so to speak, I got a grip on myself.

"At the end of the first day I was as weary as I had been nervous at its beginning, but I had run the engine steadily, inducing it to stand up nicely to its work, and I forgot my grimness and weariness in the consciousness I had actually accomplished what I had started out to do."

For eighty-three summer days, richer by three dollars at the close of each one, Henry Ford steamed about the local fields and woodlands. "It was hard work. I had to fire [345] myself and the fuel most generally was old fence-rails, though it would burn coal the few times coal was to be had." Coal, imported from Pennsylvania or Ohio, was something of a luxury in that heavily forested world.

"I became immensely fond of that machine," and by summer's end was its "complete and expert master. I have never been more satisfied with myself than when I guided it over the rough country roads of the time."

Ford's amazing magpie memory preserved the fact that 345 had eventually been sold to somebody in McKean County, Pennsylvania. So when, in 1913, he decided to go after it, at least he had a place to start. He found it, too, derelict on a Pennsylvania farm, only its builder's plate, which bore the 345, still in active service as a patch on the farmhouse stove. The farmer wanted ten dollars for it. Ford thought this was pretty stiff for some rusted-out plumbing, and stipulated that he must get the builder's plate, too. The farmer complied, and Ford paid over the ten. Then he sent the man a new Model T.

CHAPTER 3

Clara

"He's a thinking, serious person"; winning a dead man's job; electricity; a baby and a seventh home; the Christmas Eve engine.

Ford had many reasons to feel closely connected with 345. For one, during his summer labors, he apparently fell for its owner's daughter, Christine Gleason. Her contemporaries described her as a "beauty queen," and her brother said that Ford asked her to marry him. Instead, she chose Joseph Sheffery, who was both older and richer. Sheffery owned a blacksmith shop, and maintained horses and a carriage. Did Ford, who developed an increasingly powerful vindictive streak as he aged, ever take satisfaction in his career's having extinguished his old rival's job along with his equipage? Perhaps not, since 345 also brought Ford into contact with John Cheeney, the Westinghouse road agent in southern Michigan. Cheeney came and watched Ford at work and hired him to repair and run Westinghouse engines throughout Michigan and northern Ohio. This kept him happily and profitably busy during the summer months. He was in the farming country that he liked, and using machinery to make benign the chores that he loathed.

When winter and its snows put an end to the seasonal labor, Ford would return to the farm and his workshop there. Clouded accounts survive of his trying to build self-propelled vehicles during the cold, short days, but although he would later sometimes insist that they ran, it is all vague. Not time wasted, though, for his efforts seem to have persuaded him that steam power would always involve mechanisms too heavy to propel the vehicle he was beginning to envision.

In early December of 1884 he left his workbench for Detroit once again, this time not to tend a lathe but to enroll in Goldsmith's Bryant & Stratton Business University, in a substantial-looking building on Griswold Street.

All we know of the school's influence on Ford is that for a little while it had him producing clear, even elegant handwriting. That didn't last, and Ford's notes and letters have always frustrated his biographers. Sidney Olson, a shrewd, witty, clear-eyed chronicler of Ford's early years, said that when "the Goldsmith influence wore off . . . his handwriting lapsed into an illegibility that almost rises to grandeur, a magnificent nonpenmanship in which every simple-looking word can be construed in ten different ways." By way of example, Olson cites the entries in the "jotbooks" (Ford recorded the fate of his school fence in one) where he noted everything that caught his interest. Music often did and, Olson says, "In over thirty-odd years of jotting down 'Tales of the Vienna Woods,' he never spelled the title the same twice, and never once correctly."

No record survives of what courses he took at Goldsmith's, and he wasn't there very long—back with his steam engines by summer—but it is interesting to speculate whether he might have brushed up against some unsung Carnegie or Rockefeller there. Whatever happened to him at the school was the only formal business training this supremely capable businessman ever got.

Amid all the steam engines that came his way in 1885, he received one prophetic assignment. Back when he had been cutting metal at Flowers', a brass fitter recently arrived from Britain loaned him a copy of a magazine called *English Mechanic and World of Science*. In it he read that a German named Nikolaus August Otto had developed a "silent gas engine." Ford recalled, "It ran with illuminating gas, had a single large cylinder, and . . . as far as weight was concerned it gave nothing like the power per pound of metal that the steam engine gave, and the use of illuminating gas seemed to dismiss it even as a possibility for road use. It was interesting to me only as all machinery was interesting." He kept up with the Otto in the technical magazines, though, and "most particularly the hints of the possible replacement of illuminating gas fuel by a gas formed by the vaporization of gasoline."

So he was not wholly unprepared when the Eagle Iron Works in Detroit called him to repair an Otto, even though it was the first gas engine he had ever seen. "No one in town knew anything about them. There was a rumor that I did and, although I had never been in contact with one, I undertook and carried through the job. That gave me a chance to study the new engine at first hand."

An equally consequential encounter had taken place on the first day of 1885. Ford had begun to get interested in dancing—"There were no teachers in those days," his sister Margaret said, "he just learned at the parties"—and he went to a New Year's Night celebration at a hostelry called Martindale House.

In the dance hall a fiddler was calling out instructions like, "Last gentleman lead to the right, around that lady with a grapevine twist," and Ford joined in. During a quadrille he found himself next to a second cousin, Annie Ford, and across from a graceful dark-haired girl. Annie introduced them: Her name was Clara Jane Bryant.

Clara would have seen a slender young man a couple of years her senior, with wide-set blue-gray eyes. He stammered out a few commonplaces, so obviously fascinated and distracted that his cousin mildly scolded him once a partner had taken Clara off into the crowd.

The girl had pretty much the same effect on Ford as that self-propelled traction engine did. He spent futile months going to other dances hoping to meet her. Nearly a year passed before he managed to track her down. It was Christmastime again, and they ate oyster stew together and later Ford gravely demonstrated a watch he'd acquired that simultaneously told the newly instituted standard railroad time with steel hands, and the locally observed "sun time" with brass ones. This disquisition went over better than he had any right to expect. When Clara got home she told her parents that she liked Henry Ford: "He's a thinking, serious person—serious minded."

That quality might have appealed to Clara because she shared it, and not all of her large family did. She had nine younger siblings. Her two sisters were smart and pretty, but mercurial, somewhat random, and one of them, Eva, was already known for her bad temper.

As so often in his life, Ford went after what he wanted. He at once bought a sleigh so he could drive Clara about the winter landscape. By Valentine's Day of 1886 he could write her a confident letter (the script still tidy from Goldsmith's, the orthography a bit uncertain): "I again take the pleasure of writing you a few lines. It seems like a year since i seen you. It don't seem mutch like cutter [sleigh] rideing to night does it but i guess we will have some more sleighing. . . . i think as the weather is so bad you will not expect me tonight, but if the weather and roads are good you look for me. . . . Clara Dear, you can not imagine what pleasure it gives me to think that i have at last found one so loveing kind and true as you are and I hope we will always have good success."

He pursued that success so vigorously that, a few days after Clara's twentieth birthday, the two became engaged on April 19. But Clara's mother believed, engagement notwithstanding, her eldest daughter was too young to get married.

Months passed by while Ford remained something of a permanent suitor. The long courtship followed the rituals of the time and place: quadrilles at Martindale House, summer picnics at one or another's family farmstead, moonlight husking bees where the shucker who uncovered a red ear earned a kiss. This all sounds sweet with Currier & Ives placidity, but of course it was a molten, yearning, anxious time for Henry Ford.

The uncertainty came to an end when William Ford offered Henry the use of an eighty-acre tract he had bought from a neighbor named Moir who lived three-quarters of a mile to the west. Half the land was cleared, the other half still thick with timber.

Henry's first job would be to cut down the trees, but once that was done his father hoped he might take up the prosperous farming life William Ford found so miraculous an improvement over his early years on a few acres of Irish soil owned by somebody else.

Henry saw an opportunity here, if not quite the one his father did. He could clear the forest—behind a steam engine, not a plow—and sell the lumber. The old Moir residence was Spartan but perfectly habitable. He would have land, and an income, and a house a few miles from where his fiancée had grown up.

Surely Mrs. Bryant couldn't further postpone the wedding now. She didn't. Clara Bryant and Henry Ford were married in the Bryant home on April 11, 1888.

———∿∿∿∿∿∿∿———

They seem to have been at ease with each other from the start. Margaret thinks that a turning point, or at least a profound deepening of her brother's feelings, came before the engagement when William Ford asked his son to get rid of some stumps that were still stubbling already cleared land. Henry borrowed John Gleason's engine—345 back again in his life—and urged the girls to come see it at work.

Margaret and Clara did, and jolted with Henry across the fields, looked on while he and steam power wrenched obdurate stumps out of the ground. Number 345's flashing metal and occasional spew of sparks did not intimidate Clara in the least. Margaret wrote that her brother "was so enthused at that time with this way of taking so much hard work out of farming that he could talk of little else. Clara and I were 'good listeners,' but, I must confess, all the talk meant little to us at the time. I am sure, however, that Clara's willingness to ride on this engine and to go into the field, and watch Henry at his work further convinced him she was the proper girl for his wife."

"All the talk" may have made a deeper impression on Clara than Margaret realized. Clara had listened to her beau's explanation of his dual-purpose watch and gone home to tell her parents about it. She saw the casual expertise with which he ran 345, and knew he was the only man in Detroit who could be trusted to fix the near-occult Otto engine. She came to trust his mechanical judgment so completely that Ford happily began to refer to her as "the Believer." But so did he trust her: He was a Believer, too.

When, after a few months together in the Moir house, the two were speaking about building a better residence, Clara wrote a note:

Kitchen 12 x 18

Sitting-room 14 x 14

Parlor 18 x 14

Bedroom 10 x 14

"Henry, the above figures are the best that I can do. But use your own judgment about it."

He used hers, and at once started cutting and drying lumber for what they were calling the Square House. With the help of an expert carpenter, the little house, thirty-one feet on a side, a story and a half high, took shape. It was a wonderfully amiable-looking building, with almost a postmodern feel to its chipper symmetry—a cube for the first floor, a mansard roof above it punctuated by a single emphatic dormer window, and graceful with ample porches and three tiers of lathe-turned balustrades. Some Ford family members thought it was the most appealing home Clara and Henry ever owned.

They moved in during the spring of 1889, and stayed long enough for Clara to have established an herb garden and acquire the impressive domestic accessory of a pump-organ by the time her husband was summoned to Detroit to heal another Otto engine.

This one, in a bottling works, was smaller and suppler than the first Ford had seen, and he returned home distracted. He sat and brooded over some technical magazines. After a while he interrupted Clara, who was at the organ, mentioned the engine he'd spent the day with, and said he believed it could be used to power a horseless carriage. Clara was puzzled, and Henry took a piece of sheet music and sketched the vehicle while he explained it (in his magisterial biography, Allan Nevins remarks, "To judge from other drawings made by him, there was probably more explanation than sketch"). As soon as Clara understood what her husband was talking about, said Margaret, "She had complete confidence that he could do it."

There was more. Ford knew all about forging and turning metal, he knew all about steam. But the Otto engine was fired by an electric spark, and he didn't know much about electricity. To learn, he would have to move to Detroit and get a job with a power company—he told Clara he hoped that it might be at the Edison Illuminating Company.

This was disingenuous. Ford already had the job. He'd gone into Detroit a few days earlier and enjoyed the following brisk transaction from those robust days before HR departments.

He went up the steps of Edison Illuminating—which, founded five years earlier, was now feeding power to one thousand homes and five thousand streetlights—and ran into an "elderly man" who was just leaving.

"Who's in charge here?" Ford asked him.

Charles Phelps Gilbert said, "I am. What can I do for you?"

"I'm an engineer. Have you any work I can do?"

"How much do you know about the work?"

"As much," Ford boldly replied, "as anyone my age." Half true: He had enough understanding of electricity to know that the generators that produced it were spun by steam engines, and there was nothing about a steam engine he couldn't handle.

That was the interview. Phelps said, "Well, I do think we have a place for you. A man was killed last week down at our substation and we need someone in his place right away." Hours, 6:00 p.m. to 6:00 a.m.; salary, forty dollars a month.

Clara was horrified. Henry may not have told her he was leaping into the shoes of a dead man, but she saw clearly enough what his plan meant. She'd be leaving her family, the countryside she had lived in her whole life, the house she had helped design, the garden. Margaret said, "It almost broke her heart."

She was the Believer, though. The Fords left the Square House on the morning of September 25, 1891, and Henry started his job at Edison Illuminating that same day.

Gone with the couple was William Ford's last hope of seeing his son settle down and work the family acres. Henry summed up his final departure in a sentence that, although just six words long, is spacious enough to show he had never for a moment intended to make the transition from working his engines to farming: "The timber had all been cut."

———————∿∿∿∿∿∿∿∿———————

Clara and Henry Ford rented the right half of a double house at 618 John R Street, ten blocks from the substation where Ford was replacing the killed worker. Detroit would have seemed more alien to Clara than the Edison substation did to Henry, for it contained a one-hundred-horsepower Beck steam engine that he knew well. On the other hand, the familiar Beck stood in company with two total strangers: a Rice dynamo and an Aldington & Sims generator, machines that generated the electricity about which Ford had yet to learn. It was his good fortune that the Beck broke down first, less than a month after he'd arrived.

Detroit Edison had managed to win contracts for supplying the city's churches. Demand was, naturally, heaviest on Sundays, and at the end of one of them the Beck collapsed under the strain. Ford immediately knew the damage was bad: a piston rod snapped, a broken valve, a hole in the cylinder block. Charles Phelps Gilbert, looking over the wreckage with his new hire, saw a trying and costly future of experts called in from everywhere, and dark churches that might well seek out rival power companies.

Ford surprised his boss by saying he could fix the engine himself. Phelps didn't believe it, but said to go ahead and try. Ford made on his own a pattern from which to cast a new cylinder block, took care of the valve and the piston rod, and rearranged the engine's vitals so that it could withstand the pressures of future Sundays. During this there was no sign of the winning slacker who got his friends to do his work and disappeared after going for a drink of water. Ford was at the engine all the time, and by the following Sunday the Beck was in good shape and the Detroit churches had all the electricity they needed.

Gilbert gave Ford a five-dollar raise immediately, and another one shortly after.

Clara Ford would have been gratified by this victory, but even as her husband was getting his second raise from Detroit Edison, the couple was moving to Washington Boulevard and, shortly after that, to Cass Avenue. During the coming decades the Believer would pack up and soldier forward into ten different rental houses.

They were in one on Forest Avenue when their son and only child was born.

The doctor attending was named David O'Donnell. He was a year out of medical school and there because Clara's brother Harry had met him in a Detroit cigar store and thought he might do a good job with Harry's wife's impending childbirth. He had, and so, on November 6, 1893, the Fords called him to their home on Forest Avenue. Still so new to his practice he couldn't afford the horse and buggy that was a professional necessity for physicians in those days, O'Donnell arrived with his doctor's bag dangling from the handlebars of a bicycle.

"I didn't run into any difficulty," he said. "Mrs. Ford didn't give me any trouble at all. She never complained. Mr. Ford was in the house. He didn't get excited and he didn't bother me. Most young fathers bother the life out of a doctor."

If the doctor liked the father, the father liked him. Once there was a Ford automobile company, and once Dr. O'Donnell could afford a car, the Ford company repaired it free for the rest of his life.

The visit's outcome couldn't have been more satisfactory. The couple named the boy after Henry's school friend and Clara's family: Edsel Bryant Ford.

—————~~~wwwwwwwww~~~—————

Henry Ford had been promoted from the substation to the Main Station of the Edison Illuminating Company less than a week before his son was born. Edsel was ten days old when Detroit Edison nearly doubled his father's salary, to ninety dollars a month, and in December raised Ford to an even hundred and made him chief engineer. This meant he was on constant call, around the clock. Many would have hated this; Ford did not. He had managed to climb to a place he wanted to be, and would stay there for the rest of his life. The fact that he could be summoned to the now familiar dynamos at any hour also meant that he had no fixed hours. In the absence of a crisis, he could appear and leave when he chose. He was good at the latter, having mastered what Sidney Olson termed "the art of the short call": stopping by, taking an interest in this armature or that condenser, joking easily with the men who'd be doing the actual fixing, and then—gone. "He always seemed to be leisurely," said Olson, "and he always seemed to be leaving."

He might be leaving for yet another evanescent appearance at one of the dozens of machine shops that supplied his continuing education.

Mostly, though, he would go to 58 Bagley Avenue, where the Fords had relocated—the seventh move of their marriage—on December 15. This was a solid, comfortable two-family brick house. The twenty-five-dollar-a-month rent included use of the woodshed out back, which was more substantial than that sounds: It was a good-sized outbuilding, also of brick, that Ford shared with his neighbor.

The neighbor was Felix Julien, and nobody ever had a better one. A calm, amiable older man, retired from the coal business, he soon noticed that the newcomer was not storing wood or coal in the shed, but rather had set up benches and machinery to begin building something.

Julien moved his own coal into his house, took down the brick wall that divided the two areas, and said Ford was welcome to the whole shed: Clearly he had a better use for the room than fuel storage. Julien's only request was that he be allowed to look on sometimes; he found this metalwork fascinating.

A few days after he'd moved his family to Bagley Avenue, Ford was at the Edison plant watching a boilermaker—his name has come down to us, as it happens: James Wolfenden—cutting and brazing some pipes in the engine room. His repairs finished, Wolfenden found himself with a length of leftover tubing too awkward to carry around on the Christmas errands he was eager to get to. He was heading toward the scrap pile that disfigured every industrial establishment in those days when Ford told him to leave the pipe there; he'd take care of it.

In Wolfenden's rubbish, Ford had seen a cylinder for his gasoline engine.

Over the days that followed, he bored out the pipe to a one-inch diameter, made a piston to slide in it, and scavenged other parts: a discarded handwheel from a lathe could serve as a flywheel. Cam, exhaust valve, cloth-wrapped stub of wire to ignite the spark necessary to fire these elements into life. . . . He put them all together, and presented the result to his wife as what may have been 1893 Detroit's least agreeable Christmas surprise.

On the evening of December 24, Clara Ford was getting ready to entertain the cascade of Bryants the holiday always brought when her husband stepped into the kitchen with his new machine. It was not imposing. He had mounted the piece of pipe on a board, and from this cylinder a frail-looking steel rod connected the piston inside it to a crankshaft a few inches away. A second rod—again, not much thicker than a wire coat hanger—reached back to the side of the pipe. When the first rod moved, so would the second, opening and closing an exhaust valve. Both rods would be kept in motion by the lathe handwheel that had been promoted to flywheel status.

Here was Henry Ford's first gasoline engine. But it was an engine in barely fetal form, and that's why it had appeared in the kitchen. If the device was to work at all, it needed two people to tend it, one to feed fuel into the narrow throat of the intake, the other to spin the flywheel to get it started. Most of all, it needed electricity, available in the kitchen but not in the shed. Ford had run a wire into the cylinder; as the piston moved, it brought another wire, embedded in it, into contact with this one. When the piston kept moving the wires would draw apart and, given the application of an electric current, a spark would jump between them, igniting the gases that had been squeezed out of the fuel by the pushing piston.

Edsel was asleep in the next room; family was looming; it was likely the busiest evening of Clara Ford's year. If ever the Believer had justified her husband's epithet it was now, as she stood aside while Ford fastened his engine to the kitchen sink and wormed the other end of the cylinder wire into the ceiling fixture that held the kitchen's overhead light.

He handed his wife an oilcan full of gasoline, and issued instructions: She was to squirt the gas into the thimble-sized cup that stood on top of the machine's intake, and then adjust a screw that would let the gasoline into the cylinder quickly or slowly, depending on the virgin engine's thirst.

Henry put a hand on the wheel, and Clara upended the oilcan. As the clear fluid dribbled into the little cup, the kitchen filled with a smell that would have puzzled and alarmed almost every American alive in 1893, and that within a generation would be familiar as the scent of woodsmoke. Henry rotated the wheel, the piston sucked in air and gas from the cup, and the kitchen light dimmed in protest as the spark jumped and the cylinder emitted a sharp little bark.

Ford spun the wheel again, and his engine exploded into strident life. The flywheel spun, the cam did its job, spikes of blue flame jetted from the exhaust valve. The sink shook on its moorings, exhaust further dimmed the kitchen light, and surely the racket disturbed Edsel.

But not for long. After thirty seconds of clamor Henry indicated to Clara that she could move away from the sink. The engine drank off the cup and went silent. It never ran again. "I didn't stop to play with it," Ford said years later. His assemblage of cast-off metal oddments had taught him what he had needed to know.

He was thirty years old, far from young to be gambling his and his family's future on a raucous novelty he'd improvised in time stolen from a respectable and promising job.

Clara knew that was what he was going to do, though. She rinsed the gasoline off her hands and returned to her holiday cooking.

CHAPTER 4

Working from the Ground Up

Making a car in a world without any; "a colorless, limpid, innocent-appearing liquid"; the Bagley Avenue woodshed; America's first car race; Henry Ford's first car.

The Christmas Eve engine was the seed from which Ford's first car grew, but the growth was a slow one, because every screw and bracket needed to be thought through, and many made for the first time. Ford was working in a world that contained no automobile parts.

When he had to consider so basic an element of his engine as a carburetor, the all-important device that blended fuel with the proper amount of air before breathing it into the engine, he couldn't draw on literature discussing float valves and chokes. He had to figure out the entire mechanism for himself: how to get just the right mix of air and gas to cause the strongest combustion in the cylinder; and how to get the fuel flowing (from wherever it was going to be kept) to the carburetor; and how to adjust that crucial fuel-air mixture so it would work equally well in winter and summer, on dry days and wet ones; and how to connect the future carburetor to the future driver, who would have to control it to control the vehicle. Ford probably didn't have even the word "carburetor" to help sustain him: It would not appear in print in an automotive sense for another two years.

———∿∿∿∿∿∿∿∿∿———

In 1922 when, with Theodore Roosevelt gone, Henry Ford was the most famous living American, he published an autobiography called *My Life and Work.* This was written, the title page says, "in collaboration with Samuel Crowther." A capable journalist, Crowther found himself almost alone in the lopsided collaboration. If it had been hard to keep Henry Ford standing still in the Detroit Edison days, it was all but impossible a quarter century later. The book needs to be read with caution, for what information Crowther did manage to snatch from his subject on the fly was often wrong (Ford asserts, for instance, that he got his first car on the road three years earlier than he actually did). Nevertheless, there are many passages where one does seem to hear the actual voice of Henry Ford, astringent and direct.

About his Bagley Avenue days he says, "I had to work from the ground up—that is, although I knew a number of people were working on horseless carriages, I could not know what they were doing."

Despite the demands of his Detroit Edison job, the up-from-the-ground automaking didn't wear on him. "I cannot say that it was hard work. No work with interest is ever hard." Then he adds, engagingly, "But it was a great thing to have my wife even more confident than I was. She has always been that way."

He says next to nothing about the actual work he was doing. Here, in its entirety, is his description of two and a half years of unremitting effort: "The hardest problems to overcome were in the making and breaking of the spark and in the avoidance of excess weight. For the transmission, the steering gear, and the general construction, I could draw on my experience of the steam tractors."

One can get a clearer idea of what was going on in the Bagley Avenue woodshed from a contemporary of Ford's named Hiram Maxim,

who was struggling with his own self-propelled vehicle in equal isolation in West Lynn, Massachusetts. Neither man had heard of the
other (although Ford may have been familiar with the name Maxim,
because Hiram's father had already become well known in technical journals for developing the modern machine gun), but both were
groping their way through the same labyrinth.

Maxim had been lured into it by a woman. Late on a summer
night in 1892, pedaling his bicycle along a country road the five miles
between West Lynn and Salem, which was home to "an attractive
young lady" who had him "pretty much up in the clouds," he was
struck by a thought: "It would be a wonderful thing if a little engine
were to be devised which would furnish the power to drive a bicycle."
Creating one "did not appear to be a serious problem," because he
wasn't "expending more than a sixth or a quarter of a horsepower, and
that would not mean much of an engine."

Forty years later, Maxim recounted what followed this revelation in
a delightful, detailed memoir called *The Horseless Carriage Age*. Maxim
was six years Ford's junior, an easterner, and unmarried, but their sit-
uations were similar. Maxim, too, was superintending a substantial
industrial operation—an armaments factory—and like Ford he had
decided that gasoline should drive his vehicle.

"At the start," Maxim said, "I knew engines pretty well but I did
not know much about gasoline. That it was bought in paint shops,
that it was about as temperamental as dynamite, was very volatile,
would remove grease spots from clothing, and was a petroleum deriva-
tive was about the total of my knowledge."

He started out by going to a paint shop and buying an eight-once
bottle. "It was a colorless, limpid, innocent-appearing liquid," and
Maxim studied it fondly: "Gazing at the bottle and its fascinating contents, I saw in my mind's eye thousands of drops. Each one of these
little drops, vaporized and mixed with air, could develop ten times the
thrust against my bicycle pedals that I could develop with my legs.
The contents of that bottle could develop enough power to take me
to Salem."

Maxim brought his magic fluid back to the factory and began to experiment with it. He got a brass artillery shell casing—there were plenty at hand—a couple of inches across and a foot high. In it he put a single drop of gasoline and shook the cartridge to mix the gas with air. Then he stood back and tossed in a match.

After a brief pause, there came a "terrifying explosion, fire shot up out of the cartridge-case, and the match I had thrown went hurtling to the ceiling. It was evident that there was about a thousand times more kick in a drop of gasoline than I had pictured in my wildest flights of imagination."

Maxim tried it with two drops, then three, and was surprised to find that the more gasoline he put in, the slower and weaker the explosion.

Thus educated, he went in search of a vehicle to carry the engine that would live on the unpredictable liquid, and found, in Salem, a secondhand tandem Columbia tricycle. Despite the sound of its name, it had been designed for husky adults. With great trepidation—"thirty dollars was a lot of money"—Maxim bought it.

After he'd wrestled his tricycle back to Lynn and put it in a room next to his office in the factory, it silently urged him on: "There it stood, ready to take to the road. All I needed was an engine to drive it."

This he worked on every spare hour, from six o'clock quitting time until midnight on weekdays, Saturday afternoons, Sundays: "I strove mightily at first to design the general layout—the chain drive, the clutch, its operating mechanism, a change-gear system, gasoline tank and support, engine mounting and engine. But every effort resulted in something that would require an express wagon to contain it."

So he turned to the engine, which seemed to him an altogether easier proposition. "I laid out a light three-cylinder, four-cycle, air-cooled machine, three inches bore by three inches stroke, with mechanically actuated exhaust and automatic inlet valves . . . I passed up the carbureting arrangements, muffler, manifolds and lubricating systems, as minor details, the designing of which could be tossed off at any convenient time!"

The engine turned out to devour his convenient and inconvenient time alike. "It required months of night-work to finish the . . . design and make all the working drawings. It took months more to get the patterns, castings, and machine work done here, there, and everywhere."

Maxim finished the engine late in 1894, and thought it "the most ravishingly beautiful bit of machinery the hand of man had ever created." But what he called his "little darling" needed some of the fundamental things he had earlier shrugged off designing.

He improvised a carburetor from a kerosene can and tried to start it. Nothing doing: "The whole future looks black and forbidding after spending a week unsuccessfully cranking a cold engine." He worked and worked on "the beautiful creation that seemed perfect in all particulars except its prime object." At last, after hooking the recalcitrant machine up to the "electric-light system in the factory"—at almost the same time his unknown co-revolutionist was doing the same thing in a kitchen eight hundred miles away—and fastening it to one of the shop's lathes to turn it over, he was ready to try again.

A colleague wondered "if it were necessary for a self-propelled road vehicle to carry around an electric factory lighting system and a lathe and the power to run the lathe, did it not appear that the thing would become a bit top-heavy?"

This is only research, Maxim replied—nervously, because an audience of his fellow weapons-makers had gathered to watch the demonstration.

Maxim started the lathe; the engine turned, gasoline smell filled the room—so the fuel was flowing properly—but the little darling lay silent. Maxim stopped the lathe and closed off the gas supply to the engine. Perhaps the same thing was happening that had with the cartridge experiment: the more gas, the less bang. By starving the engine of gas, Maxim was also cutting down what the future would know as a "rich mixture"—a heavy ratio of gas to air.

He started the lathe again. It "turned a few times when, without the slightest warning, what seemed like the most frightful machine-gun fire cut loose. I had never heard such a terrible clatter. Noise came from everywhere. Something was buzzing around under my nose at tremendous speed, fire was spitting out of everything, and smoke, smell, and confusion reigned supreme."

His coworkers were frightened by this clamorous glimpse into the next century, and so was Maxim. He had expected his prodigy to sound like "a sweet-running little sewing machine," not a battle. He was discouraged for a few days, then he began to think about a muffler, exhaust pipes, a carburetor, and the necessity of putting some sort of load on the engine so it wouldn't race until it thrashed itself apart.

The big tricycle would provide the drag he needed. He mounted the engine on it, and liked the way it looked. It would probably be a good idea to have a clutch, he thought, but that could come later. For the moment, he connected the engine directly to the wheels with a bicycle-like chain-and-sprocket arrangement, happy in the thought that he could pedal it into life without any tedious hand cranking, let alone a lathe.

After a while, he summoned the nerve to attempt a road test. Wanting no onlookers this time, he took the tricycle (or automobile; it was surely more than a tricycle now) out into the streets of West Lynn just after sunrise.

He found that with the engine yoked to the wheels, it was too cumbersome to pedal. Maxim disconnected the chain, pushed his creation to the brow of a hill, and reattached the chain. Even pedaling downhill was stiff, slow progress with the wheels turning the silent engine, and the road was about like any other one in America at that time: a stretch of parallel troughs dug by wagon wheels and filled with stones.

Maxim set the gas-air mixture rich and pushed along; then, beginning to run out of hill, shifted it to lean, just as it had been in the artillery shell on his very first try. Immediately "there came a terrific snapping noise and what seemed to be a rear-end collision. . . . The tricycle gave a lunge ahead and started for the bottom of the hill hell-for-leather, regardless of loose stones, rocks and gullies, at a speed nothing less than horrible . . . I suppose the run lasted ten seconds. It seemed to me ten minutes."

The front wheel locked itself in a rut, and when Maxim tried to steer free shed its tire and collapsed, flinging the tricycle and its driver into the air.

Maxim landed a life-saving distance from the overturned machine and got to his feet to assess the damage. He was abraded but intact; the tricycle looked a total wreck, emitting a few final hiccups of blue smoke and "the smell which goes along with all new gasoline engines." But "to my astonishment, nothing was damaged beyond repair excepting my trousers."

Maxim spent the last days of 1894 trying to devise a clutch. The next summer he went to Hartford, Connecticut, and visited the Pope Manufacturing Company, the nation's foremost bicycle producer, whose owner, Colonel Albert A. Pope, was beginning to be intrigued with the idea of horseless carriages. So were many Americans at the time, but Pope was in a position to do something about it, and he hired Maxim to be in charge of a department that would build a horseless carriage named the Columbia (which would have four wheels; Maxim was through with tricycles). This new operation was to be called the Motor-Carriage Department. The forward-looking Colonel Pope felt that even the word "horseless" was beginning to sound antiquated.

—————⌇⌇⌇⌇⌇⌇—————

Hiram Maxim and Henry Ford had spent 1894 engaged in nearly identical tasks. Maxim had made mistakes that Ford avoided, mostly in the latter's approach to his work. Ford had figured out how to control his engine before trying to take a ride with it. "I draw a plan and work out every detail in the plan before starting to build," he said, "for otherwise one will waste a great deal of time in makeshifts as the work goes on and the finished article will not have coherence. It will not be rightly proportioned. Many inventors fail because they do not distinguish between planning and experimenting."

The similarities between the two inventors, however, were greater than the differences. Maxim had risked his life trying to prove his machine. Ford was to do that. Both shared the frustrations that came from the fact that in the automobile's earliest days, there was little difference between experimenting and planning. Most of all, Ford would have sympathized with Maxim's ceaseless search for parts and castings. "The largest building difficulties that I had," Ford said, "were in obtaining the proper materials. The next were with tools. There had to be some adjustments and changes in details of the design, but what held me up most was that I had neither the time nor the money to search for the best material for each part."

Money was a problem, but not a misery. Ford was drawing a good salary, and his wife was an excellent manager. The Strelinger hardware store gave him a credit of fifteen dollars a month—not an enormous sum but, considering Maxim's worry over committing thirty dollars to his tricycle, not negligible. And at Bagley Avenue the Fords were able to buy a player piano, the single most expensive domestic machine before the advent of what Ford was trying to create.

Ford worked all that late winter and spring, often under Felix Julien's fascinated gaze. His neighbor had become so interested in the project that he sometimes would sit alone in the woodshed, waiting for Ford to return from Detroit Edison. Others visited the shed: Ford had several friends who were willing to help him and capable enough actually to be helpful. One was James Bishop, who worked at the Edison plant, and who liked Ford even though he'd been the butt of one of his practical jokes. This form of humor was far more prevalent a century ago than it is now, but even by the standards of the day Ford relished it to an unusual extent. When another Edison employee left his work shoes in the middle of the room, Ford jimmied up a floorboard, fixed the shoes to it with spikes driven through the soles, hammered the points of the spikes to a right angle on the bottom of the plank to make sure the marriage was solid, and then nailed the board back in place.

Ford's joke on Bishop was equally subtle. His colleague was repairing an engine in one of the plant's older buildings when Bishop and the other men on the job began to have difficulty breathing. What air they could draw in was vile. Bishop discovered his superintendent outside, with a small bellows and a shovelful of glowing coals. He was dropping sulfur on the coals and pumping the resulting stench into the room through a knothole.

It says something about Ford's personality in those days that despite this sort of thing, Bishop was fond of him. So, too, was a man five years his junior who would have a decisive effect on his work.

At about the time Ford moved to Bagley Avenue, Charles B. King rented space in a new building on St. Antoine Street that housed the Lauer Brothers machine shop—one of the best in the city—in which he hoped to develop an automobile of his own. The son of an army officer, Charles King first came to Detroit, his mother's hometown, when his father retired as a general. He spent two years studying science at Cornell before his father's death brought him back to Detroit and into a draftsman's job at the Michigan Car Works. His tenure there was happier than Ford's had been.

King invented a brake beam that was adopted by the entire railroad industry, and a pneumatic hammer, which won him a high award at the 1893 Chicago World's Fair. When he moved into the Lauer building he planned to develop, along with his automobile, the pneumatic hammer and marine engines. Lauer, just one floor below him, would do his manufacturing.

Ford knew the Lauer Brothers shop well; he often came there on Edison business. On one of his visits he met King and discovered that they were both interested in building a motorcar. King was friendly, enthusiastic, and possessed formal training and real patents. Ford wanted to know whether his new friend might help him. "He asked me to give him a hand," King said decades later. "Of course, I was willing."

Soon after opening his office, King hired as his assistant a seventeen-year-old named Oliver Barthel. He had been born in Detroit, but raised in Germany, where his father represented a stove company. His mother brought him back to Michigan to study engineering in high school, but like King he had to break that off and go to work when his father died. Despite his truncated education, his new boss found him a first-rate engineer. Moreover, his complete command of the German language could get Lauer's largely German-American workforce to hurry King's projects along. For his part, Barthel adored King—"I never worked so well with anyone"—and he, too, became close friends with Henry Ford.

So King, Barthel, and Bishop often stopped in at the woodshed to help with the engine. Seventy years later a handful of elderly men in Detroit still remembered as schoolboys sneaking down the alley by 58 Bagley to catch a glimpse of Mr. Ford and his friends and the thing they were making.

The woodshed was by no means open to all comers. Clara was highly protective of her husband and his work. When, early in 1894, her sister Kate and niece Nettie, both in their early twenties, came for a weeklong stay, she neither showed them the shed nor let them in on what was happening there. All she would say was, "Henry is making something and maybe someday I'll tell you."

"Well," Nettie said tartly long after, "she didn't tell us."

Clara's secretiveness about the project reflected her husband's. The affable, gregarious Ford, welcome in any machine shop in the city, was always closemouthed about what exactly he was doing there.

Fred Strauss had by now opened a machine shop on Shelby Street where he made gasoline engines for boats. Ford liked to drop by, give him a hand, and even sold two engines for him. He also got Strauss to help him build a crankshaft. It was not until years later that Strauss learned that it had been destined to be part of an automobile.

But if the busy inventor chose not to show his visiting in-laws what was going on in the woodshed, he did manage to find the time one day to smear butter on all the doorknobs in the house. A few days later, as they were tiptoeing quietly up to their room after a late party, the sisters were alarmed by a vaguely human-looking thing flapping and thumping toward them down the darkened staircase. It was a bundle of clothes, weighted with bricks and flung, of course, by their host. (Henry Ford would change in many ways during his life, but not in this one: Thirty years later, he'd be garnishing Harvey Firestone's soup with wooden croutons.) The girls got their own back by filling Henry's shoes with finely ground pepper, which so discomfited the wearer that he had to come back in the middle of the day from Detroit Edison to wash off his feet and change his footwear.

There were few practical jokes in the woodshed, though, where Ford was pushing his way through the thicket that has entrapped most inventors, a thorny place of false leads, real setbacks, and will-o'-the-wisp successes.

A decade later, Ford described his routine in those days: "Most of the iron work was got from a firm by the name of Barr & Dates; they were located at that time on the corner of Park Place and State Street, Detroit. The wheels I made; the seat I got from the Wilson Carriage Company, and from C. A. Strelinger & Co. bolts and screws and nuts; I made the handle myself; I don't know where I got the balance wheel from; I made the pattern and got it cast; I made the braking device; the springs from the Detroit Steel and Spring Co."

When he says he made things like the wheels and handle himself, he almost always means that he supervised their making. Ford was a fine machinist, but he had a rarer skill than that, the one his sister noticed so early, which was his ability to draw work out of friends and keep them happy while they did it. For the most part, other hands than his fitted the spokes to the wheel rims. "I never saw Mr. Ford make anything," said one of his Bagley Avenue helpers. "He was always doing the directing." And the helpers he found, first-rate engineers like King and Barthel, always took the directing gladly. Fred Strauss said of Ford that in those days "he had the magnet."

There was plenty to direct. His cylinders—he'd decided to have two—were easily gotten, born like their little predecessor in a length of scrap pipe. This pipe, which had once served as the exhaust for a steam engine, was larger. Ford, working with the close tolerances that internal combustion demanded, increased its bore from 2.5 inches to 2.565 inches. He made the cylinders eleven inches long; their pistons would have a six-inch stroke. He fretted over the flywheel, trying to find the right recipe of weight (to keep the pistons moving) and lightness (to keep them as free as possible in their motion). This all went well enough, but he had little luck with the ignition, and none at all with the valves.

—————〰〰〰〰〰〰〰—————

Eighteen ninety-four passed in filing and fitting, cutting and testing. Edsel's first birthday came and went and not long afterward so did Christmas—this time with no combustive visitor to the holiday kitchen—and then it was 1895.

Two things that were to have powerful consequences for Henry Ford's life happened that year. Of one he knew nothing; of the other, a great deal.

The former was not spectacular. A Rochester, New York, man named George B. Selden moved forward on a long-pending patent claim, and on November 5 was issued U.S. patent No. 549,160.

"Long-pending" understates the case. Selden had first submitted his claim on May 8, 1879. It was for a horseless carriage.

Selden had been trying to build an internal combustion engine. He hadn't had any great success, but he could imagine his unfinished motor placed in some sort of vehicle—he never did try to build that—and he wanted his patent to cover what he might one day achieve.

Neither Selden nor anybody else in America was prepared to build such a thing in 1879, but Selden knew the law—he was a patent attorney—and he knew how to use it to put time on his side.

Under the existing statutes, having submitted his claim Selden could postpone the beginning of its seventeen-year life by making amendments to it. These he scrupulously filed at regular intervals. Some were substantive, others as finicking as changing a "the" to an "a" in the wording of his application, but they kept the claim alive. The law let him spend seventeen years on such refinements; then he had to accept the patent or withdraw it.

Selden evidently did want to build an automobile, but he had a haughty, rebarbative nature that drove away investors. At the end he had no investors, no car, and only a few months left him.

Eighteen ninety-five was a far more promising year for automobile making than 1879 had been. Selden finally pulled the trigger and got his patent for "the production of a safe, simple and cheap road-locomotive light in weight, easy to control, and possessed of sufficient power to overcome any ordinary inclination." It would have a steering mechanism, he said, either one or several cylinders, a clutch, passenger seats, a brake, and so forth. None of these was described in any great detail, and didn't need to be. Selden had sought—and, amazingly, got—a patent on the *idea* of the automobile.

Although Henry Ford had no inkling of this, if he wanted to build a motor carriage, United States law now said he would have to get George Selden's permission.

———————

If Selden's patent made not a ripple in the embryonic American automotive world, another event that same November transformed it.

In the summer of 1894 the motorcar had progressed sufficiently in Europe—nurtured by roads that had been good since Roman times—for a race to be run the eighty-odd miles between Paris and Rouen. Reports of the contest inspired a young newspaperman named Frederic Adams to approach his boss, Herman Kohlsaat, the owner of the *Chicago Times-Herald*, and suggest that he sponsor a similar race in their town.

Kohlsaat resisted. Surely there couldn't be enough vehicles in America to hold such a race. There will be in a year, Adams said, and Europeans will send some machines if the prize is sufficiently enticing. Kohlsaat thought it over. He was monitoring a confident city in an era that liked machinery, and he decided to put up a five-thousand dollar purse. The race would be held on the inevitable date of July Fourth. Once committed, Kohlsaat sent Adams off around the country to scratch up possible contestants.

Adams did well. Thirty entries came in from Chicago, six each from Indiana and Pennsylvania, five from New York. Just one came from Detroit. Charles King filed it.

Many were from widely scattered places where one might not have expected to find mechanics capable of building automobiles from scratch doing just that: Skowhegan, Maine; Sisterville, West Virginia; Center Point, Iowa; *two* from Pine Bluff, Arkansas. Clearly Adams was fanning isolated sparks that were heating toward a general blaze.

But as spring came to Chicago and no cars did, the July Fourth date began to seem too optimistic. The *Times-Herald* moved the race back to November.

In France that June there was another automobile race, this one from Paris to Bordeaux, eight hundred miles, ten times the distance of the Paris–Rouen contest of less than a year earlier.

The meet reignited interest across the Atlantic. By September Americans had filed five hundred automotive patents. The *Times-Herald* set the date of its race for Thanksgiving Day, and as autumn blew in from the lake, entrants began to show up in Chicago. Adams put their cars on public display in a store on Wabash Avenue, and people turned out to see the automobiles—without, it occurred to Adams, knowing exactly what to call them.

Reassured that he really did have the makings of a race, Kohlsaat let his paper announce another automotive prize: five hundred dollars for giving the horseless carriage a horseless name. Hundreds of entries came in, endless reiterations of "motor" and "auto," "wagon" and "carriage." The prize was divided among three entrants who, visited by the same muse, offered up: motocycle. The *Herald* gamely stuck with the word until the race was done and then, along with the rest of the English-speaking world, abandoned it.

Adams had drummed up nearly ninety entries for the race itself, but by mid-November the list of those who promised to be there had dwindled to eleven. Kohlsaat, already stung by the merry sarcasm of the *Herald's* rival newspapers, wanted to cancel the event. Adams prevailed, and for his pains got to spend a miserable Thanksgiving Eve watching an early snowfall deliver eight heavy, wet inches before turning to sleet.

The race was scheduled to set out at 7:30 from the 1893 fairgrounds, ghostly and radiating no festivity whatever in the gray, stormy morning. By 8:30 six motocycles had managed to make their way to the starting line: two electric-powered ones, the Sturges and the wonderfully named Electrobat, what a reporter described as the "Benz, a gasoline wagon of German make entered by H. Mueller Manufacturing Company," two other Benzes, one entered by Macy's department store, and "the Duryea, a gasoline wagon of Duryea Manufacturing Company."

The Duryea company had been founded in Springfield, Massachusetts, by two brothers, Frank and Charles, and they had made a good machine. Frank would drive; Charles would follow behind with a team of horses to offer whatever support he could.

The automobiles faced a course from Jackson Park to Evanston and back, and what even today would not be an easy drive: fifty-two miles over bad roads heavily drifted with snow and glazed with ice.

Charles King was aboard the Mueller Benz. Like so many other hopeful entrants, he hadn't finished his machine on time. He had, however, been chosen as one of the umpires assigned to accompany each contestant, and would be sitting beside the driver, Oscar Mueller, son of the Mueller company's owner. King's friend Henry Ford had wanted to enter, too, but knew he had no chance of getting ready by Thanksgiving. He stayed behind in Detroit, confident in getting a full report from King.

The race got under way an hour late: The Duryea was waved off at 8:55, the Mueller Benz eleven minutes later. The electrics made a brave start, but the cold and the course soon drained their batteries. The Duryea churned along steadily for the first hour, and then the steering gear broke. "The rules forbid outside help," Charles reported, "but did not forbid borrowing facilities. Being a holiday the [blacksmith] shops were closed and it took a good deal of looking to find any open, but finally one was found and the damage repaired in short order. . . . Fifty-five minutes after the stop, the wagon was off again with a steering that steered, even if it was not perfect. In the meantime the Macy wagon had passed us and gotten thirty-five minutes ahead while a third wagon [no "motocycle" for the Duryeas] had rolled into sight several blocks back." Frank Duryea left it behind and overtook the Macy Benz at Evanston.

All this in gray, gloomy weather, but in midafternoon the sun showed itself and the sudden onset of a fine winter day brought the Chicago gentry out in their sleighs to enjoy the first snowfall of the year. They heard an unfamiliar crackling noise and reined their horses aside to let the Duryea pass, and to get a good look at it. Here was the nineteenth-century equine world at its most appealing, the horses' breath steaming in the clear air, the sparkle and chime of sleigh bells, men and women waving from beneath blankets and furs above the hiss of the runners, all of them in orbit around the dour nucleus of the noisy little motor carriage.

The sky clouded over, and the cheerful allegorical scene dissolved. The day again turned cold and drab, and the sleighs headed for home. Duryea couldn't: He had to keep his wagon banging forward through the snowy dusk.

He crossed the finish line at 7:18. The Mueller Benz, the only other competitor still running, got in an hour and a half later. Charles King was driving, holding the tiller with one hand and supporting his fellow motorist with the other. The rigors of the day had made Oscar Mueller pass out.

Shortly afterward, Charles Duryea wrote about the race in *Horseless Age*, a magazine just founded in response to the excitement over Paris-Bordeaux. "We had run the first road contest in America. We had proven the motor wagon to be superior to the horse on roads decidedly unfavorable to wheels. We had forever answered the objections of the *ultra* conservative people to the effect that the motor wagon could not be of use except on good roads; we had opened a new era; we had let forth a new type of vehicle. No contest or trip over summer roads, or under pleasant skies could have demonstrated our claim for our vehicle as did this trip."

This none too modest assessment was premature. Bellamy Partridge, a pioneer motorist who years later wrote spirited popular histories of the American automobile, pointed out that although in its reporting of the event, the *Times-Herald* "could not have spread itself any more had Chicago been the target of an invasion from Mars," the eastern press was restrained: four column inches in the *New York Herald,* even fewer in the *Times.*

Yet in the end, Duryea was more right than wrong. That race, the wretched conditions under which it was run, the victory of an American car over European competitors, and a sense of the motor carriage leaving horses behind in the winter twilight seeped through the national consciousness.

A Chicago man who had run his sleigh beside the Duryea for a few minutes said something that kept being passed from newspaper to newspaper: "No horse on earth could have made those fifty-four miles."

Less than three months later, the Duryea brothers made a sale, thereby becoming not only the first American carmakers to capitalize on a racing success, but the first to sell an automobile.

———∿∿∿∿∿∿∿∿———

Later on, when Henry Ford liked to toss out provocative and extravagant statements, he sometimes said that he had built the first automobile seen on the streets of Detroit.

The closest this approached the truth was that he had *seen* the first automobile ever seen on the streets of Detroit.

Charles King had made it. He'd returned from his adventure in Chicago to go back to work on his car and had got well along—the engine finished, the chassis taking shape—when the United States Rubber Company let him down: The three-inch pneumatic tires he'd ordered failed to appear.

In their absence, he accepted an offer from Emerson & Fisher, Cincinnati wagon builders who, like so many of their competitors, were beginning to sniff out the promise in the horseless carriage.

Emerson & Fisher, King said much later, "had been considering self-propelled vehicles without arriving at any practical result, and in the hope of getting somewhere loaned me an incomplete, experimental, iron-tired wagon with full privileges to reconstruct it for testing." King transplanted his nearly completed engine into this body. "That wasn't a car," said Barthel, "it was a testing wagon. We merely built it to have something to test the engine in."

Nevertheless, in early March the *Detroit Free Press* reported, "The first horseless carriage seen in this city was out on the streets last night." A newsman from the *Journal* added that "when in motion, the connecting rods fly like lightning, and the machine is capable of running seven or eight miles an hour."

Another witness was Henry Ford, who rode behind his friend's machine on a bicycle, carefully noting the behavior of the first gas-driven vehicle he had ever seen moving under its own power.

Ford went back to his shop. If he felt at all crestfallen that King had beaten him to the street, he has left no record of it. King had strong patents to his name, and the Duryeas were starting to build cars: They were to sell twelve of them that year, America's first automotive production run.

But Ford had a steady job; he had a steady wife; and he seems to have had a steady faith that no matter what the automotive world might serve up, he could better it.

He also knew he was doing something different from King. As Barthel pointed out, King's machine had been given a chassis that King had not chosen. Still, King's inaugural car was a true horseless carriage—or, more accurately, wagon. It weighed thirteen hundred pounds.

The automobile would descend not from the horse-and-wagon, but from the bicycle: lithe, supple, mechanically sophisticated, and, above all, light. "The most beautiful things in the world," Ford said a quarter century later, "are those from which all excess weight has been eliminated." The car he was working on would weigh five hundred pounds.

The engine, the thing that would actually replace the horse in the equation, was Ford's most urgent concern, and the one that made the greatest demands on him.

He had decided on a four-cycle engine. The first gas motors, following the example of their steam predecessors, were two-cycle. In the steam engines of the day, every stroke of the piston was a power stroke. That is, the steam, fed in from outside the cylinder, entered under pressure and pushed the piston from one side and then, once the piston drove its distance, gave it a second punch from the other.

This turned out not to be good enough for the gasoline engine. As it began to reveal its properties, the gas engine demanded that the power come from an explosion inside the cylinder—rather than being pumped in from the outside—and that driving the piston on every stroke fouled the mechanism. The two-cycle system didn't allow enough time to exhaust the burned gas, or to draw in a fresh mixture of gas and air.

Everything happens so quickly with gasoline. As Maxim had discovered, it's a powerful elixir, vigorous enough to give the piston a push that would carry the crankshaft to which it was connected around twice before the next push had to come.

Henry Ford explained this economically and well: "'Four-cycle' means that the piston traverses the cylinder four times to get one power impulse. The first stroke draws in the gas, the second compresses it, the third is the explosion or power stroke, while the fourth exhausts the waste gas."

But how to ignite the compressed gas without the help of a ceiling fixture? That would mean a battery, which could be bought from the outside rather than designed—like the doorbell Ford would mount on the front of his vehicle to warn of its approach (although considering how noisy the engine was likely to be, this seems a redundant precaution).

For the ignition mechanism itself—the "sparking device," Ford called it—he drew on two more of the helpers he so easily recruited. An electrician named George Cato came up with an "ignitor" that would explode the gas, and helped Ford build two of them. Edwin S. Huff, who went under the irresistible nickname of "Spider," helped him on other parts of the engine—and would stick by Ford in some scary places in the years to come.

The ignition was difficult. The transmission was difficult, finally evolving into a combination of belts and a chain drive to the rear wheels. Everything was difficult. But the work went forward.

Valves proved particularly vexing, until King gave Ford four steam valves that he'd been working on, and Ford figured out how to adapt them to serve a gasoline engine. He avoided the problems of inventing a carburetor by not trying. Instead, he mounted the gas tank above the engine, so that gravity would do the job of getting the fuel to the intake where it blended with the air.

He took his car body off the sawhorses that had supported it for months; he had the machine on its wheels. He had eliminated so much excess weight that he could lift the front or rear end by himself until he put the engine in. Even then, the thing was easy to push back and forth, and needed to be because it had no reverse gear.

It never would. In May the Indianapolis Chain and Stamping Company delivered an order—put in for Ford by Charles King—for ten feet of $1^1/8$-inch "bright" at twenty-five cents a foot. This was what would finally transmit the power to the wheels.

Ford threaded it into place, fitting the sprocket teeth between the pins that held the links together, and tightened it, and that was that. What he was already calling his Quadricycle was finished. There was nothing left to do except take it for a drive.

Gleaming with promise and moody with its capacity to wreck its builder's highest plans, the Quadricycle stood in its brick shed. Ford's benevolent witness Felix Julien had probably gone to bed; it was after two o'clock in the morning. Clara was there carrying an umbrella, for it was June now—most likely, the fourth of June—and a spring rain was falling.

Henry Ford almost never expressed anxiety, but he was frank about having not been able to sleep for the last two nights.

There is another indication of his worry, as well as of the intensity with which he had pursued his project. Only when he began to push the Quadricycle toward the door did he realize it was too wide to fit through.

The man who had spent so much painstaking time with small, cunningly cut pieces of metal took up an ax in the woodshed, and in a few minutes had splintered the doorframe and knocked a gap-toothed opening through the brick wall that surrounded it. He and Bishop pushed the car out into the alley.

Clara went back into the house to bring a sleepy Edsel to the front steps so the three-year-old could see his father carry off the triumph in which her faith had never lagged.

Ford and Bishop got the car pointed in the right direction. Ford set the current running from the battery and spun the flywheel. The engine took: The Quadricycle transformed itself from plumbing into creature.

Ford climbed up on it. The small carriage seat he'd ordered either hadn't arrived or had gotten there too late. He perched on a bicycle seat.

Bishop wheeled out in front of him—he'd be cycling ahead to warn any horse-drivers that might be out so late that drizzling night. Ford pulled back on the lever that tightened the driving belt. The Quadricycle ran along the alley to Bagley, and then Ford turned onto Grand River Avenue, moving forward into his future and ours.

CHAPTER 5

What Edison Said

*Ford's first sale; "There's a young fellow who has made a gas car";
Ford's first company; a winter drive with "civilization's latest lisp";
dissolution: "Henry wasn't ready."*

Ford had just started up Washington Boulevard on his maiden voyage when a metallic snap and a clatter on the wet cobbles told him something had failed. The car rolled to a stop. Bishop cycled back and Ford figured out that a nut holding the spring on a valve stem had jumped off. The Edison plant was a few hundred yards away. The two men pushed the car over to it and Ford got the needed part from his colleagues. Watched by a few night owls from the nearby Cadillac Hotel, who were grateful for such a diversion at this hour, Ford, working in the spill of light from the plant's tall windows, screwed on the new nut and got the Quadricycle started again. Then, Bishop preceding him, he made his way back to Bagley Avenue.

The two men got a couple of hours of sleep, and Clara made breakfast. Despite his successful trial run, Ford was worried about the shed. He drew again on the bounties of the Edison plant and persuaded two bricklayers to come restore the mutilated door.

They had barely begun when Ford's landlord, a prosperous wholesale meat dealer named William Wreford, stopped by to collect the June rent and demanded to know what was going on with his shed.

Ford said it was being repaired, and in a couple of hours would be good as new. Wreford was not placated. "What did you do it for?"

Ford explained that he'd had to get his motor carriage "out to see if it would run."

Wreford immediately saw that this was more interesting than anything his other tenants might be up to. "You ran it?"

"Yes, sir."

"Let me see it."

Ford at his most engaging explained his car to the landlord, who concluded his visit with a thought that possibly had not yet occurred to the inventor. "Say! If these fellows put the wall back up, how are you going to get your car out again? I've got an idea. Tell the bricklayers to leave the opening and then you can put on swinging doors. That will let you in and out."

By the end of the day William Wreford owned what was almost certainly the first purpose-built garage in America, and Ford was back at work on his car.

The Quadricycle ran, but its brief nocturnal trial had revealed a host of weaknesses. "The original machine was air-cooled—or to be more accurate, the motor was simply not cooled at all," Ford said. The engine ran so hot that after a while it began to bleed silvery drops of solder, "striking the ground and looking like dimes." Ford took care of this: "I very shortly put a water jacket around the cylinders and piped it to a tank in the rear of the car over the cylinders." But the chassis was all wood, and that wasn't going to serve.

A few weeks after his first drive, Ford made an opportune—indeed, opportunistic—hire at Detroit Edison. A Scottish-born mechanic named David Bell came to the chief engineer and said he was looking for work as a blacksmith.

"What kind of blacksmith are you?"

"A carriage blacksmith."

"You come to work," Ford said.

Bell reported for duty, and discovered that most of it involved the Quadricycle. He fabricated sturdier wheels, a better steering arrangement, substituted iron piping for wood throughout the body, with at least some help from his boss (Bell is the recruit who said, "I never saw Mr. Ford make anything").

The buggy seat replaced the bicycle seat, and Ford began to take Clara and Edsel for rides. One autumn day, he felt confident enough to try a run out to the family farm in Dearborn.

His sister Margaret remembered his arrival there for the rest of her life: "My first sight of the little car was as it came west along what is now Ford Road. The wheels on one side were deep in the rut made by the farm wagons while the wheels on the other side were high in the center of the road. Henry had built the car in such a way that the distance between the wheels was less than that of the wagons and carriages, thus it was driven in this way on a road which had ruts. Clara and Edsel were with him and all of them were sitting on the slanted seat. . . .

"Henry took all of us for rides during the day, and I well remember the peculiar sensation of what seemed to be a great speed and the sense of bewilderment I felt when I first rode in this carriage which moved without a horse. Henry particularly enjoyed explaining the mechanical details to his younger brother, and I am sure that he enjoyed scaring the life out of his sisters."

Henry's father, Margaret said, "was as interested as all of us in the fact that here was the horseless carriage about which we had been hearing. He looked it all over and listened with interest to Henry's explanation of it, but he refused to ride in it." Nevertheless, "Father was very proud of Henry's achievement. He talked to us at home and he told his neighbors about it."

Charles King has left a more somber account of that first ride out into the country. "I could see that old Mr. Ford was ashamed at a grown-up man like Henry fussing over a little thing like a quadricycle. We'd gone and humiliated him in front of his friends. Henry stood it as long as he could, then he turned to me and said, in a heartbroken way, 'Come on Charlie, let's you and me get out of here.'"

This bleakly satisfying picture of the inventor as solitary visionary, scorned even by those closest to him, seems in Ford's case to be untrue. Margaret flatly denied it. "I do not believe the story which has been told of a visit of Henry and Mr. King to the homestead and of their talks with Father. Neither my brother William nor myself can remember any such incident. We are both sure that if any such incident had occurred, Father would have talked about it at home. Clara also did not recall any such visit." If William Ford was too cautious to take a ride that day, the reason was not shame about what Henry was up to. Once a week or so William liked to go into Detroit, stop at Jimmie Burns's saloon for some whiskey and a sirloin steak (he never shared his son's strong views about the evils of drink), and then seek out Henry and ask him how the car was coming along.

Coming along fine, Henry would have answered, for he kept improving and testing it. He drove it, he said, about a thousand miles around the streets of Detroit. In the beginning, he remembered, it caused such a stir that if he stopped it "anywhere in town a crowd was around before I could start up again. If I left it alone even for a minute some inquisitive person always tried to run it. Finally I had to carry a chain and chain it to a lamppost whenever I left it anywhere."

Not one of those curious bystanders had ever driven a car, so it is hard to see how they could have started it running, let alone motored off in it. But Detroit was a city full of able mechanics and engineers, and perhaps just a few moments looking at the trim, cleanly designed four-horsepower engine—for the first months of the car's life fully exposed to view—would have revealed its secrets to them.

In time Ford covered the engine and completed all the improvements he thought his Quadricycle could bear. Then he was through with it. His first car, the object of years of steady work, had served its purpose and, as with the Christmas Eve engine, Ford "didn't stop to play with it." He sold it for two hundred dollars. "That was my first sale. I had built the car not to sell but to experiment with. I wanted to start another car. Ainsley [actually, Charles Annesely, a wealthy

Detroit friend of those days] wanted to buy. I could use the money and we had no trouble in agreeing upon price."

By the time the Quadricycle left its builder's hands it had become an impressively capable automobile, as Ford learned in the spring of 1899 when he got a letter from a bicycle dealer named A. W. Hall, an acquaintance of his who had bought the car from Annesely.

Friend Ford—

. . . You will be surprised when I tell you that the little carriage is still doing its usual duty. I disposed of it this spring and the little rig was still in fair shape after all the banging around that it has had and I guess you know that was considerable; I ran it almost two years as you know and about the only trouble I had was that one tire and the springs on the sparkers working loose, but you know how they were fastened and there was nothing to prevent them from doing so, until I put on a binding bolt and after that I never had any more trouble with it. . . .

I was out in Chicago all last fall and looked over the few horseless rigs there and among them all I did not see one I would of rather had had than that little rig for when it comes right down to simplicity they were not in it. . . .

Hall could not know it, but his praise for the car's "simplicity" was powerfully prophetic.

Henry Ford bought the Quadricycle back, for sixty dollars, probably in 1905. By then he had made himself known, had founded a motorcar company, and possibly was beginning to believe that his experimental gas buggy might someday be a historical artifact that could stand alongside the frigate *Constitution* and the Liberty Bell.

———∿∿∿∿∿∿∿———

Less than a month after his trial run, Ford got a new boss. The highly competent Alexander Dow had given up running Detroit's municipal lighting system to become manager of the Edison operations in the city. He soon learned that his superintendent had a second job that he carried on in a number of satellite workshops: the Bagley Avenue woodshed, a basement across the street from Detroit Edison that he had rented for the friendly tariff of seventy-five cents a month (the magnet at work again), and any Edison plant machinery that happened to be idle at the time he needed it.

These arrangements would not have pleased every new employer, but Dow thought highly of Ford, as is evidenced by the manager's immediately asking him to come to New York for the seventeenth annual convention of the Association of Edison Illuminating Companies. Only one other Detroit employee, the company's attorney, got invited.

The convention was held on Coney Island—or, as the report of its proceedings made clear, "Manhattan Beach, Brooklyn." Manhattan Beach was on the island's eastern end, where three immense frame hotels stretched their verandas along hundreds of yards of Atlantic shorefront. Their operators were careful to emphasize the location's distance, in tone at least, from the raffish district to the west where, amid jovial violence, the modern amusement park was busy being born.

Henry Ford would not have visited the district's ample offering of saloons, but surely he would have enjoyed its amusements: for instance, that mechanical incarnation of the practical joke, the roller coaster, invented here a decade earlier.

There is no record that he rode one, but he did encounter something that interested him more than any roller coaster, and perhaps even more than the automobile itself: Thomas Edison.

Henry Ford's career is so thoroughly brined in myth—much of it tended by the carmaker himself—that his meeting with Edison might seem like folklore, but in fact that August he spent three days with the man who played much the same role in the nineteenth century that Ford would in the twentieth.

The conference took place beneath the confection of vaguely pagoda-like towers that complicated the roof of the Oriental, classiest of the hotels. The delegates heard papers read through several sessions—Dow spoke on "The Selection of Alternating-Current Apparatus for Central-Lighting Stations"—and then gathered together again for dinner.

Dow had much faith in Ford, but little in the internal combustion engine. He was an electricity man. Edison had set up his Pearl Street Station, the first central power plant in the country, in Manhattan just thirteen years earlier, and that was modern enough for Dow. On the second night, August 12, he and Ford were seated at Edison's table. The group had been discussing batteries that day, and the talk turned to their use in powering automobiles.

Dow pointed across to Ford and said loudly—everyone spoke loudly around Edison, because he was half deaf—"There's a young fellow who has made a gas car!"

Ford believed the perfectly accurate statement contained a barb of mockery. Possibly Dow hoped that here, next to the man who might as well have invented electricity, Ford could be laughed out of his fixation on gasoline.

Dow went on to tell how he had looked out his office window one day to see his superintendent, wife, and little boy "pop pop popping" past beneath. He made fun of the engine noise because electric cars ran silently.

Servants of electricity though they all were, everyone at the table turned to Ford with interest, including Edison himself, who was clearly struggling to hear. Noticing this, the man next to him got up and gestured Ford into his chair.

"Is it a four-cycle engine?" Edison at once asked. Ford said it was. What ignited the gas in the cylinder?

"I told him that it was a make-and-break contact that was pumped apart by the piston and drew a diagram for him of the whole contact arrangement." He was going to improve this on his next car, Ford said, and went on to draw "what today we would call a spark plug; it was really an insulating plug with a make-and-break mechanism, using washers of mica. I drew that too."

Edison kept asking questions, and Ford kept drawing, "For I have always found that I could convey an idea quicker by sketching it than by just describing it."

When he was finished Edison banged a fist on the table so hard "that the dishes around him jumped," and said, "Young man, that's the thing; you have it. Keep at it."

He went on to dismiss the competition: "Electric cars must keep near to power stations. The storage battery is too heavy. Steam cars won't do either, for they have to have a boiler and fire. Your car is self-contained—carries its own power-plant—no fire, no boiler, no smoke and no steam. You have the thing. Keep at it."

Edison finished by telling Ford "that for the purpose any gas motor was better than any electric motor could be—it could go long distances, he said, and there would be stations to supply the cars with hydro-carbon. That was the first time I ever heard this term for liquid fuel."

Remembering the evening some thirty-five years later Ford said, "That bang on the table meant the world to me." He went on with an extremely rare mention about having entertained doubts: "I had hoped that I was headed right, sometimes I only wondered if I was, but here all at once and out of a clear sky the greatest inventive genius in the world had given me a complete approval."

While Ford made his way back from New York, Clara waited for him with her family in Greenfield, where she'd taken Edsel to get away from the city, simmering in a bad August. "The heat was so great we could hardly stand it," she wrote her husband the day after his talk with Edison. ". . . And then the dreadful storms. I thought surely we would have a Cyclone that day. . . . It is 5 PM now and the baby is having a glorious time on the lawn . . . I asked him if he would like to send Papa a kiss and he said yes paper him over one. Just like one of his speeches. . . . I suppose you have seen great sights. . . . I hope things will be all right at the Station so that you can come out. For I want you awful bad."

Things were fine at the station, and Ford went out to Greenfield. He told Clara: "You are not going to see very much of me until I am through with this car."

Ford recounted this remark decades later with the implication that Edison had inspired him to persevere. Although of course he was pleased to have had his project so magnificently anointed, he would surely have kept pursuing it even if Edison had delivered a sermon on the primacy of the horse. And his wife had long ago learned not to count on seeing him too much.

Ford started on his second automobile. The work went slowly, because he kept improving the car while it took shape—something more easily done with, say, an oil painting than a transmission. Years later Bell remembered making the handrails for the seat and the radius rods and "a small device to form the spokes for the four wheels." But "I made many other things which were not used—because Mr. Ford had some other thought in mind that might work better. He was still experimenting."

Bishop helped, and so did Spider Huff, who had a more intuitive and inventive grasp of electrical systems than Ford. He also had a host of interests his friend did not share: tobacco, hard liquor, serial divorce (Huff would marry seven times). He was no roisterer; he was always quiet and thoughtful. Always dependable, too, except when some internal spur would drive him into an unannounced exile in his native Kentucky. Ford paid the bills he left behind, and always welcomed him when he returned.

On April 7, 1897, Ford filed a patent application for a carburetor. Forty years later a man named R. W. Hanington still had a clear memory of speaking to him about it, and wrote to tell Ford so in 1939.

Hanington, an engineer, had come east from Denver to work with Charles Duryea, who was building cars on his own in New Jersey. Not long after their Chicago triumph the brothers had squabbled and split up, and for the rest of their lives would be running separate operations, thereby very possibly robbing themselves of standing in history with Chrysler, Ford, and General Motors. Hanington found the factory a disappointment—indeed, "a total failure"—and after a few months decided to go home. Along the way, though, he ambitiously set out "to see every motor wagon that was being attempted."

Half a lifetime later he told Ford that "the last stop was Detroit where . . . I had the pleasure of an hour's interview with you in the engine room of a large electric plant. . . . You were working on an ingenious device for feeding gasoline into the cylinder."

During his visit, Hanington also conducted a bit of industrial espionage, sending a highly detailed confidential report on Ford's second car to a friend who was interested in the new industry.

Ford never knew of this document, but he would have been pleased by what it contained: "The design of the motor is excellent . . . similar to that of the Springfield Duryea's [Charles's brother Frank] wagon. The sparker is better, however. . . . The carburetor is good. . . . The design of the gearing is compact and well-balanced. . . . The whole design strikes me as being very complete, and worked out in every detail, and . . . the carriage should be the equal of any that has been built in this country."

Hanington was obviously a capable and observant engineer. The conclusion of his report is a succinct summary—still sound today—of what would, in little more than a decade, enable Henry Ford to sell more cars than all the rest of the American automakers combined: "It is apparently a first-class carriage, well thought out and well constructed, but embodying no *novel* feature of great importance. Novelty, rather than good design, has been the idea of most of the carriage builders.

"Simplicity, strength and common sense seem to be embodied in Mr. Ford's carriage, and I believe that these ideals are essential ones for a successful vehicle."

Hanington sent off his report shortly after the Christmas of 1898. The next July, on a bright Saturday that promised good weather, Ford drove his second car into a prosperous Detroit neighborhood and parked in front of a house there. He went up to the door and spoke to the owner, William H. Murphy. "I am ready to take you on that ride," he said.

Murphy was ready to go on it. He got into the car, and Ford set off. They drove through the summer afternoon to Orchard Lake, and then returned to Detroit by way of Pontiac. All during the eighty-mile excursion Murphy made notes in his lurching seat about how much gasoline the car was consuming, how it behaved on good roads and bad. The car did well throughout, bringing them back to Murphy's house in three and a half hours—a lightning run, considering the roads of the era and the capriciousness of any motor carriage that traveled them.

Murphy climbed down from his seat. "Well," he said to his driver, "now we will organize a company."

Murphy was a rich man. Lumber had made him rich. Born in Bangor, Maine, when there was still first-growth timber to cut down there, he had both followed and helped push what loggers called "the big clearing" west to Detroit. Henry Ford found the time, while bringing his genial presence to welding shops and metal turners, to cultivate people like Murphy, the people who ran Detroit.

Later, cleaving to the familiar inventor myth, Ford liked to suggest that he kept his flame burning despite the indifference of the mighty, and even in the face of their efforts to extinguish it. In fact, he had been careful to make friends with them. He used the same techniques that worked in the foundries—Henry's here! He's lively; he's helpful; oh, he's gone—perhaps to greater effect in the turn-of-the-century years that followed the completion of his second car than ever again. His habits, says Sidney Olson, who has tracked him with the most scrupulous care through that time, "are the despair of biographers." Ford was then "a real slippery creature. He is elusive, baffling, protean; submerged, he slides along for a month or two and then pops up in a dozen places at once, like a whole school of dolphins."

He's getting Fred Strauss to machine the mysterious camshaft, he's making himself agreeable to James McMillan, who gave him his first job in the Michigan Car Works, and who has joined his brother Hugh to establish the Detroit Car Wheel Company to make sure the cars have a steady supply of something to move on. The brothers command the largest industrial operation in Michigan, as is suggested by the spacious name of the railroad they own most of: the Duluth, South Shore & Atlantic.

He's making friends with a younger McMillan, William, who not only supervises his father's and uncle's finances, but sits as secretary and treasurer on the ten boards, four of their names beginning with "Detroit": Iron Mining Company; Iron Furnace Company; Railroad Elevator Company; Transportation Company.

William C. Maybury, the city's popular new mayor, likes the motor carriage enthusiast. He amiably gives Ford an official "chauffeur's license"—as official, that is, as an orally issued license can be.

These were some of the people Henry Ford had been making himself agreeable to when he wasn't busy thinking through a new flange or bolt to replace one that his shop helpers believed was already perfectly satisfactory.

To whatever Goldsmith's business school had taught Ford, his duties at Edison had added knowledge about how corporations work, how a big enterprise is organized and how capital gets fed into it. Alexander Dow thought his employee had learned a great deal, and at about the time of Ford's drive with Murphy, Dow recorded in his notebook that he'd "had a talk with Henry as to what part he cared to play in some big plans we were about to carry out."

The plans included Ford: He would become general superintendent of the Detroit Illuminating Company, with a nearly doubled salary of nineteen hundred dollars a year. But it was a demanding job, and would not allow time for automotive experimentation. Dow was friendly and conciliatory: "I offered him the best I then had, in the work upon which my heart was set." Dow's heart, though; not Ford's.

"I had to choose between my job and my automobile," Ford said. "I chose the automobile, or rather I gave up the job—there was really nothing in the way of a choice. For already I knew that the car was bound to be a success. I quit my job on August 15, 1899, and went into the automobile business."

The automobile business was waiting for him. Ten days earlier the papers for the Detroit Automobile Company had been filed: It was capitalized at $150,000, with $15,000 in actual money already put up by a dozen solid Detroit citizens. Henry Ford was superintendent, had some stock in the company, and a salary of $150 a month. Ford and his backers had been shown a suitable factory building, on Cass Avenue, earlier that spring.

Here is Henry Ford the planner working at his shrewdest. When he left Detroit Edison, writes Olson, "We watch Henry leap from security to security. The new job is well in hand before he quits the old; everything is carefully set, with artillery preparation laid on, before he moves."

True enough, but so is what Ford said about his new job. "It might be thought something of a step, for I had no personal funds. What money was left over from living was all used up in experimenting. . . . There was no 'demand' for automobiles—there never is for a new article."

That his move actually was a tremendous gamble is suggested by the fact that not one of his Detroit Edison friends, these men who thought nothing of staying up all night long milling and welding on Ford's behalf, would risk joining his new concern.

He urged Bell, rebuilder of the Quadricycle, to come along: "Dave, Dave, you'll go with the business."

Bell said, "Henry, I've got a wife and family and I can't take the chance."

Ford said he couldn't pay Bell "wages, but he would keep a record. He'd give me a paper for it."

Decades later, Bell said with matter-of-fact rue, "It would have made me rich."

In the end, of all Ford's old friends, only Fred Strauss joined him. Strauss had come with Ford to see the Cass Avenue factory, and only then discovered that Ford was interested in automobiles.

One associate followed without hesitation: "My wife agreed that the automobile could not be given up—that we had to make or break."

Clara Ford's first two decades with her husband seem a study in unassuming courage. In 1897 they'd moved from Bagley Avenue to an eighth home, and now—with the seven-year-old Edsel just starting out in public school—they'd be moving again, to Second Boulevard near the Detroit Automobile Company.

The backers were far more confident than the Edison Illuminating crew. They signed a three-year lease on the factory, and announced that the first cars would be finished by October first. Frank Alderman, secretary of Detroit Automobile, said, "We have several new devices in connection with the construction of our automobiles, on which patents are now pending, which will make them as near perfect as they can be made. We have solved the problem of the bad odor [of half-burned fuel] by securing perfect combustion, and with our improved method of applying power to the rear axle and keeping all the machinery hidden from sight, we will have a fine motor carriage. We expect to have 100 to 150 men employed before the year is past."

October came and went, and so did November and December, and no motor carriage left the gates of the Detroit Automobile Company. It was not until mid-January that the first car emerged.

It wasn't a car; it was a "delivery wagon," perhaps chosen by Ford to demonstrate the versatility of internal combustion: Here was no toy; this can take an honorable place in the working world.

The delivery wagon, a glossy cube riding high above four pneumatic tires, could not have had a more auspicious advent. Just a little over a month into the new century Henry Ford took a reporter from the *Detroit News-Tribune* for a ride. The man was fascinated by his adventure and wrote an account of it that took over the front page of the paper's second section on the first Sunday in February.

"Swifter Than a Race-horse It Flew Over the Icy Streets," the headline ran. The text beneath offers a glimpse of Ford as promoter, and a feel of the tug of his magnet.

The reporter came into the factory out of a bitter day when, the story's subhead says, "Mercury hovered about zero." Inside was the wagon, "smooth-covered, box-topped, with black enamel sides, red wheels, and running gear, nothing but the absence of the proverbial horse revealed that the motive power was to come from within."

Ford said hello, and filled the tank with three gallons of gasoline—

enough, he explained, to "run the automobile 100 miles or more at the rate of a cent a mile."

He yanked the engine into life, a worker pushed open a factory door, and "with incomparable swiftness the machine picked up its speed and glided into the wind-blown street. . . .

"The puffing of the machine assumed a higher key. She was flying along at about eight miles an hour. The ruts in the road were deep, but the machine certainly went with dream-like smoothness. There was none of the bumping common even to a streetcar."

"Hold on tight," Ford told his passenger. "When we strike the asphalt we will have a run."

"How fast?"

"Twenty-five miles an hour."

"Hold on!" yelled the reporter in delighted mock-terror. "I get out."

Instead he spotted an approaching milk wagon whose "horse shivered as though about to run away."

"Ever frighten horses?" he asked Ford.

"Depends on the horse." Which might have seemed answer enough during a freezing ride along a busy street, but which Ford eagerly expanded: "A low-bred, ignorant horse, yes; a high-born fellow, no. There's as much difference between horses as between dogs. Some are wise, some otherwise. The other day I was passing down in front of the Majestic building in the big crush; along came a man with a speeding cart and racer. Alderman, who was with me, told me to slack down, as there would surely be trouble. The racer came flying right by us and merely gave a side glance. He was too wise to show any emotion."

In return, the reporter embarked on a meditation on the aural forces of history.

"Whiz! She picked up speed with infinite rapidity. As she ran on, there was a clattering behind—the new noise of the automobile.

"There has always been, at each decisive period of the world's history, some voice, some note that represented for the time being the prevailing power."

Once "the supreme cry of authority" had been the lion's roar. Then came the "hammering of the stone axe" and "the slapping of oars in the Roman galleys." Wind against sails next, and the all-transforming concussion of gunpowder and then, for generations, "the shriek of the steam whistle has been the compelling power of civilization."

But now the reporter is hearing "in the streets of Detroit the murmur of this newest and most perfect of forces, the automobile, rushing along at the rate of 25 miles an hour.

"What kind of a noise is it?

"That is difficult to put down on paper. It was not like any other sound heard in the world. It is not like the puff! puff! of the exhaust of the gasoline in a river launch; neither is it like the cry! cry! of a working steam engine; but it is a long quick mellow gurgling sound, not harsh, not unmusical, not distressing; a note that falls with pleasure on the ear. It must be heard to be appreciated. And the sooner you hear its newest chuck! chuck! the sooner you will be in touch with civilization's latest lisp, its newest voice."

Ford's visionary passenger watched a couple of horses hearing the "new voice" for the first time, but before it could register on them, "the auto had slipped like a sunbeam around the corner."

At one point during this perfect jaunt Ford pointed out a storefront to the reporter. "See that harness-maker's shop? His trade is doomed."

Not yet, though, and not by the Detroit Automobile Company's delivery wagon.

It ran well enough that cold day to light the flues of the reporter's imagination, to give him a taste of the exhilaration that would seize so many people in the next ten years. Here was an engine of liberation, an epochal break with the past.

Many of the men who worked on the delivery wagon, however, said that far from cornering like a sunbeam, it could barely crawl around the block. In a tone quite different from that of Ford's passenger, Fred Strauss remembered, "We did get one of the engines to run on this car, but we had an awful time doing it." Its flywheel was too heavy; all of it was too heavy; and it took far too long to build.

Ford was looking toward quantity production, but didn't yet know how to do it. Every day in the factory was a frustrating lesson in stasis: Engines stood inert on sawhorses until they were tapped and filed and worried into completion, then moved to a chassis. That is, if the components of the chassis had arrived. Almost everything came from outside manufacturers. Meanwhile bodies were being built at the rate of violins, cosseted in every stage of their development.

Nobody knows how many cars came out of the Detroit Automobile Company. Perhaps no more than a dozen; possibly fewer than that.

Part of the problem was the scattered state of an enterprise that was still too nascent to properly be called an industry. Part of it was Ford's perfectionism. But there seems to have been something else that was holding back the best-financed automobile company of its day. Ford disliked working for backers, even though he understood the necessity of having them, and this may have slowed his pace, though by all accounts during that time he was working steadily and hard. Surely he would have felt an increasing frustration at being unable simply to will speedier production.

One gets a sad glimpse of this in Fred Strauss's summary of the sinking Detroit Automobile Company. "Henry wasn't ready. He didn't have an automobile design ready. . . . Henry gave me some sketches to turn up some axle shaftings. I started machining these axle shafts to show them we were doing something . . . but they didn't belong to anything. We never used them for the automobile. It was just a stall, until Henry got a little longer into it."

But busy pointless machining and, later, gears laid out in gleaming patterns on worktables could not forever divert the backers from seeing that none of this enterprise was coalescing into cars.

A few months after his confident predictions, Alderman glumly observed, "You'd be surprised at the amount of detail about an automobile."

By the summer most of the directors were beginning to get disgusted with Ford, although Murphy remained loyal to him. At one point the backers convened a meeting that Ford, who by now had managed to persuade himself that he was being ill-used, refused to attend. "If they ask for me," he told Strauss, formulating a fib he would use again and again down the years, "tell them that I had to go out of town."

The day after the meeting, Alderman told Strauss the company was going to move out of the big factory and lay off most of its workers. Strauss could keep a few of them to run a much smaller experimental shop.

The show table of pretty machinery would have to go, said one particularly hard-nosed director. "Throw all that stuff out, bury it, get rid of it."

Strauss was especially saddened by the condemnation of four truck bodies that "were as elaborately built, designed, painted and finished as are pianos." There was no reprieve. "We put them in the boiler room. Charlie Mitchell our blacksmith, and I took sledge hammers and busted all those beautiful bodies. Then we burned them under the engine-room boiler."

To this desolate scene, said Strauss, "All at once Henry came in one morning and came into the experimental shop." He had Spider Huff with him and they got right to work on what Strauss called a "little car."

If Ford felt any grief for his fast-as-a-racehorse delivery wagon and its beautiful woodwork, he never said a word about it.

The little car—which seems to be what the directors wanted from him in the first place—was a regular automobile and, according to Strauss, "It ran pretty good."

Not good enough for its creator, who kept making improvements while autumn turned to winter and the stockholders fretted and then began to pull out. Mayor Maybury, now running for governor, stood by Ford, and even bought more shares, bringing his holding up to five hundred. So did Murphy, who continued meeting the bills. He had met eighty-six thousand dollars of them before the Detroit Automobile Company filed notice of dissolution in January 1901.

Still Murphy stuck. The lumberman and a handful of the original shareholders bought up the remnants of the company at a receiver's sale and kept financing Ford.

No record remains of how generously they were backing him, but perhaps there is a hint in the fact that in January Henry and Clara moved into their tenth home, with Henry's father and sister Jane, who themselves had recently left the family farm to spend the winter in the city. William Ford paid the rent.

His son wasn't there as much as Clara would have liked. The diary she kept for a few months at that time is full of entries like the one in which she recounts her surprise and pleasure at having "met Henry on the crowded streetcar coming home." On February 1 she "spent half hour with Henry, then took the train to Kate's"—her sister, in Jasper, Michigan, who was about to have a baby. On February 3, "Snow all day. Wrote a letter to Henry. Felt pretty lonely."

Her husband must have, too. He was spending nights on a cot he'd set up in the small patch of the Cass Avenue factory that his backers had saved for him. But the shadowy galleries around him, hired for a production run that never materialized, seemed to depress him not at all. He and Spider Huff and Oliver Barthel were working steadily. So, too, was a twenty-two-year-old newcomer with the Byronic name of Childe Harold Wills (he never used the Childe, but did pass it on to his son).

Wills's father was a master mechanic. His son wanted to be a painter—when he was seventeen the *Detroit City Directory* listed him as an "artist boarding at home"—but the next year he was working as an apprentice toolmaker while studying metallurgy in night school. Within three years he had not only gotten a job in the engineering department of what would become the Burroughs Adding Machine Company, but was its superintendent.

Automobiles interested him more and more, and he sought out Henry Ford. The two men discovered an instant affinity that went beyond Ford's ability to charm good people into working for him.

Like Ford, Wills was happy to work two jobs, or at least indifferent to the pressures of doing so. Unlike Ford he was a brilliant draftsman. Where the former could instinctively know the strengths and weaknesses of any machine he could look at and touch, the latter could envision the machine, put it on paper, and see whether it would work well or not, all without going near a lathe.

What they—Ford, Wills, Huff, Barthel—were trying to make that spring of 1901 had nothing to do with the "little car" that, if ever produced, might sell to a public that was growing more confident in the future of the automobile. In fact, it was that car's antithesis.

CHAPTER 6

"Glory and Dust"

*"We had to race"; Smiling Billy's World's Championship Sweepstakes;
Ford vs. Winton: "A thin man can run faster than a fat one"; the
Henry Ford Company; "The materialization of a nightmare."*

"I never thought anything of racing," Ford said long afterward. This seems true: He had grown up without once seeing that then ubiquitous American diversion, a horse race. But now he was building a race car.

Ford later explained that he'd had no choice: "The public refused to consider the automobile in any light other than as a fast toy. Therefore we had to race."

It is true that the public had become interested in auto racing. Rich Americans were buying heavy, expensive European machines. William K. Vanderbilt, an early and loyal enthusiast, brought over the "Red Devil," a thirty-five-horsepower Mercedes so costly he had to pay seven thousand dollars on it just in customs duties. He raced it, and won, and generated headlines across the country. There was prize money to be made as well: The Chicago races run the September before had offered a purse of ten thousand dollars.

Still, there seems something disingenuous in Ford's insistence that this spectacular road was the only one open to him. He was still getting support to build a motorcar for regular folks, not moneyed daredevils, and if only he could bring the "little car" to a point where he could say: There; that's it; this is how we'll build it, he had a far better chance than most would-be car builders of getting into production.

He couldn't say it. Possibly he sensed launching his car on the seas of trade as some final surrender of control. Perhaps he still was not confident he could produce cars in any quantity. The great advantage of a race car was that you could enjoy a famous success making only one.

The drawback was that it had better *be* a success. Once Ford had committed himself to the racer, he was quite right about the importance of racing, at least as far as Henry Ford was concerned. If his car failed, that was the end of even tenuous financial support for his automaking ambitions. He could try to get his Edison job back, and then tinker with the little car as a hobby for the rest of his days.

———～～～～～～———

Ford put into the racer all the energy his backers urged him to devote to the car they wanted to produce. The one they didn't diverted Ford from his love of lightness. It took shape at sixteen hundred pounds, which was not heavy for racing cars of the day, but three times the weight of the Quadricycle. Barthel worked closely with Ford—so closely that, fifty years later, he claimed to have "designed the car from the ground up," and its engine, too. The latter had two seven-inch cylinders, lying horizontally, mounted beneath the driver. This was the traditional place, but out ahead of the engine coils of thin copper cooling tubes serving as a radiator were strung across a sort of maw in the front of the hood. For, unlike most automobiles and any that Ford had yet built, this car *had* a hood: It looked like a car. Its machinery was not encased in the shell of a horse-drawn carriage (some of the first automakers were so respectful of tradition that they mounted sockets for buggy whips on their machines).

Scientific American admired the completed car in an article not about technology but aesthetics called "Style in Automobiles." The author, a motoring enthusiast named Hrolf Wisby, complained that "comparatively little is being done by the automobile makers toward guiding the public taste." Instead, they were pandering to "horsey people" with "horseless carriages of a horsey style." This is "a silly combination. An automobile is not merely a vehicle bereft of horses."

Only the racing car, said Wisby, "is progressing toward a definite style," and is showing "a distinct improvement over the most graceful French patterns."

And "the latest American racing automobile, the Ford, possesses features entitling it to credit as being the most unconventional, if not the most beautiful, design so far produced by American ingenuity.

"It is a model that commends itself strongly to the automobile experts because of the chaste completeness and compactness of its structure. In this rarefied type of racer, the . . . chauffeur seat has been shaved down to a mere toadstool perch . . . the carriage arrangement so detrimental to a clear, unsophisticated style, has been avoided. . . . No matter how we may choose to view this machine, it is an automobile first and last."

But this tribute appeared in November, when the car had become a celebrity. In the early spring it was still a half-furtive, half-finished cipher.

As always, Ford was grasping for things to improve it even as he was building.

One day a Norwegian immigrant entered the much-dwindled Cass Avenue factory and introduced himself. He was Peter Steenstrup, he said, and he represented the Hyatt Roller Bearing Company of Newark, New Jersey. He didn't speak English very well, but he spoke it well enough to tell Ford why Hyatt's were the roller bearings he needed.

Of course Ford knew what a roller bearing was. Together with ball bearings, they made the automotive industry possible. On a nineteenth-century wagon the turning axle would be supported by a housing that was kept from sawing through it only by the lavish application of grease. This wouldn't work with cars; their axles turned too swiftly.

But if between the hole in the mounting and the axle there is a circle of steel balls, the friction is so radically reduced that it might as well have disappeared. That's how ball bearings work.

Roller bearings do the same thing, and provide far more support. Roll a marble between the flat of your hand and a tabletop, and you'll instantly feel what a tiny amount of surface the ball is touching at any time. That's a "point" bearing. Now roll a pencil between your hand and the table: that's a "line" bearing.

Roller bearings are line bearings, clustered in a ring like the ball bearings, but each—at least the ones Steenstrup was promoting—perhaps five inches long. They circle the axle and let it turn freely. Even if a machine won't actually ruin itself without them, Steenstrup told Ford, the savings in energy are tremendous. And there was more: Hyatt made roller bearings not just out of solid metal cylinders, but out of strips of cold steel twisted into a tube like a long spring, and cut to length. Given their flexibility, they adjusted themselves to any irregularities in either the turning axle or its housing.

Steenstrup was a salesman. He had begun his American career as a bookkeeper at Hyatt, but when a big machine tool company in Providence, Rhode Island, had turned down Hyatt's salesman, he had begged to go and try himself.

This not surprisingly annoyed his superiors, and his boss said, "We can't have fresh guys around this plant. Since you're so smart, Steenstrup, you can go to Providence. Don't come back unless you get an order."

He came back with the order, explaining with some pride that he'd finally gotten it by bursting into tears.

He didn't have to cry for Ford, who liked him, and was sold. The racer would have ball bearings on its front axle, and roller bearings—Hyatt roller bearings—on its rear.

The axles carried thirty-six-inch wire wheels and four-inch tires. The ignition, as always, was a problem. Huff and Barthel talked it over and decided that an igniter might be far more effective if it were insulated by porcelain, which, along with glass, was used to make insulators for power and phone lines. But who knew anything about porcelain? Barthel suggested Dr. Sanborn, his dentist, who fashioned replacement teeth out of it. Huff and Barthel drew up a spark coil, and Barthel took it to Dr. Sanborn, and a few days later emerged from his offices with the first modern spark plug. This morning time of the industry could bring forth something new and tremendous at any moment.

By summer, the car was ready to try out. The engine was so loud that Ford thought it prudent to have a team of horses pull it to the outskirts of town before opening it up. When he did, on West Grand Boulevard, he claimed he burned through a half mile at seventy-two miles per hour. This would have broken every record of the day. Who knows? Barthel said the car was capable of that speed.

In any event, the machine was done. Ford wanted to go east and challenge Henri Fournier, the French driver—the most famous of the time—who had won a Paris–Berlin race in his Mors, and was now knocking down speed records in America. But as it happened, Ford's opponent turned out to be an American, and came to him.

—~~~~~~~—

In 1901 Alexander Winton was the best-known carmaker in America. Part of his reputation came from publicity, but most rested on the fact that, unlike Ford, he was actually building and selling automobiles, and racing them, too.

Born in Scotland in 1860, he trained as a marine engineer on the River Clyde before following a married sister to Cleveland, where he established first a bicycle repair shop and then, in 1892, a bicycle factory. His business did well enough to finance the interest in automobiles that overtook him almost immediately. By July 1897 his brand-new Winton Motor Carriage Company had produced a car capable enough to carry its maker from Cleveland to New York. This considerable feat—eight hundred miles in slightly less than seventy-nine hours—attracted some mild interest in the press but to Winton's

event is the talk of Detroit's smart set," wrote the *Free Press*. "The boxes are almost engaged and the display of feminine finery is expected to attract quite as much attention as the speedy machines.

"One of the most promising contesters is the Detroit chauffeur, Henry Ford."

The day started with what the press called, and what almost certainly was, the largest parade of automobiles ever seen in "the West." "There were more than 100 machines in line and not a horse in sight!"

Grosse Pointe was a summer resort then, and already buttoned up for the empty winter months, but even there automobiles crowded the track. "The horse was forgotten. All around the horse were other things, large, small, white, black, red, yellow. . . . Outside along the fences where usually are found tally-hos and coaches with their gay parties, were long rows of these things instead."

The event was a sellout, the mile-long track's grandstand full and, said the *Free Press* reporter, "A crowd on the lawn in front and a row of railbirds clear down past the three-quarter pole."

Rain had been forecast, but instead it turned out to be a fine tall blue October day.

Unfortunately the race was boring. At the start, anyway. The five preliminary events before the main one, contests of steam cars, electrics, and so forth, were all wan: The one-mile race for the electric cars was won by Walter C. Baker of the Baker Motor Vehicle Company at 4:49, more than thirty seconds slower than the record for the mile run by a human on foot.

Responding to the crowd's rumblings of jocose disgust, the flexible Smiling Billy immediately improvised a "special event." Alexander Winton would "try to break the world speed record."

The obliging Winton got behind his wheel and took three turns around the track, in one of them clocking a mile at $1.12^{2}/5$. This indeed was a new world record. But even while Winton was setting it in Detroit, at the Empire City track in New York Henri Fournier was warming up his Mors to run the mile in $1:06^{4}/5$. The next day the *Evening News* headline ran, "Glory Soon Gone."

This casual demonstration of the Winton's ability cannot have been encouraging to Ford. It perked up the onlookers, though, and prepared them for the climactic event of the day, the World's Championship race. This was open to all comers, and Smiling Billy had said there would be twenty-five contestants.

Three made it to the starting post: Ford, Winton, and a Pittsburgh sportsman named William Murray, who had bought one of Winton's heavy racers. At the last moment Murray's car started bleeding oil from a cracked cylinder, and its owner had to withdraw.

The earlier events had consumed far more time than had been allotted them. This (and perhaps the desire to avoid a grisly and tiresome embarrassment in which the world's speed record holder lapped the failed local carmaker time after time) caused the promoters to trim the twenty-five-mile race back to ten.

Ford started his car. Spider Huff, who would ride with him, crouched down on the narrow running board, taking hold of a pair of brackets that looked about as substantial as filing cabinet pulls. Charles Shanks, publicist, sales manager, and punch bowl advisor, apparently as versatile and daring a man as Huff, would serve as Winton's riding mechanic.

Ford knew his car was fast. What he didn't know was how it would corner on the track's turns. He'd not yet put it through a turn at all. And the car had no brakes.

Winton's car vibrated next to his, potent with seventy horsepower and its newly won speed record. Ford's engine could put out twenty-six horsepower.

"A fat man cannot run as fast as a thin man," Ford had said. Nevertheless, Winton's physical and moral advantages immediately made themselves clear: He took the lead at once, and easily held it for the first five miles.

The turns frightened Ford. He did fine on the straightaway, but lost ground when he backed off on the gas to skid into another of the endless successions of hard lefts. At each one, Spider Huff would coolly swing himself out from the body of the car, acting as a counterweight, and then crouch back down. The two men, who had never done anything like this before, began to develop a rhythm. Ford got through the turns more quickly. The gap between the cars narrowed.

Now Ford's care with every aspect of the mechanical showed its value. His engine did not begin to pump out smoke, and Winton's did. A reporter wrote that Spider Huff "hung far out in his effort to ballast the car. After three miles Winton was a fifth of a mile to the good. . . . Then Ford on the sixth lap shot up perceptibly. A thin wreath of blue smoke appeared at the rear of [Winton's] machine and it gradually increased to a cloud." Winton pushed hard, and so did Shanks, who squirmed around on the bucking car to pour oil on the running gear, but it did no good.

Clara Ford, watching in the stands, wrote her brother, "Henry had been covering himself with glory and dust . . . I wish you could have seen him. Also had heard the cheering when he passed Winton. The people went wild. One man threw his hat up and when it came down he stamped on it, he was so excited. Another man had to hit his wife on the head to keep her from going off the handle. She stood up in her seat & screamed 'I'd bet fifty dollars on Ford if I had it!'"

Afterward, Ford stood exhausted by his car while it cooled down in the October dusk. He told one of his hundreds of new fans, "Boy, I'll never do that again! That tight board fence was right here in front of my face all the time! I was scared to death."

The punch bowl eventually shed its anomalous splendor on a landing in Clara Ford's new rented house on Hendrie Avenue—a modest place, but one she did not have to share with in-laws.

———∿∿∿∿∿∿∿———

A little more than a month after the race Clara Ford wrote her brother Milton, "We are keeping house again and are very happy to be alone. We have a very nice cozy little house. We did not build on account of Henry building the racer. He could not see anything else. So we will have to put up with rented houses a little longer. We got Edsel a bicycle for his birthday. He rides it to school and thinks it fine. He and Henry have raglan overcoats."

These luxuries—bicycle, raglan coats, in-lawless home—all happened because however reckless Ford had been to gamble everything on winning the first race he'd ever seen, he had redeemed himself thrillingly and publicly.

His backers saw this. Murphy had been at the race, and immediately began preparing to form another carmaking operation, this one wearing the new celebrity's name: the Henry Ford Company.

Murphy had already spoken to Ford about this when Henry, feeling flush, went to New York City in early November to have a look at the second Madison Square Garden automobile show (the first had been held the November before).

Ford paid the fifty-cent entrance fee and walked into a barking, fuming, boisterous arena.

The early auto shows were far more strenuous for their stars than the modern ones are. This exhibition was more like the horse shows that had preceded it, because the cars were not merely on display: They had to prove they could move around nimbly under their own power.

Automobiles banged into noisy life and circled the arena, ran obstacle courses, bumped over little bridges, and did everything their sellers could devise to show the machines' abilities. Up on the roof of the Garden, promoters of the Mobile Steamer had built a tall, moderately steep ramp that led to empty sky so that people could watch the Mobile hiss up it, then complacently roll back down.

Henry Ford wasn't intimidated by busy machinery, but there was a lot to take in, and he was getting tired when he heard someone call his name.

He turned to see Peter Steenstrup waving to him from the railing of the stand behind the Hyatt Roller Bearing exhibit. Ford went over, shook Steenstrup's hand, took off his derby, and wiped his forehead with a handkerchief.

"Come in," said Steenstrup. "Where could you find a better place to rest? Sit down at the railing and see the show from a box seat."

Steenstrup introduced Ford to his partner, a young engineer named Alfred Sloan. He and Steenstrup had been spending the day watching from their perch to see which cars drew the most attention from the crowd: the Lane, the Lozier, Col. Pope's Toledo Steamer, the Autocar, the Stearns, the Locomobile, and the Oldsmobile, Ransom Olds's popular little one-cylinder runabout, which was the closest existing exemplar of what Ford's backers wished he would build.

Sloan wrote, "So we three sat and watched the cars go round in the show ring below and talked, for hours I guess." He remembered his guest in a pose that would be characteristic of the man for the rest of his life: "Mr. Ford was tilted back in a chair, his heels caught in the topmost rung, his knees at the level of his chin."

Sloan liked his partner's client, but had little idea that "much was to come from our association with Mr. Ford: fabulous orders for roller bearings." Even less did Sloan "suspect that I was talking with a man who was to take a foremost place among the industrial leaders of all times."

Nor did Ford suspect, as he waded back into the melee of exercising cars and the fog of exhaust, that he had met, in this agreeable twenty-seven-year-old, his Nemesis.

———∿∿∿∿∿∿———

On November 30, 1901, Murphy and several of his original investors filed incorporation papers for the Henry Ford Company. Ford was named chief engineer, and given a sixth of the stock. The company acquired a factory on Cass Avenue where Ford was going to create the car that it would produce. Ford and Barthel began working on a two-cylinder runabout.

And then the company's namesake began to make himself scarce. Barthel, who had joined the firm as a designer, soon discovered where Ford's true enthusiasm lay. "He did not seem inclined to settle down to a small car production plan. He talked mostly about wanting to build a larger and faster racing car. This, together with some dissatisfaction as to the amount of interest he was to share in the company, led to a considerable amount of dissension between himself and Mr. Murphy."

Surely the tone of grievance in a letter Clara wrote her brother Milton just two days after the incorporation papers were filed belongs at least as much to her husband as it does to her: "Henry has worked very hard to get where he is. That race has advertised him far and wide. And the next thing will be to make some money out of it. I am afraid it will be a hard struggle. You know how rich men want it all."

Ford had nothing to say about a small-car production plan in his own letter to Milton, written on imposing new stationery headed "HENRY FORD COMPANY" and bearing, next to the hopeful legend "BUILDERS OF HIGH-GRADE AUTOMOBILES AND TOURIST CARS," a portrait of the victorious racer that is as crisp and authoritative as the engraving on a stock certificate.

In his note, Ford speaks of his continuing desire to get Henri Fournier to race against his car. "If I can bring Mr. Fournier in line there is a barrel of money in this business . . . I don't see why he wont fall in line if he don't I will challenge him until I am black in the face. . . . My Company will kick about me following racing but they will get the advertising and I expect to make $ where I can't make ¢s at manufacturing."

He was quite right about his management kicking. Murphy told Barthel that if he helped Ford with his race-car designs he'd be fired. The dutiful Barthel continued to work surreptitiously on the racers at night.

Not for very long, though. A little over four months after its formation, Henry Ford left the Henry Ford Company.

His backers had finally grown sick of what could be seen as six straight years of procrastination. For his part, if Ford thought his sixth share in the enterprise too meager, he may also have been vexed by the appearance at the factory of a gaunt, white-bearded man who looked like an El Greco saint, only less jolly.

This was Henry Leland, grim, acerbic, deeply pious, and one of the finest machinists in America. His shop, Leland and Faulconer, could cut parts to $^1/100,000$ of an inch. Now he was making engines for Ransom Olds, and Murphy wanted his opinion on what Henry Ford was doing.

Leland's opinion wasn't high. Having played a crucial part in the success of the one-cylinder Oldsmobile, he advised that the two-cylinder engine Ford had been working on was needlessly complex. The company should drop it: Leland had just developed a greatly improved motor that could squeeze ten horsepower out of its single cylinder.

Leland asked the directors to keep the factory alive for long enough to try out his engine. Such was his reputation that the discouraged men agreed to give it one more shot. Leland's engine went in the prototype body that Ford and Barthel had built.

In his autobiography Ford groused about his time at the company. "I could get no support at all toward making better cars to sell the public at large. The whole thought was to make to order and get the largest price possible for our car. And being without authority other than my engineering position gave me, I found that the new company was not a vehicle for realizing my ideal but merely a money-making concern—that did not make much money. In March 1902, I resigned, determined never again to put myself under orders."

Despite Ford's insistence on their venal obtuseness, once Leland gave the backers something to sell, they produced it quickly, and in increasing volume.

Ford left with nine hundred dollars, the half-done plans for his new racing car, and the assurance that the enterprise would cease using his name. The firm chose a new one: the Cadillac Automobile Company.

All that remains today of the Henry Ford Company are a few sheets of its handsome stationery. And, of course, the Cadillac.

———~~~~~~~———

What of Ford, carrying nine hundred dollars and his sheaf of unfinished plans out into the raw Detroit March? As when he left Edison, his quitting was not quite as reckless as it might seem. A photograph of a family picnic he took a few weeks later shows a relaxed and smiling Clara Ford, the stress-gained "fleshiness" her sister had written of melted away. Nine hundred dollars sounds skimpy today, but it could support Ford and his family for half a year. More important, in jumping, he had carefully chosen where he was going to land.

Among the spectators at the October race were two professional bicyclists. During one of the event's many longueurs, Smiling Bill Metzger had urged them out onto the track, but the crowd was interested in automobiles that day, and paid little attention.

They were named Tom Cooper and Barney Oldfield, and they were famous. Bicycle racing was for a while as big a sport as prizefighting or the horse track, and offered purses just as fat. But the "bicycle craze"—and it really did approach the dimensions of a craze for many years—had in 1897 begun to shrink with a suddenness as unexpected as it was inexplicable.

Hundreds of thousands of bicyclists remained, of course, and always would. But Cooper and Oldfield, not long before the objects of fervid national attention, felt themselves drifting toward irrelevancy while still in their early twenties.

Like the bicycle industry itself, they were drawn toward the motorcar. The Grosse Pointe race fascinated them, and Tom Cooper spoke with Ford during that day.

Then, while Ford was working erratically with his second round of backers, Cooper and Oldfield invested in a coal mine and went to Colorado to run it. This is slightly less surprising than if they had gone west to found a literary magazine, but it was an odd enough choice. What is not surprising is the speed with which they discovered they detested the work.

In February 1902, Cooper was back in Detroit, and talking to Ford again. He wanted a racing car, and he'd done so well at bicycling that he had something like a hundred thousand dollars set aside to invest in it. This was more than sufficient, as Ford's first race car had cost about five thousand dollars. The bicyclist and the mechanic struck a deal: Cooper would pay the bills; Ford would build two racing cars; and one would belong to his partner.

Ford rented a modest workshop on Park Place and Oliver Barthel came to help. He was still working for what was now Cadillac, and later said that Ford offered him 10 percent of all his future profits if Barthel would come on full-time. Barthel agreed to help in odd hours, but he was too cautious to leave Cadillac, and thus joined the many who were brushed by the tail of Henry Ford's comet but failed to take hold of it.

Harold Wills did, apparently working free in exchange for a share of whatever would emerge. And Spider Huff, between bouts of the remorse or whatever it was that occasionally drove him back to Kentucky, was there, too.

Wills and Ford worked together fluently and without friction that season. Although Wills could draw up a plan with a speed and precision that Ford never approached, the two men were similar in temperament. Both liked to discover whether things would work by building them. When told there was a book that offered clear instructions on a project he was attempting, Wills said, "If it's in a book, it's at least four years old and I don't have any use for it."

These men spent the cold spring of 1902 (Ford and Wills would sometimes pull on gloves and box just to warm up) building the two biggest, most powerful automobiles yet made in America.

The machines, all but identical, were well over ten feet long, with a wheelbase of nine feet nine inches, and the yard-high wheels set more than five feet apart. The chassis rode low on the wheels, probably at Cooper's suggestion. The cars carried absolutely nothing that wasn't essential to their being able to move.

In September, with the racers nearly finished—in good time for the second annual Grosse Pointe race, to be run on October 25—a *Detroit Journal* reporter wrote, "All the machinery is exposed. Oilcups and polished wheels gleam alongside of black wires which lead to entirely exposed batteries. Being racing autos they are 'stripped.'" They were nothing but chassis: The engine, whose four cisterns of cylinders displaced eleven hundred cubic inches, was bolted directly to a suspensionless frame made of two long planks fortified with steel.

The *Automobile and Motor Review* reported, "Built for speed and speed alone, the two new racing machines . . . are first-class examples of how an automobile may be simplified by the 'leaving off' process. This most recent addition to the ranks of racing monsters has power and means to apply it; it has few conveniences, no luxuries and not the slightest indication of a frill or decoration. Not even an attempt has been made to hide the machinery, for a motor-bonnet is not necessary to speed, and no other considerations matter."

Another magazine account, in the *Automobile*, was harsher. "Technically [the racer] . . . is an automobile, practically it is an engine on wheels, a machine in which brute strength and disregard for all the essentials of modern automobile construction are embodied."

Ford had one of the cars painted red, and one yellow. The red one he named the *Arrow*, the yellow the *999* after the New York Central locomotive whose tall driving wheels had carried it to a world speed record of 112.5 miles per hour in 1893.

That paint required plenty of maintenance. The reporters weren't exaggerating about the cars' being stripped down, nor about their being primitive even by the automotive standards of 1902.

Not only did the cars lack a hood over the engine, but every single piece of running gear—valves, flywheel (all 230 pounds of it), and transmission—was unshielded. The cars boiled along in a thunderstorm of their own making, a cloud of flung oil at whose heart blue lightnings of exhaust flickered. The noise alone, said Ford, was "enough to half kill a man."

The *999* was finished first, and on September 17 Ford drove it around the Grosse Pointe track, although not against any competitors: He'd said he'd never do that again, and he never did. A reporter from the *Journal* was there and told how the car treated its driver. "Mr. Ford was a daub of oil from head to foot. His collar was yellow, his tie looked as though it had been cooked in lard, his clothes were spattered and smirched, while his face looked like a machinist's after 24 hours at his bench."

Ford had wanted a fast car, and he got one. The *999*, propelled by perhaps as much as one hundred horsepower, had come awfully close to the automotive grail of a mile a minute on an oval track—1:08—but the car had scared its builder: "I cannot quite describe the sensation. Going over Niagara Falls would have been but a pastime after a ride in one of them [the two cars]. I did not want to take the responsibility of racing the *999*."

Neither did Tom Cooper, once he'd spent some time at the throttle. But, as the year before, Ford *had* to race.

Cooper thought of his friend Barney Oldfield who, after his brief, joyless immersion in the mining business, had moved to Salt Lake City. "He lived on speed," Cooper told Ford. "Nothing would go too fast for him."

Cooper sent a telegram and Oldfield came to Detroit. He was tough, sanguine, and good-natured. He'd never driven a car, but he was philosophical about the risks. "I may as well be dead as dead broke," he told Spider Huff.

Still, he was startled when he first saw the racers.

"We didn't build these for looks," Cooper said.

"You sure as hell didn't. They're ugly as sin!"

A lot of contemporary observers felt the same way. One British reporter said the racers were "the materialization of a nightmare."

In fact, the *999* is an example of Ford's dictum about the most beautiful things: They are "those from which all excess weight has been eliminated."

The massive block of an engine up front, the low frame, the gallant confidence of its single ("one life to a car was enough," Ford said) bucket seat, the big, wire-spoked wheels—all combine to give the 110-year-old *999* a look of sculptural modernity. And, for all its essential brutality, of lightness: "Weight may be desirable in a steam roller but nowhere else," Ford said. "Strength has nothing to do with weight. The mentality of the man who does things in the world is agile, light, and strong." It is the *999* and not the previous year's racer that most closely approaches the *Scientific American*'s description of being the first automobile truly to look American.

Nevertheless, Cooper and Ford were wise to be wary of it. Oldfield, though, expressed no qualms, even when Ford told him why the car was steered not by a wheel, as his first racer had been, but rather by a fork-shaped tiller a little like a vertical pair of bicycle handlebars. Oldfield didn't record what Ford said, but another racing driver who asked about the steering did: "You see, when the machine is making high speed, and for any reason the operator cannot tell at the instant because of dust or other reasons, he is going perfectly straight, he can look at this steering handle. If it is set straight across the machine he is all right and running straight." Grosse Pointe was, of course, an oval track. If Oldfield recognized the absurdity of the anodyne explanation, he didn't say so.

"It took us only a week to teach him to drive," Ford wrote. "The man did not know what fear was. All that he had to learn was how to control the monster. Controlling the fastest car of today was nothing as controlling that car. . . . On this car I put a two-handed tiller, for holding the car in line required all the strength of a strong man."

Oldfield remained confident. Ford apparently did not. Here, at another point that could have made his career, he withdrew. The cars were proving fussy; sometimes they wouldn't start. In the middle of October Ford in effect shut down his new business by selling both of them to Cooper (or, more accurately, selling one, since the cyclist already owned the other by the terms of their agreement). Cooper paid eight hundred dollars, which sounds like a small price until one considers that he had covered all the expenses, and that Ford was leaving with enough money to support his family for another half year.

But if Ford had wished to shield his reputation from the caprices of the untried automobiles by shedding his ownership of them, he failed. The press was greatly interested in the cars, and invariably referred to them as the "Ford racers."

Whatever strains may have accompanied his break with Cooper, Ford said he was there at the Grosse Pointe racetrack on October 25. Indeed, he fired up the 999 for Oldfield that day: "While I was cranking the car he remarked cheerily, 'Well, this chariot may kill me, but they will say afterward that I was going like hell when I hit the bank.'"

There were four contestants in the five-mile race: Oldfield; Alexander Winton, back with a bigger, more advanced race car that he called the Bullet; a driver named Buckman; and the doughty Charles Shanks in another Winton.

It was Oldfield's race from the start. Winton kept up for a while, but the speed of Ford's car, coupled with its driver's swashbuckling indifference to the laws of physics, dominated. Oldfield wrenched the "steering handle" from side to side, but kept it hard left on the turns, which he slewed through like a motorcyclist, the rear wheels cutting arcs in the dirt before they again dug in.

Winton's old trouble returned: His car started misfiring, and he had to withdraw after the fourth mile. Oldfield lapped Buckman, then Shanks. He boomed past the finish line having devoured the five miles in 5:28, a record he topped the next spring when he circled a mile track in a third of a second under a minute.

Cooper took his cars, and Oldfield, and together they campaigned around the Midwest staging exhibition matches. When Oldfield won at Grosse Pointe the crowd had pulled him from the car and carried him around. His fame only grew, and even today strikes a faint chord in the national memory, the only name from the heroic age of American auto racing to hold that residual power.

Everywhere he and Cooper appeared, the press spoke of the "Ford machines."

Cooper was killed in New York City—a car accident in Central Park—in 1906, but Oldfield kept on going. By 1910 he was able to charge four thousand dollars for an appearance.

Toward the end of his life (long, for a racing driver of those days: He lived until 1946), Barney Oldfield liked to tell people, "Henry Ford said that we made each other." Then, his victories and prize money far behind him, he'd add, grinning, "I guess I did the better job of it."

CHAPTER 7

The Seven-Million-Dollar Letter

Malcomson's gamble; from a toy printing press; the Dodge brothers; the
Ford Motor Company; "This business cannot last"; the (first) Model A;
"BOSS OF THE ROAD."

After Clara Ford died, on the last day of September 1950, some-body inevitably asked, "I wonder if Mr. Ford left any papers."

He had. He'd left virtually every piece of paper he'd ever handled. Nineteen-fifties industrial archaeologists entered Fair Lane, his last, big house in Dearborn, with the same wonder and surprise that Howard Carter and Lord Carnarvon had entered Tutankhamen's tomb thirty years earlier.

As Henry and Clara Ford had aged, they'd given over one after another of the house's fifty-six rooms to stacks and drifts of memorabilia, and papers, papers, papers. Today the Ford Archives, among the greatest of all such American repositories, hold ten million of Ford's papers: a newsboy's forty-five-cent bill for delivering a month of the

Detroit Evening Journal to 58 Bagley Avenue in 1894; receipts for the payments the couple kept up on that player piano; a 1919 telegram from Henry Ford to the Chase National Bank releasing $175 million to the company's stockholders.

There with all the other paper—the letters from Franklin Roosevelt and Calvin Coolidge and a relative who had made a ten-dollar deposit on a toupee and couldn't come up with the thirty-five-dollar balance (Ford sent it to him)—is a bill for five dollars' worth of coal, which Ford paid on May 28, 1895, to Alexander Young Malcomson. This may have been the day Ford first met Malcomson. If so, it was one of the most important days of his life.

Alexander Malcomson, a short, powerfully built man in his mid-thirties, had been born in Scotland and immigrated at the age of fifteen to Detroit, where he found a job as a grocery clerk. Within five years he not only owned a grocery store but had gotten bored with it. Energetic himself, he became interested in the nation's prime source of energy, and sold his store to enter the coal business.

He began with a single wagon and zeal, like so many entrepreneurs of the day. But he also had an idea about the industry: The real money lay not only in selling the product, but in its speedy delivery. The zeal before long got him 110 wagons and a half dozen coal yards. The idea made him Detroit's leading coal supplier.

Most coal wagons were heavy, laboring along behind six-horse teams. Malcomson hitched three horses to lighter wagons and lesser loads and got faster and more regularly to his customers. These grew to include housewives and steamship lines and factories. He was scrupulously fair: He never took advantage of the occasional coal strike and its accompanying fuel scarcity to gouge his clients. The whole city knew his company's motto "Hotter than Sunshine" (it may have sounded catchier to the 1900 ear).

The coal business seems steady, even stolid; but Malcomson had a restlessness of spirit evident in the quick, darting raptor's glances with which he raked every conversation. He was, as his son would put it, "the plunger type, a man who did not hesitate to take chances."

He was fascinated by the plunger's favorite machine, and he owned a Winton. He had probably seen Ford's Grosse Pointe racing victory; if not, he knew about it within hours.

The two men struck up a friendship when Ford was buying coal from Malcomson for the Detroit Edison boilers. During early 1902 Ford talked with him about how they could start a motorcar company.

Ford was still involved with his racing behemoths then, but once again, despite the seeming recklessness of abandoning them, he had carefully cleared the way for his next step.

He didn't talk to Malcomson about racing cars: He wanted to build the will-o'-the-wisp that had lured on his previous investors, a low-priced runabout.

On August 20, 1902, the two men went to the offices of Malcomson's lawyers, John W. Anderson and Horace H. Rackham, and signed a partnership agreement. Ford would contribute his tools, plans, and experience, and henceforth concentrate on building a prototype of the new car. Malcomson would give him five hundred dollars right away to get things started, and pay what was needed as the project went forward. The prototype, Ford assured him, would cost no more than three thousand dollars. Once it was finished, the two men would form a manufacturing corporation in which their combined shares, split evenly between them, made them the majority stockholders.

The enterprise, Ford and Malcomson, hired one significant employee, Childe Harold Wills. Although he would be a bulwark of Ford's success, and become the nation's foremost metallurgist, Wills made one early contribution that everyone recognizes today. The company was trying to come up with what we would now call a logo, and nobody liked the various blocky FORDs that draftsmen offered. Wills remembered that when he was in his teens he had a toy printing press from which he made some money by striking off business cards for neighbors.

He still had the set, and his type case yielded up a script *FORD* with a little break in the O and the top of the F sweeping confidently toward the D. This looked pretty good to everyone back then, and you'll see it if you go outdoors today.

————~~~~~~~~~~————

Malcomson was true to his word, and Ford would get his money, but somewhat on the sly. In building his business the coal dealer had stretched himself to the limit. He didn't want his bankers to know he was veering into a risky and wholly unconnected enterprise. Before long, Detroit banks would be notorious for shoveling money toward almost anybody who was able to say "car company," but not now, not in 1902.

To keep his credit intact, Malcomson paid Ford through an account he had set up in the name of his office manager, James Couzens. Though Ford could have no idea of it at the time, this was another tremendous stroke of good fortune for him.

It is almost unnecessary to say that the prototype didn't cost three thousand dollars. By November Ford had gone through seven thousand dollars and Malcomson was feeling badly pressed. In August he'd had the sunny idea that once he started selling cars, the influx of money would take care of the overhead, and the business would pay for itself. But in November, Malcomson—in charge of business matters, as Ford was of technical ones—decided he had to form the company. It would issue 15,000 shares of stock, at ten dollars each. Ford and Malcomson would split 6,900 shares as compensation for their efforts thus far, and pay cash for 350 more. That left 7,750 shares, which, once sold, would bring in plenty of working capital.

Sold to whom, though? Nineteen oh three had dawned, and the year would see fifty-seven new automobile companies struggling to get born, all of them thirsting for capital. Ford had already mined out the richest strata of Detroit investors. He tried his old boss Alexander Dow, who received him cordially, but had not changed his mind about the gasoline automobile. Years later, he said, "I didn't know then, of course, that he was going to make millions of the blame things."

It was left to Malcomson, then, to badger his friends and associates as winter turned to spring.

Two early believers were the lawyers who had helped draw up the original agreement, John Anderson and his partner, Horace Rackham. They were different in many ways: Rackham, forty-five, was a stern prohibitionist; Anderson, some years his junior, liked a drink and a cigar and a noisy restaurant. But both men shared qualities that, however appealing in many human beings, are not entirely helpful to lawyers. They were timid, shy, and gentle.

Their little office was struggling. Unable to afford either a secretary or a typewriter, they spent their pinched days writing longhand letters either gingerly inquiring whether clients might be interested in paying the fees they'd incurred, or mildly rebuking the people the clients were sore at.

But on June 4, John Anderson sat down and wrote a long letter that turned out to be well worth the wrist-cramping amount of effort he put into it, for it eventually netted him $17,435,700.

The letter was to his father, a Civil War surgeon who was now the mayor of La Crosse, Wisconsin, asking him for five thousand dollars to invest. It is clear, persuasive, and largely honest—a fine selling letter. It is also the best firsthand account we have of the birth of the Ford Motor Company.

"Dear Father," John began, "Horace and I have an opportunity to make an investment that is of such a character that I cannot refrain from laying the details before you for consideration.

"Mr. Ford of this city is recognized throughout the country as one of the best automobile mechanical experts in the U.S." There follows a summary of Ford's racing history and (this is as close as the writer came to fantasy) a wonderfully benign account of his dealings with Leland: "Several years ago he designed, perfected and placed on the market a machine. A Co. was organized, but not long after, desiring to devote his attention to a new model entirely, he sold out his patents and interest, and retired. The machine is known as the 'Cadillac' (you will see it advertised in all the magazines). . . ."

He then turned his entire attention to the designing and patenting of an entirely new machine. Mr. Malcomson, the coal man, backed him with money and the result is they have now perfected and are about to place on the market an automobile (gasoline) that is far and away the best of anything that has yet come out. . . .

Having perfected the machine in all its parts, and demonstrated to their complete satisfaction and to the satisfaction of automobile experts, and cycle journal representatives from all over the country who came here to inspect it that it was superior to anything that had been designed in the way of an automobile, and that it was a sure winner, the next problem was how to best and most economically place it on the market. After canvassing the matter thoroughly, instead of forming a company, with big capital, erecting a factory and installing an extensive plant of machinery to manufacture it themselves, they determined to enter into contracts with various concerns to supply the different parts and simply do the assembling themselves.

So, they entered with the Dodge Bros. here to manufacture the automobile complete—less wheels and bodies—for $250. apiece, or $162,500, for the 650 machines, which were to be delivered at the rate of 10 per day, commencing on July 1st. if possible, and all by Oct. 1st. I drew this contract, so know all about it.

———∿∿∿∿∿∿∿———

So the Dodge brothers came into Henry Ford's life, and he could scarcely have found two colleagues more different from himself.

Alfred Sloan once wrote, "I saw nothing of the mining camps of the West and nothing that happened when oil was struck, but I did see Detroit." The gasoline engine and its myriad promoters, from gifted engineers to "manufacturers representatives" living out of their suitcases, were giving the long-established city something of the feverish evanescence of a boomtown. Into this volatile brew of hope and money and opportunism, John and Horace Dodge brought a whiff of the all-but-vanished violence of the frontier.

Now in their late thirties, the Dodges had been born to a blacksmith in southeastern Michigan, and gone to Detroit in the 1880s to become expert machinists. Horace worked two years with Henry Leland and then the brothers went across the river to Canada and set up a bicycle factory. It prospered enough for them to move back to Detroit, open a machine shop, and win the contract to make engines for Olds.

As against this admirable rising professional arc, they were both loudmouth saloon brawlers. The brothers were inseparable: They dressed even more identically than men of business usually did in those days, and shared the red hair that folklore ties to a quick temper. Horace was the slightly less aggressive of the two, and his wife always blamed John for the scrapes they got into. But Horace clearly needed little encouragement. One time they smashed all the light bulbs in the chandeliers of the Cadillac Hotel; once, in a scene truly reminiscent of Tombstone days, John pulled a pistol on a saloon keeper and made him "dance" on top of his bar while using his free hand to fling glasses against the mirror. There must have been a lot of glasses, because this particular spree cost John Dodge thirty-five thousand dollars in damages.

But to continue with John Anderson's pitch to his father, what he wrote next is also true: "Now Dodge Bros. are the largest and best equipped machine plant in the city. They have a new factory, just completed and it is not excelled anywhere. . . . Well, when this proposition was made them by Ford and Malcomson, they had under consideration offers from Oldsmobile, and the Great Northern automobile Co. to manufacture their machines, but after going over Mr. Ford's machine very carefully, they threw over both offers and tied up with Mr. F. and Mr. M.

"Now in order to comply with this contract, which was made last Oct. Dodge Bros. had to decline all outside orders and devote the entire resources of their machine shop to the turning out of these automobiles. They were only paid $10,000/on account, and had to take all of the rest of the risk themselves. They had to borrow $40.000., place orders for castings all over the country, pay their men from last October (they have a large force) and do everything necessary to manufacture all the machines before they could hope to get a cent back."

Most of the car accounted for, Anderson enumerates the rest: bodies and cushions from the C. R. Wilson Carriage Company (suppliers of the seat to the Quadricycle); the wheels from a firm in Lansing at twenty-six dollars per set of four; the tires "by the Hartford Rubber Co. at $46.00 per set (4 wheels)."

Where would the wheels from Lansing join with the Hartford tires and then with the Dodges' chassis and the Wilson company's cushions? "They found a man from whom Mr. M. rents a coal yard on the belt-line R.R., with a spur track running into it. He agreed to erect a building designed by Mr. Ford for their special use, for assembling purposes (which will cost between 3 & 4 thousand dollars) and rent it for three yrs. to Mr. F. and Mr. M. at $75. per month. This building has been all completed and is a dandy. I went all through it today. It is large, light and airy, about 200 feet long by fifty ft. wide, fitted up with machinery necessary to be used incidental to assembling the parts, and all ready for business."

Amid all that light and air "the workmen, ten or a dozen boys at $1.50 per day, and a foreman fit the bodies on the machine, put the cushions in place, put the tires on the wheels, the wheels on the machine and paint it and test it to see that it runs 'o.k.', and it is all ready for delivery. Now this is all there is to the whole proposition."

It might not sound like much of a proposition: a "dozen boys" in a seventy-five-dollar-per-month wooden factory patching together parts pulled in from various works around the countryside and offering the result as an automobile. But given the immense amount of capital necessary to create a factory that could accommodate the whole job of building a car under one figurative roof, the independent supplier and his piecework were almost inevitable. For a while, budding car companies even argued for the system's superiority: The Cole, one of the hundreds of hopeful automotive brands that lived its mayfly life in those years, boasted about the clear advantage its "assembled" cars enjoyed over "manufactured" ones. With the former, the fortunate motorist was drawing on the long-refined skills of any number of different machinists; the latter was by necessity a sloppy and hastily improvised orchestra of metalworkers doing many things a little beyond their abilities.

There is some truth to this with the Dodge brothers. They had all the business that they could handle with Olds, but Ford's two-cylinder engine that Leland had thought excessive evidently sold them on the idea that Henry Ford was the man to go with. The shift involved a good deal of expensive retooling on their part, but in the end they were willing to bet their company on it.

Anderson sided with the short-lived Cole and the now 110-year-old Ford operations. His letter continues: "Now, as to the investment feature. You will see there is absolutely no money, to speak of, tied up in a big factory."

He goes on to speak about product. The "tonneau" he mentions is actually a backseat. The basic model car was a two-seater, with a sloping rear. If the plunger wanted the tonneau, he would pay another hundred dollars. Tonneaus are described in the literature of virtually all cars of the day with words like "effortlessly attached with seven latches." Fat chance.

Here's where Dr. Anderson will get his returns: "The machines sell for $750., without a tonneau. With a tonneau $850. This is the price of all medium priced machines and is standard. It is what the Cadillac and the Great Northern sell for here, and what other machines elsewhere sell for. Now the cost, figured on the most liberal possible estimate, is as follows."

Machine...................*$250.00*
Body...........................*52.00*
Wheels..........................*26.00*
Upholstering...................*16.00*
Tires...........................*40.00*
Cost of Assembling...........*20.00*
Cost of Selling................*150.00*

Total cost...................... *554.00*
Cost of tonneau.............. *50.00*
                        604.00
Selling price
With tonneau.............. *$850.00*
Cost price..................... *604.00*
Throwing off $46
(for any possible
contingency) *46.00*
                        $200.00

Anderson adds a couple of notes to his triumphant summary: Even without the tonneau, the car will net $150; and the rather stiff-looking "cost of selling" includes "advertising, all salaries commissions, etc. 20% on each automobile (it will really be nearer to 10 or 12)."

And now the money will flow in: "On the seasons output of 650 machines it means a profit of $97,500 without a tonneau, and more in proportion to those sold with tonneaus, and of course the latter is almost always bought, as it adds to the capacity of vehicle."

Now, the demand for automobiles is a perfect craze. Every factory here (there are 3, including the "Olds"—the largest in this country—and you know Detroit is the largest automobile [manufacturer] in the US.) has its entire output sold and cannot begin to fill their orders. Mr. M has already begun to be deluged with orders, although not a machine has been put on the market and will not be until July 1st. Buyers have heard of it and go out to the Dodge Bros. and inspect it, test it, and give their orders. One dealer from Buffalo was here last week and ordered twenty-five: three were ordered today and other orders have begun to come in every day, so there is not the slightest doubt as to the market or the demand. And it is all spot cash on delivery, and no guarantee or string attached of any kind.

Mr. Malcomson has instructed us to draw up articles of incorporation for a $100,000.00 limited liability company, of which Mr. Ford will take at least $51,000 (controlling interest) and the balance he is going to distribute among a few of his friends and business associates, and is anxious that Horace and myself go in with him. Mr. Couzens is going to leave the coal business, for the present at least, and devote his entire time to the office and management of the automobile business—and he is a crackerjack. He is going to invest, as he expresses it, "all the money he can beg, borrow or steal" in stock. Mr. Dodge, of Dodge Bros, is going to take 5 or 10 thousand, and two or three others, like amounts. Horace is going to put in all that he can raise, and I do want to do the same if I can, because I honestly believe it is a wonderful opportunity, and a chance not likely to occur again. Mr. M. is successful in everything he does, is such a good business man and hustler, and his ability in this direction, coupled with Mr. Ford's inventive and mechanical genius and Mr. Couzens's office ability, together with fixed contracts which absolutely show what the cost will be, and orders already commencing to pour in, showing the demand that exists, makes it one of the very most promising and surest industrial investments that could be made. . . .

I went into the Dodge Bros. plant and the assembling rooms today, and even into the room where the half dozen draughtsmen are kept under lock and key, (all the plans, drawings and specifications are secret you know) making drawings and blue-prints of every part, even to the individual screws, and was amazed at what had been accomplished since last October. Not another Automobile Co. has started and got its product on the market inside of three years before this.

―――――∼∼∼∼∼∼∼∼∼――――――

Dr. Anderson read his son's letter and headed for Detroit, spurred on not by enthusiasm but by caution. John had once gotten him involved with a Chicago fire-sprinkler company that had eaten a good deal of Dr. Anderson's capital before expiring as though poisoned by it.

What he found in Detroit did not reassure him. His first stop was at the "large, light and airy" new plant.

> I came to see the factory which I had heard so much about. It was nothing prepossessing . . . just a little building on Mack Avenue in which the cars were being assembled from parts made elsewhere.
>
> James Couzens was at the plant when we were there, and he offered to drive us to town in his first Ford car. On the way he attempted to drive through a small park, but the car stalled on a small hill. After frequent attempts to cross the little hill, Mr. Couzens was forced to detour around the block. That was my first auto ride.

Dr. Anderson could have saved himself some trouble and anxiety simply by staying put in La Crosse after receiving his son's lengthy plea. He was evidently a fond father for, after having looked with dismay upon the Mack Avenue factory and gotten stuck in the park in its sole product, he gave his son the five thousand dollars he'd asked for.

All the fund-raising went like that—slowly, the money arriving in painfully extracted dribs and drabs.

Despite his dismal ride with Dr. Anderson, James Couzens remained convinced that this was the one great chance of his life. As he'd told John Anderson, he was going to put all the money he could "beg, borrow, or steal" into it, but this came to $400. His schoolteacher sister Rosetta had managed to save $200 over her lifetime. Couzens, now every bit as much a believer as Clara Ford, told her to throw all of it in with Ford. She said she couldn't do that without asking her father's advice. This would have vexed Couzens; he deeply disliked his father. But instead of saying something like "don't you dare gamble a dime on those devil wagons," the elder Couzens reasonably suggested she halve the risk by putting in $100. This she did, and by 1919 had cleared $355,000 on her gamble.

Charles Bennett, president of the Daisy Air Rifle Company, was combining two errands when he stopped in at his tailor's to order a new suit while on his way to buy an Oldsmobile. He was chatting with the tailor about his future car when another customer peered out through the curtains of the adjoining booth.

"Pardon me," said Alexander Malcomson's cousin Frank, "I couldn't help overhearing your conversation. Have you heard about the Ford car?"

Bennett had not, and amiably allowed himself to be hustled over to Mack Avenue to see the prototype and its builder.

He met Henry Ford at his most charming, and the car on its best behavior, and forgot about the Oldsmobile. For a heady few days it looked as if this industrialist might combine his highly successful company with Ford, but his board pointed out that Daisy's bylaws did not permit it to merge with another enterprise. Still, Bennett said he was good for a five-thousand-dollar investment.

The most cash came from the banker John S. Gray—$10,500. He was Malcomson's uncle, and it was the family tie alone that brought him in. "This business cannot last," he told friends, and refused to ask anyone he knew to invest in Ford, even when, three years later, he had gotten back his ten thousand and fifty thousand on top of it.

The Dodge brothers were in a position to drive a hard bargain, and they did. It was their demands that pried the $10,000 loose from the deeply reluctant Gray.

As John Anderson pointed out, they'd agreed to abandon their other automotive business to make Ford's cars. They gave promissory notes for $10,000, thus acquiring fifty shares of stock each. Then they said they had to have $10,000 in cash, too. Gray supplied it and mournfully added an extra $500 for operating expenses.

On a humid, unseasonably warm Saturday night in mid-June of 1903, the shareholders got together in Malcomson's ramshackle office, which looked more like the domain of an 1880 small-town depot master than the crucible where the twentieth century was being born.

The eleven men there (Gray was evidently too mortified to attend) gave over their money or their promises of money. Couzens had scrambled successfully enough to be able to pledge $2,500. The Ford Motor Company—the name was Malcomson's suggestion—started in business on June 16. Two days later it absorbed what had been the Ford-Malcomson limited partnership.

John Gray was president, Henry Ford vice president and general manager—at $3,600 a year—Couzens treasurer. The company had issued $100,000 in stock. $28,000 had been paid in. Or, its pledgers assured, soon would be.

———wwwwwwww———

The Dodges started delivering in July, the chassis pulled from their Monroe Street shop by dray horses. Ford's dozen workers would put on the wheels, thread some wiring to the batteries, test the engine, clean it up, fix it to the body, and send the machine out to an eager public.

So John Anderson had envisioned the process, but it didn't go that way.

The sanguine view of "assembled" cars, in which each contributor does his best work on his own specialty, might have made perfect sense with steam locomotives or windmills or anything else that had been around for a while. Automobiles hadn't.

The Ford car was nothing like the Olds the Dodges had been working on. The chassis the brothers had signed up to deliver was composed of scores of parts that had never before existed in quite the same form.

This meant that every intricacy of the car—which may look like a naïve little antique to us today, but was one of the most complicated things in the world in its time—had to be designed and, most important, drawn perfectly so the Dodge mechanics would know what to do.

Here Ford's career depended on Wills. Ford knew what he wanted, but he couldn't draft a plan. Wills could, superbly, and he turned out hundreds of them.

Nobody could have done it better, but still it was all new. Further complicating the process was that the Dodges paid by piecework— that is, the more engines you make in a day, the more money you get. The result was reflected in an encounter between Ford's tester, a man named Fred Rockelman, and the Dodges. Rockelman had a fierce temper—all his life Ford attracted bad-tempered associates—and when Rockelman found that the flywheels coming in did not fit tightly enough on the crankshafts, he went to the Dodge works and expressed his dissatisfaction in such a manner that John Dodge told him to get the hell out of his shop and stepped forward to slug him.

"Go ahead!" shouted Rockelman. "Throw me out! But that won't make us accept engines with loose flywheels!" Rockelman grabbed up a finished crankshaft from the shop floor, and easily slid it into a nearby flywheel.

The Dodges, demonstrating the frontier ability to leap from fury to camaraderie, laughed, said the joke was on them, and promised they'd do better. Everyone shook hands, and the Dodges did do a little better.

Still, the problems seemed to multiply themselves even as the cars came together.

The car was given the name Model A, with its hopeful suggestion of being the progenitor of a long run of alphabetical successors. Wills had done an immense amount of the work that brought it into being, but it was wholly the product of Henry Ford's mind.

It was light. Later he said "it was lighter than any car that had yet been made." He knew better than that: At 1,250 pounds it weighed 400 pounds more than the Oldsmobile. But in a way, Ford was justified in his hyperbole, because the Model A was a great deal of car for the money. Ford had hoped to sell it for $500, but in the end the cost came to $750—and another hundred with the tonneau. That was nonetheless a very good price for an automobile that had an eight-horsepower, two-cylinder engine that pushed it along at thirty miles an hour while running more smoothly than any single-cylinder could.

The body contributed to the car's relative lightness. One of those first dozen workers, Fred Wandersee, who had been hired to sweep the floors of the place, described fitting it to the chassis. "The body came on a hand truck and they picked it up and put it on. The fellows could lift a car body easy enough. After the car was assembled one fellow would take hold of the rear end and one the front and lift the whole thing up." It had been painted a single color: crimson.

Final fitting included the attachment of vestigial fenders. One of the workers said, "You could wear them as a luck charm, they were so small."

The car itself was small—a wheelbase of just six feet. Clearly this disturbed its creator's sense of proportion. When shown an accurate rendering of the car in profile for his company's first advertising efforts, Ford told the illustrator to "stretch it out. It looks too short."

The Model A appeared at a slightly more dignified but still plausible length in magazine ads that July: "BOSS OF THE ROAD," read one that ran in *Frank Leslie's Popular Monthly.* "This new light touring car fills the demand for an automobile between a runabout and a heavy touring car. It is positively the most perfect machine on the market, having overcome all drawbacks such as smell, noise, jolt, etc., common to all other makes of Auto Carriages. It is so simple a boy of fifteen can run it."

"Always ready, always sure," another ad said. "Built to take you anywhere you want to go and back again on time. Built to add to your reputation for punctuality; to keep your customers good-humored and in a buying mood. Built for business or pleasure—just as you say."

It could go fast, "without acquiring any of those breakneck velocities which are so universally condemned." This from the father of the *999,* and somewhat contradicted by another advertisement: "It is your say, too, when it comes to speed. You can—if you choose—loiter lingeringly through shady avenues or you can press down on the foot-lever until all the scenery looks alike to you and you have to keep your eyes skinned to count the milestones as they pass."

Finally, always, the company promoted the Model A's "exceedingly reasonable" price, "which places it within the reach of many thousands who could not think of paying the comparatively fabulous prices asked for most machines."

All these virtues—simplicity, reliability, dependability, cost—were portents of what would make the Ford Motor Company the Ford Motor Company, and they struck a chord with potential car buyers below the Vanderbilt level.

The *Leslie's* ad finished with a mildly preposterous claim—"for beauty of finish it is unequalled" (at the time the body was being painted by a couple of guys in what Wandersee described as "a barn down the alley")—followed by a bravely preposterous one: "—and we promise IMMEDIATE DELIVERY."

There were no cars to deliver when the advertisements were written. Ford's handful of workers struggled heroically ten hours a day to rectify this as soon as the Dodges sent the first of the 650 chassis mandated by the initial order. Working two or three to a car, some adjusted the carburetors, some made sure the brakes gripped, some pulled out faulty valves and ground them on one of the few machines in the Mack Avenue factory. One of them remembered, "We used to try to get out fifteen cars a day. We would work our hearts out to get out fifteen cars a day."

Getting out even fifteen cars a day cost money, and none was coming in. The company was struggling before the first chassis appeared.

On June 26 the Ford Motor Company had $14,500 on hand. The next day John Anderson turned over his (father's) money, and now there was $19,500. Ten thousand of that went at once to the Dodge brothers. Then $640 was sent to Hartford to buy the tires. Five thousand more to the Dodges; $7 for the charm-bracelet fenders; $22 as per order of C. H. Wills for "sundry bills." By July 10, after being in business for less than a month, the Ford Motor Company had a bank balance of $223.65.

Five days later the starving newborn received sustenance in the form of a check drawn on the Illinois Trust & Savings Bank. A Chicago dentist named Pfennig became the company's first customer. As Anderson had optimistically predicted to his father, Dr. Pfennig had ordered the tonneau, so the check was for $850.

By summer's end, the Model A had proven itself a success. "The business went almost by magic," Ford said. "The cars gained a reputation for standing up." During its first fifteen months, the Model A found seventeen hundred buyers.

Not all of them thought that the Boss of the Road deserved any reputation for standing up. Those early models could set their radiator water on a boil when the car was running through a cool day in high gear on a good road. The brakes were serviceable, but not if the Dodge workers had hurried the job, and rectifying their sloppiness meant tearing apart the rear axle. The carburetor, originally a Dodge contribution, was bad, and continued to be until Ford and Wills designed a better one. The spark plugs fouled. Even when the brakes were properly adjusted, their fragile cast-iron drums often shattered.

A very early dealer sent from Los Angeles a sheet of urgent recommendations that can be read as a sort of free-verse summary of the state of the Model A—actually, of the entire automotive industry—in 1903:

> *Make brakes more sensitive and powerful by shortening and*
> *adjusting eye-bolt.*
>
> *See that the lubricator glasses have large enough hole.*
>
> *Put in Schebler carburetor.*
>
> *Get the valve in the gas tank out of the way of carburetor.*
>
> *Make strut rod end adjustable for wear.*
>
> *Put battery terminals outside battery box.*
>
> *Front wheels turn wrong. Steering knuckles should be bent*
> *differently.*
>
> *Radiator too small; more radiator tubes needed.*
>
> *Steering rod eye-bolt wears out too quickly.*
>
> *Cast iron in which plug is screwed is too long.*
>
> *Pins in steering wheel should be upset at each end.*

Henry Ford was every bit as sensitive to the faults of his car as was his most angry customer.

Had William Murphy been in the room when Ford told the illustrator to make the Model A longer, he might have given a sour grin of recognition and thought: "It's going to happen again." Ford was perfectly capable of deciding to make not only the portrait of his car longer, but the actual car, too. That might hold up production for a month, and then Ford could decide to tackle the carburetors once they'd revealed their shortcomings, and then the brakes would need attention . . .

That Henry Ford didn't follow this all too familiar pattern is due to the combative persistence of one man.

CHAPTER 8

Ford Finds His Greatest Asset

"Who in hell are you?"; Couzens bosses the boss; the cars get shipped; the importance of dealers; an earthquake proves the Model A; parasites; who was Malcomson?

Early in the negotiations between Malcomson and Ford and the Dodge brothers, John Dodge suggested—probably too mild a word—certain changes in the contract.

A dough-faced but sturdy-looking young man scarcely out of his twenties, wearing over hostile blue eyes round wire-rimmed glasses that were at least a decade too old for him, said, "I won't stand for that."

John Dodge looked at him in astonishment. "Who in hell are you?"

"That's all right," said Malcomson, trying to hurry past a potentially ugly impasse, "Couzens is my advisor on this."

James Couzens had not particularly wanted to advise his boss on this Ford Motor Company, but he'd been with Malcomson long enough to know how swollen and thin-stretched the Malcomson coal enterprises were. If Ford failed, so would they. But if Ford could be made to succeed, Malcomson would handle its business and the coal operations would fall to Couzens. This interested Couzens greatly.

—〰〰〰〰—

James Joseph Couzens, Jr., seemed to have been looking for an important job all his life. He had been born in the small town of Chatham in Ontario, Canada. His father—who for some reason could not manage to get along with his own father—was heading to America but ran short of money four hundred miles shy of the border and Detroit. He got off the train in Chatham equipped with a grocery clerk's training and the peculiar vein of arrogance that would show up pure in his son.

The senior Couzens did not seek a lofty job—he found work as a handyman in a hardscrabble general store—but he spoke with a studied elegance that would have made his neighbors think he was "above himself."

Chatham, municipal nonentity that it was, had an interesting history. Its citizens played a large part in capturing Detroit during the War of 1812, and half a century later abolitionists decided it should be the last stop on the Underground Railroad. John Brown convened a meeting there in 1858 calling for an invasion of the United States. By the time John Couzens arrived, the town was still so predominantly black that once he'd married a woman he'd brought over from England and the two produced a baby, neighbors liked to joke that James Joseph Couzens, Jr., was "the first white child born in Chatham."

Before the boy was in his teens he had dropped the Junior—he wasn't going to be anybody's junior—and the Joseph, because he had already established another generation of paternal hostility in the Couzens family.

The father in time had been accepted by Chatham townsfolk as a cheerful and polite neighbor despite his airs, and charmingly deferential to his wife. To his son, he was savage. "I have been panned ever since I was born," Couzens said once.

The results showed up early in James. In elementary school he yanked the principal's beard for no good reason, getting himself suspended. Later he said he "guessed" he did it because to him the principal's beard represented "authority."

A surprise fifteen-hundred-dollar inheritance allowed Couzens Senior to move from the job he'd gotten working in a soap factory to establishing the "Couzens Steam Soap Works, James J. Couzens, Prop."

The consequent change in family status that his son perceived helped convince him you gained manhood by making money, and he set about doing so. He pumped the organ in his father's Presbyterian church for ten cents a week, bolstering this with a dollar a month lighting Chatham's four gas streetlamps every evening.

His personality solidified early. The mother of one of his classmates, a neighbor, complained to Mrs. Couzens that when her daughter called hello to James from across the street, he "deliberately snubbed" her. Chided for his unsociable behavior, the schoolboy explained that "if a girl wishes to speak to me, she should come across the street and do it properly."

He wasn't a schoolboy for long. At the age of twelve he found an ad in the *Chatham Planet* seeking a bookkeeper for a flour mill. High school would be a waste of time, he decided, and applied for the position and (although the circumstances are almost impossible to imagine) got it.

Over his father's vigorous objections he went to work, and did about as well as could be expected from a preadolescent with no training whatever. He was fired and found he didn't like failing one bit. He went back to high school for two years and then, still stinging from his short-lived career, entered a local business college to study bookkeeping.

By 1890 he'd run out of patience with business school and Chatham, and went to Detroit where, just eighteen, he got a job as a car checker on the Michigan Central Railroad at forty dollars a month. Couzens had to note down the numbers on the freight cars that entered the yards, check the seals on their doors, and tack a confirmatory card to the side of each car. This was merely tiresome work in August, but in December, when the cars might roll in carrying a couple of inches of ice on their sides, it was a true ordeal. During bad weather his fellows often glanced at an encrusted seal and simply wrote down "indistinct." Couzens never shirked, always chipping away the ice until the seal yielded up its secrets to his kerosene lantern. Bundled against the Michigan winter, he couldn't fumble in his pockets for tacks, so he held them ready in his mouth, where sometimes the searing cold froze them to his tongue.

All the time, even in the stormy midnight yards, he dressed like a banker. He made few friends in his ramshackle boardinghouse, and his eyes already looked, as they would for the rest of his life, forbidding as gun sights beyond those round lenses.

Railroad bureaucracy rarely moved swiftly, but the car checker's superiors saw what sort of worker they had in Couzens, and when he turned twenty-one and asked for a promotion, they jumped him over several men who'd been with the road years longer to make him the head of the freight office.

Couzens was not a popular boss. Stern, distant, and always cross—his employees began to say that his sole annual smile signaled the spring breaking of the ice on Lake Erie—he nonetheless was grudgingly regarded as a fair one. "He never tried to shift responsibility upon others to shield himself," said a man who worked for him in the freight office. "If he made a mistake, he would own up regardless of what the result might be."

And if Couzens was intemperate with his underlings, he was every bit as abrupt with his superiors, and even with his customers. "The way Jim Couzens talked with these patrons on the telephone," another employee remembered, "giving them holy hell, was just astounding."

He had plenty of opportunity to dispense holy hell because the Michigan Central had just imposed demurrage charges on its clients, which were in effect fines for taking too much time unloading one of the railroad's cars. This angered virtually everyone who used the road, but Couzens had a bottomless capacity for returning anger with more anger.

One of the customers who often got the sharp side of his tongue was Alexander Malcomson. He had plenty of temper himself, but a few bouts with Couzens left him more impressed than annoyed by the man's utter devotion to the interests of the Michigan Central Railroad.

Wouldn't so implacable an advocate be of use to the Malcomson Coal Company?

In 1897 Alexander Malcomson offered Couzens the job of managing the coal company office, including—which surely would have pleased Couzens—all the bookkeeping responsibilities. Given the grandeur of the opportunity, he would be working for fifty-six dollars a month, only four dollars less than the Michigan Central paid for its humdrum duties.

Couzens accepted. A year later he was earning a hundred dollars a month and scrupulously saving enough to have accumulated his four-hundred-dollar hoard when his boss got together with Henry Ford.

Couzens knew nothing about motorcars, and that was fine with him. He remembered going out with Malcomson in his Winton: "Frequently he turned something on the dash board, explaining that he was changing the mixture." Couzens believed his boss meant he was fortifying the gasoline with water, "and I continued to think so for a long time."

He got more interested in automobiles when his employer told him how consumed he expected to be by the Ford operations. While Malcomson was away discussing engine compression and flywheels, he'd give Couzens greater responsibility in the coal business, a raise, and a bonus, too.

As it turned out, Couzens never got near the coal business again. During a meeting of the Ford stockholders-to-be, Malcomson explained his plan to John Gray, reluctant president of the new company. Gray was having none of it. Malcomson knew coal best, he said.

No, no, said Malcomson—no need for that: Couzens here is a wonderful manager; he can easily run our coal operations. That's fine, Gray replied: "If Couzens is so good then you can send him to the automobile business. He can watch that for you."

Malcomson protested again, but Gray shut down the debate: "I am putting up my money on you because you are a good coal man. You must stay in the coal business."

Thus Henry Ford was assigned a partner. He offered to drive Couzens home from the incorporation meeting on that close, muggy June night. In the welcome breeze generated by his car, Ford started discussing salaries with his new business manager. He said, "What do you think we should ask from those fellows?"

The simple question was heavily freighted. He and James Couzens were going to be together at Mack Avenue doing work. "Those fellows" were going to benefit from their efforts simply because they'd been able to write checks. The "we" and "those fellows" shine a light forward along the whole track of Ford's life.

In time, Ford would become consumed by his resentment of "those fellows," but in the first months of manufacturing what worried him most were the complaints of the fellows who had bought his cars. Each one stung him. Perhaps it was a shattered brake drum, perhaps one more cavil about the teakettle radiator. Whatever the particular goad, Ford started once again to voice his conviction that the customers were right, that the car wasn't quite ready yet, and had to be improved before it was sent out in the market. Another month or so should suffice.

Such scruples had already wrecked two promising companies, but those operations hadn't had James Couzens's infinite reserve of stubbornness and resource to draw on.

Couzens told Ford no. Couzens would, he said, be willing to dispatch a mechanic to anywhere in the country to fix an ailing Model A, "but stop shipping, and we go bankrupt."

Ford kept shipping. Couzens would accompany him down to the yards—and no man knew his way better around a railroad yard than James Couzens—to make sure that the automobiles were actually aboard the freight cars, and the car doors sealed shut.

Couzens exercised the same fierce vigilance over every aspect of the company's operations. He got to his office in the Mack Avenue plant at seven in the morning, and stayed there until eleven most nights.

Everything that Ford couldn't do, he did. He took care of the books, of course, he kept a constant intimidating eye on the shop floor, and he wrote lively and seductive advertising copy. He made no friends, above or below him. When Alexander Malcomson sold a close acquaintance a Model A at a discount (a practice forbidden by Couzens), the founder of the company found himself so flayingly berated that he made up the difference to the company out of his own pocket.

A few years later, managers who had authority over groups of workers the size of army divisions would sneak off into the men's room to open a communication from Couzens, so they could absorb in privacy whatever devastations it might contain.

The only people who didn't live in fear of Couzens were his family. When he was still working for the railroad, Couzens had further enraged his stringently Presbyterian father by marrying Margaret Manning, a Roman Catholic. Couzens treated his father's protests as he did those of any agitator about a Michigan Central freight surcharge. The match seems to have been a remarkably solid and happy one. He was a tolerant, even pliant father to his children, and then to his grandchildren. A decade ago his grandson Frank Couzens, Jr., wrote, "We loved him. We knew him as Daddy Jim." The harshest remonstrance he remembers receiving from the scariest man in Detroit came when Daddy Jim "observed me trying to cut my meat with my elbows up in the air. He asked, 'Are you trying to fly, Frank?'"

In the shop, though, one of the workers from the early days said, "He was a manhandler. We went in enthusiastically and he opened up the hydrant on us and chilled us off." Another colleague put it more succinctly: "I called him 'Sunny Jim' because he was so God damned mean."

Couzens was far more than just a hectoring bully. Ford R. Bryan, a historian and descendant of the Ford family, writes that "Ford by himself could not have managed a small grocery store, and Couzens could not have assembled a child's kiddie car. Yet together they built an organization that astounded the world."

——————~~~wwwwwww~~——————

The Model As came off the line—or, rather, their sawhorses—and were tuned and shined to the best of the small factory's ability, and sent out into the world to fare as well as they could despite all their imperfections. Behind them came the Ford mechanics, dozing in the smoking cars of trains that were taking them ever farther from Detroit, stepping down and checking in under the stained ceilings of railroad hotels, seeking out exasperated owners and jollying them into a better mood, fixing the cars, of course, and then reporting the problems back to Mack Avenue where Ford and Wills were quick to address them.

The steering rod eyebolt was strengthened, the eggshell brake drums made thicker, the carburetors replaced. When Ford's friend Peter Steenstrup wrote an anguished letter beginning, "You have broken faith with me!" because he found that the new cars contained ball bearings and not the Hyatts Steenstrup had promised in his advertisements, the roller bearings came into the recipe. Bit by bit, gear by bolt, Ford and Wills and their workers improved the Model A on the fly. Each month saw a more reliable product shipped forth on the implacable tides of Couzens's schedule. The Model A that went to customers in early 1904 looked identical to its predecessor sent six months earlier, but it was a different car. It had, under the steady and heeded hectoring of salesmen and customers and Wills and Ford and Couzens, been entirely reworked; even, in Allan Nevins's word, "reborn."

The Model A had grown up to be an excellent car, worthy now of the premature praise with which Couzens had varnished it. Couzens, who understood everything about the car business except how a car worked, looked at the books and they told him that during the two months ending on September 30, 1903, 215 cars had been built and (here he surely would have hazarded a rare smile) 195 of them shipped. Moreover, as Anderson had assured his father, 159 of them went out capped with the desirable and profitable tonneau.

On November 21, Couzens had the company pay its shareholders a 10 percent dividend. Ford contracted with the Dodges for 725 more chassis, wanting them at the rate of 7 a day. The Mack Avenue plant grew a second floor, another five thousand dollars' worth of faith in the company.

Henry Ford practiced none of his random disappearances during these months. He was always there, always accessible, always willing to lend a hand. One of the men working on the chassis remembered, "If there was a dirty job and he had a good pair of trousers on, he wouldn't hesitate a minute in those days to tackle any job."

His peppery tester Fred Rockelman said, "At the time we looked upon Mr. Ford as our great godfather or benefactor. We were always able to go to his office because he would have an open door and we felt he had a great sense of understanding of mechanics."

Ford's bonhomie had thorns in it, though, even then. One of those first dozen he hired was a mechanic named Dick Kettlewell, a young man whose long, grave, innocent face was so trusting that it made him the object of practical jokes. Most of them were on the exploding-cigar level, but here is one that Ford and the famously dignified Wills (well, he was in his twenties, but still . . .) worked out together. The two men fixed a live wire to the metal urinal in the shop's men's room, and waited until Kettlewell paid it a visit. Judging the proper moment, one of them threw a switch and the punch of wattage flashed up the stream of urine. A fellow mechanic, Fred Seeman, said, "Dick just gave out one yell and came running out of the toilet before buttoning his pants," while Ford could barely stand for laughing.

This is a harsher practical joke than buttering doorknobs, and far more elaborate than nailing somebody's shoes to the floor. For all the goodwill Ford shed on his Mack Avenue operation, it suggests a coarsening in the man, a nascent cruelty.

The workers who tormented the invincibly gullible Kettlewell would no more have thought of playing a practical joke on Mr. Couzens—which is what Ford himself called the man—than they would have on President Roosevelt. Indeed, they might have picked TR first as the mark, guessing, rightly, that he was better natured.

If Mr. Ford and Mr. Couzens kept a certain distance from each other—and no photograph of the two together betrays the slightest sense of mutual geniality—at first they worked in complete mutual trust.

Couzens believed from the start in the necessity of establishing reliable dealerships at a time when many would-be automobile sellers would display several different machines, knowing that one of the makers would be gone by the spring and that another one's cars wouldn't start. Couzens was pushing for a strictly organized group of dealerships before the first Model A sold, and Ford agreed with him.

Fred Rockelman remembered, "Mr. Ford was always a great believer in service. He always said that a car was never complete, that it was 75 per cent complete when it left the factory, and 25 per cent of the completion was done by the dealers. It needed gasoline, it needed tires, it needed tire repairs, it needed washing, and it needed tuning up. . . . A Ford car as manufactured plus the dealers' service made it 100 per cent in the hands of the public. Mr. Ford from the very early days pressed that the dealers should be able to give service to their cars. That was uppermost in his mind constantly."

Ford himself said, "A manufacturer is not through with his customer when a sale is completed. He has then only started with his customer. If the machine does not give service, then it is better for the manufacturer if he never had the introduction, for he will have the worst of all advertisements—a dissatisfied customer. . . . A man who bought one of my cars was in my opinion entitled to continuous use of that car, and therefore if he had a breakdown of any kind it was our duty to see that his machine was put into shape again at the earliest possible moment."

Ford went on to say that in the days when he was starting out,

"The repair men were for a time the largest menace to the auto industry." If "an unscrupulous mechanic [had] an inadequate knowledge of automobiles and an inordinate desire to make a good thing out of every car that came in his shop for repairs, then even a slight breakdown meant weeks of laying up and a whopping repair bill. . . . Even as late as 1910 and 1911 the owner was regarded as essentially a rich man whose money ought to be taken away from him. We met that situation squarely and at the very beginning. We would not have our distribution blocked by stupid greedy men."

The very beginning was William Hughson, a San Franciscan who earned his living by representing eastern manufacturers on the West Coast. In 1902 he went to a bicycle show in Chicago and there was puzzled to come upon a four-wheeled bicycle. He was examining this anomaly when a well-dressed man standing next to him asked, "Interested?"

"What is this thing?"

Hughson wrote that "the man introduced himself as Henry Ford, and the 'thing' as a motor carriage. He hadn't said five words before I began to feel he was the most interesting man I'd ever met. He was a dreamer, too. He talked about the future of his automobile, how it would help people, particularly how it would ease the farmer's burden of heavy toil. A lot of that stuff was over my head, but I felt a complete confidence in this man."

Ford asked Hughson if he might be interested in representing his cars in California. Hughson said sure: "It didn't cost money to be a representative."

That was true, but Ford told his new friend that he'd need about five thousand dollars to buy a stock of cars. This seemed not to bother Hughson in the least: "He agreed to let me know when they would be in production, and I agreed to come back with the money. We shook hands and that was the deal."

Half a year later Hughson showed up in Detroit with five thousand dollars of borrowed money. This was in that hot June when the company was forming. Ford greeted him, said that although he was soon to begin production, there were as yet no cars. Why not invest the money in the company? This seemed like a fine idea to the apparently endlessly optimistic Hughson, but not to his investors, who wired back, "You went to Detroit to buy automobiles. Now buy automobiles."

So the investors, all unknowing, said good-bye to about $35 million and hello to the dozen Model As that eventually arrived—and sat on Hughson's shelf. He "hardly sold one in three years. My partner, George Emmons was a drayman, and we'd rent one out occasionally with a driver. But no sales."

William Hughson and his wife were shaken out of bed on the morning of their fourteenth wedding anniversary, April 18, 1906, by the San Francisco earthquake.

"My cars were in a warehouse on Market Street. I started to drive there from my office at the other end of town. As I passed the Call Building, the corner fell off it. Before I got to the warehouse, flames were meeting across Market Street like a canopy."

Some of his cars were stuck in the basement, but he managed to wrestle six or seven off the main floor and turned them over to General Frederick Funston, who was in command of the riven, blazing city.

"The United States Army had marched in . . . I went to see General Funston and he assigned every automobile to Red Cross work or helping with the Army. Cars could go where horses balked. My Fords could climb hills, and kept going when others broke down."

Two hundred private automobiles were drafted into service. That it was a hard and steady service is shown by their consuming fifteen thousand gallons of gasoline donated by the Standard Oil Company. When the incandescent streets exploded their tires, the cars clanged uphill and down on their rims, steering around the bodies of dray horses dead from heat and exhaustion.

Ten days later, the *San Francisco Chronicle* wrote, "That the automobile played an all but indispensable part in saving the Western part of San Francisco and at the same time had proved invaluable in the serious business of governing the city through its greatest stress is conceded by every man who has had his eyes open. . . . Old men in the bread lines who had previously occupied much of their time on supper-table denunciations of the whiz-wagons now have nothing but praise for them. Men high in service . . . go even further and say that but for the auto it would not have been possible to save even a portion of the city or to take care of the sick or to preserve a semblance of law and order."

"It was a terrible time," said Hughson. "I lost my voice from inhaling the brick dust; that's why I still talk in this husky whisper. But you know, that was the beginning for the automobile in the West.

"It took an earthquake to show people the soundness of Henry Ford's idea."

General Funston appreciated Henry Ford's idea, and showed his gratitude by having his soldiers knock together a plywood shack at 318 Market Street right in front of the still-warm embers of Hughson's office. "We were the first business to resume on Market Street," Hughson said. "And from then on the automobile business began to grow. Cars became the workhorses in the job of rebuilding San Francisco."

Remembering back across half a century, Hughson said, "Henry Ford came out to the West Coast personally to see if he could help. He said, 'If you need anything, we'll send it out. You pay for it when you can.' Insurance companies were going broke and money was awfully tight. But Ford shipped us carload after carload of cars until we got back on our feet. I never forgot that."

If the Ford visit to the ruined city gives a vibration of the apocryphal, Hughson's feelings toward the man at that time are clearly genuine.

The dealer was, in a way, able to return the favor five years later. In 1911 someone came upon a heap of picturesque wreckage in a West Coast junkyard and recognized it as the *999*, which had campaigned its way to the Pacific and died there. Oldfield went to take a look and said it was scrap, beyond repair. Hughson didn't think so. He bought it and restored it, and today it stands in all its old pugnacious bravado in the Dearborn museum.

Perhaps Henry Ford didn't come personally to visit Hughson, but there's a good chance that Couzens did. He met all the dealers he could, and sized them up with his cold, shrewd gaze. (He clearly approved of Hughson, who eventually was responsible for 120 western Ford dealerships.) Within a decade the requirements for a Ford dealer had been codified, and were strictly enforced: twenty thousand dollars' worth of spare parts on hand; the facilities and willingness to repair any Ford car no matter where it had been purchased; at least one immaculate new model there at all times to show potential buyers; and the strong suggestion that if a disabled Ford had to be taken in to the shop, the towing should take place after dark so as not to draw attention to the car's plight.

While Couzens was building this unprecedented network, Ford's old rival Alexander Winton's advertisements boasted, "Write us direct—WE HAVE NO AGENTS." The Winton Motor Carriage Company built its last car in 1924.

—————∿∿∿∿∿∿—————

In the spring of 1905 James Couzens could tell the *Detroit Journal,* "We are now turning out twenty-five machines a day on average and giving employment to three hundred men."

His city was enjoying the same boom. That year a *Journal* headline read, "Eight Thousand Men Build Autos." Henry Ford said that the New York Automobile Show should change its name to the Detroit Automobile Show, since Detroit contributed half a dozen times more cars than any other American town. Thanks to its pool of skilled machinists, that year Detroit turned out 11,180 cars. Every part of an automobile was being made there except tires, and that changed in the spring when the Rubber Goods Manufacturing Company started building a plant on the riverfront. The company's president said, "The great industry of today is the manufacture of automobiles, and soon Detroit will be the center of the world in that business." The *Journal* fretted about the coming "Auto Famine" and said "manufacturers are swamped with orders."

Ford was, and had moved from the Mack Avenue plant to a new three-story building on Piquette that had ten times as much floor space. Here he built the Model A's successors, the B, C, and F (the D and the E disappeared with the experimental models they designated). The C and the F were essentially improved Model As, a little heavier, a little more powerful. The B was a different animal altogether. It was an imposing touring car—the term was just coming into wide use—with a twenty-four-horsepower, four-cylinder engine that could spur it along at forty miles an hour. The Model B weighed seventeen hundred pounds, and cost two thousand dollars. It was Malcomson's baby, and Ford didn't like it.

Malcomson wanted the Ford Motor Company to build expensive cars. In 1906 an Apperson two-seater sports car (although that phrase was still forty years in the future) cost $10,500, and a nice suburban house might go for $2,000. Work out that calculation today: If prices had stayed relative the house would cost $1.2 million, and a Dodge Viper would cost $6 million. Of course it was more desirable to sell something that cost thousands of dollars than something that cost hundreds.

Henry Ford believed exactly the opposite. Make the car cheaper, not more expensive; you'll do better selling lots of low-priced cars to farmers and shop clerks than you will a few lavish ones to millionaires.

In later years Ford suggested that this lightweight, inexpensive everyman's car had been his lifelong goal. In fact it is difficult to discover just when the idea took hold with him, but it was fully formed by the time he founded the Ford Motor Company. In the middle of that year, he told John Anderson, "When you get to making the cars in quantity, and when you make them cheaper you can get more people with enough money to buy them. The market will take care of itself. . . . The way to make automobiles is to make one automobile like another automobile, to make them all alike, to make them come through the factory just alike; just as one pin is like another when it comes from a pin factory, or one match like another when it comes from a match factory."

As his convictions hardened, his friction with the board increased. Couzens, who by now was siding with Ford on virtually everything, just wanted a car that he could sell for more than it cost to build. The Dodge brothers were for an expensive car, but disliked Malcomson and didn't fight on his behalf when he demanded one.

As a leading investor, Malcomson had the clout to get what he wanted. Late in 1905 the Model K came on the market: six cylinders, ten-foot wheelbase, twenty-four hundred pounds and costing more than a dollar a pound, all brass and lacquer and fragrant leather.

At the same time, Ford was feeling his way toward his vision with the Model N. Three feet shorter than the K, and weighing a third as much, it nonetheless had a four-cylinder engine, an unprecedented feature at Ford's asking price: "I believe that I have solved the problem of cheap as well as simple construction. Advancement in building has passed the experimental stage, and the general public is interested only in the knowledge that a serviceable machine can be constructed at a price within the reach of many. I am convinced that the $500 model is destined to revolutionize automobile construction, and I consider my new model the crowning achievement of my life."

Despite this ambitious, even messianic, pronouncement, the crowning achievement did not yet exist. He sent the car to the 1906 New York automobile show with nothing but vacant air under the hood, because the engine wasn't ready. His agents were forbidden to lift that hood no matter what, but the price made the ambitious little car an immediate hit nonetheless.

The Model N's success meant that it *had* to be put on the market for $500, which in turn demanded the most stringent economies at Piquette Avenue. Ford wangled the body maker down from a unit cost of $152 to $72. Some of the savings were fortuitous. One of Ford's associates remembered, "Painting the wheels was considered a highly skilled job, for stripes on the spokes gave a star effect to the center of the wheel. It was quite an expensive operation until the day we refused the painters' demand for more pay per wheel. They went on strike. That settled stripes on wheels. We gave them up, so, in a way, the painters helped us lower costs."

After the Ford Motor Company had squeezed all the excess it could

out of the car, and put it on sale for the promised price, the dealers couldn't get enough of them. So eager were they for Model Ns
that they meekly swallowed Ford's demand that for every ten Ns they
accept one Model K.

Malcomson's ideal car wasn't selling. Ford, a quiet but dedicated
gloater, likely gloated about that. He also did a great deal more than
gloat.

Even as the Model A was sprinkling prosperity on everyone
involved in its creation, friction grew among the shareholders.

Most of the discord came from the different aims of Ford and Malcomson. There was more than that to the acrimony, though. As he had
back in the Detroit Automobile Company's brief day, Ford was beginning to resent not being his own man. That Malcomson's faith and
capital had made possible his success meant less and less to Ford. He
was surely thinking of his chief investor when he said, "Anyone who
did not have a part in the manufacturing of the company was actually
not contributing and was a parasite."

For his part, Malcomson thought Ford was being both stubborn
and perverse. The trend throughout the industry was toward expensive
cars. In 1906 half the automobiles sold in America went for between
three and five thousand dollars. Why stake your business on sales a
tenth this magnitude? A decade later, such cars would command less
than 2 percent of the market. But during fractious and hostile board
meetings, Ford alone foresaw that.

When the tussling grew from shouted disagreement to an actual
corporate fight, it was Malcomson who started it.

He said, truly enough, that the original arrangement had stipulated
that Couzens would handle the car business while Malcomson got his
coal dealership in order, and then the two men would swap positions.
This had been all Couzens wanted when he joined up with Ford a
couple of years earlier. But back then he'd believed a car could run on
water. His hard-earned success with his partner made him refuse his
boss. So did Henry Ford: "I told Malcomson that I did not want him
but that I wanted his man Couzens."

Malcomson then seems to have tried to get Couzens fired. Ford in turn persuaded the board to double his business manager's salary from four to eight thousand. This was in part a provocation, and like most deliberate provocations, it worked. Malcomson protested violently at the next shareholders' meeting, despite the fact that the Ford Motor Company had enjoyed a net profit that year of nearly thirty times his initial investment.

As the claustrophobic meetings bickered on, Ford and Couzens decided on a strategy at once sly and forthright.

The Ford Motor Company had advanced to a maturity where it was no longer desirable, and possibly even dangerous, for the company to rely on a single supplier for the heart and muscle of all its automobiles. Henry Ford announced the incorporation of the Ford Manufacturing Company, which would make chassis, but only for the Model N. The Dodges would continue to build them for the big Model K. The brothers had nothing to kick about because they automatically became shareholders in the new company and recipients of all the dividends it would generate.

Malcomson, on the other hand, did not: He retained his shares in the Ford Motor Company, of course, but would get profits only on the sale of the finished cars. And who knew how much the new, housebuilt chassis would cut into that profit. They were to be supplied at an "unspecified" cost. The price ratio would make no difference to those who held shares in both companies; it would make plenty of difference to Malcomson.

He sent an angry letter to the board denouncing the "Ford Manufacturing Company [which is] comprised and controlled by the holders of the majority both of stock and directorships of the motor company, and designed . . . to sell its products to the Motor Company, presumably not without profit." The new company's allocation of shares ensures "the prospect of participating in the profits and confining the injury to those stockholders of the Motor Company on the outside.

"I consider this scheme as unwise as it is unfair."

This was a position difficult for anyone to argue against. But then the gambler's audacity that had given birth to the Ford Motor Company, intensified by indignation and bruised feelings, prodded Malcomson into taking an unwise step.

On December 5, 1905, the *Detroit Free Press* announced the establishment of a new auto plant in the city. The Aerocar Company, capitalized at four hundred thousand dollars, was building a factory on Mack Avenue that would turn out five hundred air-cooled touring cars in 1906. The company, which would be making "The Car of Today, Tomorrow, and for Years to Come," was owned by Malcomson.

That the treasurer of the Ford Motor Company would now be competing with it shifted the sympathies of the entire board to Ford. The directors demanded Malcomson's resignation, and after a few months of quarrelsome negotiations, Malcomson sold his one-fourth interest to Ford.

He got $175,000, hardly a bad return on an investment of $10,000 three years earlier. But if he'd stuck it out for a decade longer he would have gotten $100 million.

Bennett, the Daisy air rifle magnate, disgusted by the maneuver and wanting no more to do with those who had planned it, got out, too.

Ford had found that despite all his squeezing, he could not keep the Model N on the market for five hundred dollars. He raised the price by one hundred dollars. At six hundred dollars the N was not really a cheap car, but with its four-cylinder engine it was more powerful and reliable than anything close to its price. Up until September 1906, when Ford was able fully to back the N, the company had offered many models—among them, of course, the sumptuous K—and sold 1,559 cars altogether. By the end of the following September, selling only the Model N and very minor variations (one of them forthrightly described in his sales literature as "more pretentious"), Henry Ford sold 8,243.

His bruised partner Malcomson had been in earnest about his challenge, and a few Aerocars got built. Then the operation, like so many hundreds of other carmakers in those years, disappeared.

Forty years after the death of the Aerocar company in 1908, the journalist John Gunther came to Detroit to do research for the book that would become his bestselling *Inside USA*. Reading about the original Ford Motor Company stockholders, he spotted an unfamiliar name and got curious: "I would like very much to know about a man named Alex Y. Malcomson. He too had 255 shares in the original company, an amount equal to Ford's, and he was its first treasurer. It seems that he was a coal dealer, and Couzens was a clerk in his office. Ford must, of course, have bought him out many years ago, as he bought out Couzens. I was unable to find anybody in Detroit who knew further about Mr. Malcomson."

CHAPTER 9

Inventing the Universal Car

Who wanted it?; Sorensen's locked room; steering wheel on the left—forever; new experts, new engine, new steel, new car; "Without doubt the greatest creation in automobiles ever placed before a people."

When the struggle was over, Henry Ford was the majority stockholder in the company that Malcomson had paid for and to which he had given Ford's name. In the summer of 1906 heart trouble killed John Gray, and Henry Ford moved up from vice president to president of the Ford Motor Company. Nobody would ever again be in a position to tell him what kind of car he had to build.

Clara Ford's household records suggest that she was beginning to realize that her family was on the way to becoming rich. For the first time she began to buy food from catering firms: chicken salad sandwiches at ten cents each, and lobster salad for a hefty $1.50 a quart. She subscribed to magazines: the once famous children's publication *St. Nicholas, Good Housekeeping,* and *Munsey's,* a high-level general-interest monthly. Her husband seemed to be having a good time—he enjoyed going to the theater with Clara and playing with Edsel—but he was fretting.

The Model N was doing more than well. Yet every time Ford looked at one, he was goaded by the specter of a better car hidden somewhere within it.

On the evening of the day he bought out Malcomson, he asked Fred Rockelman to give him a lift home. Like the time he'd driven with Couzens after the formation of the company that was now wholly and indisputably his, he was rolling through an oppressively hot summer dusk.

"Fred," he said, "this is a great day. We're going to expand this company, and you will see it grow by leaps and bounds. The proper system, as I have it in mind, is to get the car to the people. . . . If you can get people together so they get acquainted with one another, and get an idea of neighborliness, the car will have a universal effect. We won't have anymore strikes or wars."

How to get the car to the people, though? That segment of the people who lived in the cities were already comfortable with it, and those heavy four-thousand-dollar machines went almost entirely to them. When the owners decided to take a spin in the country, they often angered their rural counterparts. Bouncing and banging down dirt lanes at fifty miles an hour, they'd leave behind a cloud of ill will, along with dust settling on lines of drying laundry and terrified livestock. Some counties passed ordinances that verged on the bizarre. One mandated that if motorists spotted a distant team coming their way, they were to stop and fire off warning flares, like shipwreck survivors in a lifeboat. (It is difficult to see how this measure would reassure the horses or oxen.)

Actually, things were trending in the other direction. More and more farmers wanted cars. Not, of course, the heavy ones that cost more than a farm, and whose weight would often immobilize them on the dire byways of the day. A 1909 census of American roads determined that only 8.66 percent of America's highways were "surfaced," which could mean covered with gravel, or possibly "corduroyed" with logs laid side by side like touching railroad ties that put the traveler in an endless purgatory of violent jouncing. The rest went where wagons had gone for year after year, cutting two ruts with a tall hummock of shale or mud or rocks between them.

These roads were the farmer's thoroughfares, and early in the century a new sort of automobile arose to carry him along them. It was called a "high-wheeler" or "western buggy"—"western" because these vehicles were born in the Midwest; "buggy" because that's what they basically were. To the buggy's frame, which rode on wheels more than a yard high, was fastened a single-cylinder engine. These cars were in a way more primitive than Ford's Quadricycle, but they were light, cheap (starting at $250), and their high freeboard let them scramble over some of the roughest ground. But their lightness and their wooden skeletons meant they could shake themselves into dilapidation in a matter of months, and the single cylinder could never give them quite enough push.

Yet for half a decade they sold well enough to support a score of companies. One farmer spoke for thousands when he explained why, for all its shortcomings, he liked his high-wheeler: All his life his horizon had been "bounded by the ten- or twelve-mile circle that my horses could go in a day and get back in good shape. I now make exploring trips of five times the distance. I can call on friends living thirty miles away who have been asking me to come for twenty years."

Henry Ford understood this. He wanted a car tall enough to successfully attack the worst roads, and strong enough for them not to crack its frame after a season. Most of all, it had to be cheap enough for the landlocked farmer to afford it.

~~~~~~~~~~~~~~

On a winter morning early in 1907, Ford walked into the pattern department of the Piquette Avenue plant and went over to a tall, handsome man in his midtwenties who looked, and was, both tough and dour. He stopped what he was doing and Ford said, "Charlie, I'd like to have a room finished right here in this space. Put up a wall with a door big enough to run a car in and out. Get a good lock for the door, and when you're ready, we'll have Joe Galamb come up in here. We're going to start a completely new job."

Charlie was Charles Emil Sorensen. He would be the longest lasting of Ford's high lieutenants. Most of them had a length of tenure similar to that of Stalin's marshals, but Sorensen could truthfully title his memoir *My Forty Years with Ford*.

He was born in Copenhagen in 1881, and came to America five years later. His father, a skilled woodworker, emigrated from Denmark because of his admiration for a professional runner named "Little Sorensen." The athlete wasn't a relative—"the name Sorensen is as common in Denmark as Smith is here," Charles wrote—but no family tie could have been more binding. Little Sorensen went to compete, with great success, against American runners, and when he wrote his fan, "This is a great country. Come on over," Soren Sorensen immediately complied. Little Sorensen eventually settled in Buffalo, and so it was there that Charles Sorensen spent a decade in public schools before leaving to become a patternmaker for a company that manufactured stoves. By the turn of the century he had moved with his family to Detroit.

Nineteen oh four was a pivotal year in Sorensen's life: He married Helen Miller, a young bookkeeper for the Sun Stove Company, and Henry Ford hired him at three dollars a day as an experimental patternmaker for his new car company.

In choosing Sorensen, Ford again ratified his affection for hardhanded, easily infuriated colleagues. Sorensen's temper was every bit the equal of that possessed by Couzens and the Dodge brothers. So was his ability.

It is not surprising that Ford should have approached a patternmaker to take the first steps toward the automobile he envisioned, for the patternmaker's work was a bridge between the blueprints of Wills and the blades of the machine tools.

Years later, and still proud of what he had mastered by 1906, Sorensen wrote, "Patternmaking is neither a profession nor a trade but an exacting, highly skilled craft which requires understanding of both."

The patternmaker would look over the drawing of the gear or cylinder, and then "translate" it—Sorensen's word—into a woodcarving. He had to be a bit of a "clairvoyant," Sorensen's word again, because he "must be able to read the most complicated blueprints, and he must have more than a cabinet-maker's meticulous skill and infinite patience to saw and plane, sandpaper and glue together an accurate representation of what the designer or draftsman had in mind." It had to be accurate because it made the mold into which was poured the molten metal that, once cooled and machined, would be the part itself.

Ford appreciated the patternmaker's skill more than he did the draftsman's; although he wasn't the blueprint illiterate a few of his colleagues later claimed, he always felt most comfortable with something he could handle rather than something he had to read.

"It was apparent," wrote Sorensen, "that Ford never quite understood what a design looked like until it was put into a three-dimensional pattern. I also discovered that he was not a draftsman and couldn't make a sketch that was any too clear."

Sorensen found out, too, that he almost always understood what his boss was looking for: "I began making sketches of his ideas and final drawings, and when I couldn't finish them on Piquette Avenue, I took them into the pattern shop." Eventually he got so he didn't need drawings. Ford would explain what he wanted, and Sorensen would pick up a piece of wood and make it ("We had the most beautiful white pine in those days," he remembered wistfully, "straight and clear").

From the shop he would bring Ford a model of the part, an accurate prophecy worked in wood. Ford would turn it over in his hands, squint along its curves and notches, and know exactly what needed doing: Shave a few millimeters off here; I think we're a little too thin here; no need for this flange.

So it was Sorensen Ford sought out when he wanted his chamber of invention, and in a few days he had it. The place wasn't much: twelve by fifteen feet, two blackboards, a drafting table at which Joseph Galamb was promptly and almost continuously installed, a few power tools, and a rocking chair imported from Ford's house; it had been his mother's, and he hoped it might bring him luck.

As in the Quadricycle days, access here was severely limited: Galamb, Wills, a machinist named Jimmy Smith who had been with Ford for years, Sorensen (although perhaps not so freely as he suggests in his memoir), and the fourteen-year-old Edsel. Spider Huff was back, too, no longer in his role as the man hanging out over the streaming track to keep the race car from tipping over, but as a brilliant electrical engineer who would give the new car one of its most crucial components.

Ford came every day to sit in the rocking chair, sometimes for hours at a stretch, while Galamb chalked on the blackboard sketches of his ideas and refinements of his drawings. Before being rubbed clean for the next session, the boards were photographed, both for future patent protection and to have some kind of record of the swift progress they recorded.

In this secret room, Ford's genius—and for what was going on here "genius" is not too inflated a word—played as strongly and steadily as it ever would. He deployed his inherent contradictions only toward a creative end. Contradictions, because the car he was building would be at once as simple as he could make it, and yet immensely sophisticated.

For example, it would have four cylinders, like the Model N. But then, not like the Model N. The engines in almost all the multicylinder cars of the day, even the grandest, were essentially a bundle of thick-walled pipes, strapped and bolted together. Even the Model N's four cylinders were a marriage of two different castings.

Fussy, complicated, unsatisfying, said Ford: We must machine our engine out of a single block of metal. While Sorensen was puzzling out how to do this, Ford had another thought: Slice off the top. That is, have the engine be a single casting, its cylinders wholly accessible and thus easy both to build and to repair, and fit a cylinder head on top of the four of them like a hat and bolt it down. And that is how car engines are built to this day.

This left Galamb struggling to find a gasket that could seal the engine to its new head without leaking the power of the endless inferno of little explosions that propelled the car. Ford rocked back and forth in his chair, radiating the calm and friendly conviction that Galamb would come through. Galamb always did.

Couzens was not calm and friendly. "Ford was always relaxed," Sorensen remembered, "whereas Couzens drove himself to the limit." Yet "Ford's patience, perhaps more than Couzens' driving, inspired the rest of us to work long hours to clear away problems."

At first, the castings made from Sorensen's patterns were mounted on a Model N chassis rolled in through the door Ford had said should be made large enough to accommodate a car. The Model N had run further through the alphabet by now, and new customers could buy the Model S, a grown-up-looking car whose hood and fenders collaborated to flow into a real running board, and that offered such refinements as umbrella holders. This car was not going to be a Model N, though, or even a Model S. It was going to be the Model T.

By the fall of 1907 two of its chassis were ready for the road. A thousand ever-shifting calculations went into the new car. Many of its components had been tried and found satisfactory on the Model N. Others were new. Wills, pondering how to keep both engine and transmission properly lubricated, settled into his bathtub and, like Archimedes, suddenly saw the solution to the problem: Encase both together and let gravity promiscuously bathe the two of them in oil.

What kind of transmission should enjoy this bath? Most cars of the day used the sliding gear that has come down to us, or at least to those of us who have ever used a stick shift. The stick shift was harder to maneuver then than now, for it demanded the driver pick exactly the right moment to shift gears, and then step on the clutch and force the shift to the next speed without breaking their teeth.

Ford tried the system out. Or, rather, he had a worker named

Charles Balough try it out. Balough drove into the thick of Detroit one busy weekday evening and found himself confronted by three streetcars. Stamping on the clutch and wrestling with the gearshift, he tried to swing around them and recalled some fifty years later, "The experimental model was completely wrecked, crushed between the street car and a telephone pole."

Balough went back to the office worried about what his boss would say, which turned out to be: "Charley, that's the best job you ever did for this company."

Ford had been willing to try the sliding gear, but he preferred the planetary transmission he had in the Model N. There was no shift lever for the driver to grapple with, because all the gears were always meshed in constant motion around the crankshaft—hence the "planetary"—and engaged by floor pedals that would tighten a band on one while releasing the band on another.

Ford at first wanted a three-speed transmission. Balough tried it out for him on the streets. This time he managed to avoid trolley cars, but the system wouldn't work. Again Ford smiled his driver's worries away: "The gear that gives you no trouble is the one you never use." The T would have two forward gears, and they had to be sturdier than their predecessors on earlier cars. He and Sorensen worked the problem through with a succession of carved wooden disks that Ford insisted—rightly, always, in those glowing days—could get much smaller.

Sometime during the deliberations a decision was made that would soon affect every American. Ford put the steering wheel on the left. He was defying the towering precedent of the railroad, where the locomotive engineer always sat on the right-hand side of the cab. Ford thought this made no sense on American roads.

Those roads also demanded considerable nimbleness. Most cars rode on springs set parallel to their bodies. Ford had his front and rear springs arch across the axles at the front and back of the car nearly from wheel to wheel. He balanced the machine on two sturdy triangles formed by radius rods that ran from close to the wheel hubs to the engine, which was fixed to the car's frame at only three points. Most cars of the day had the engine fastened to the frame at four places, and when the frame bent, the engine might shed its bolts and open like a purse.

Ford developed a chassis that could carry its engine almost anywhere, twisting over the broken, crooked roads supple as a cat scuttling under a fence.

Weight: Ford said that while attending a race at Ormond Beach, Florida, he'd gone over to look at the carcass of a wrecked French car and "I picked up a little valve strip stem. It was very light and very strong . . . I asked what it was made of. Nobody knew." He handed the stem to an assistant. "Find out all about this. That is the kind of material we ought to have in our cars."

This vivid incident may be one of the picturesque promotional fictions Ford manufactured almost instinctively. When he was in his seventies, a reporter noticed a bandage on his ankle and asked about it. Oh, Ford said casually, I was playing football with some kids. In fact, it was a blister.

"I sent to England," Ford wrote, "for a man who understood how they make the steel commercially. The main thing was to get a plant to turn it out."

Actually, he sent to Canton, Ohio, but there *was* an Englishman involved. The metal was real enough, too. It was a steel alloy called vanadium, which Wills first heard about at an engineering conference in 1905. A British metallurgist named J. Kent Smith was a strong proponent and went to the Piquette Avenue factory in 1906 to speak with Ford about it. Smith had a laboratory in Canton, which Ford visited, and came away persuaded: "Until then we had to be satisfied with steel running between 60,000 and 70,000 pounds tensile strength. With vanadium, the strength went up to 170,000 pounds." That meant "the strength of an automobile axle or crankshaft may be doubled without increasing the dimensions or weight."

Vanadium was strong, light, and easier to machine than nickel steel. It had been used in the Model N, and would be the backbone of the Model T.

Once Ford had decided on it, Wills told him that the company needed its own metallurgy laboratory, and they should hire a professional to establish it. Ford didn't like professionals. "No, make an expert of Wandersee," he told Wills, so a man who had been hired to sweep the factory floors went off for three months of tutelage at the United Steel Laboratory, and by late 1907 he had a laboratory of his own on Piquette Avenue and was ordering vanadium steel for the new car.

What with the vanadium steel and the general paring down of every part, the car would weigh only eleven hundred pounds. The engine could generate twenty horsepower, which might sound pallid now, but in 1907 American cars tended to weigh some eighty pounds per horsepower. The Thomas Flyer that in 1908 won an extraordinary race from New York to Paris (west, of course, across all North America and the Bering Straits and along the tracks of the Trans-Siberian railroad) weighed sixty-four pounds per horsepower. The Model T would weigh sixty pounds for every horsepower, and would cost just a little over a tenth as much as the Thomas six-cylinder limousine. Ford put the difference in engineering terms, and there is clearly no bluffing here: "With the Ford there are only 7.95 pounds to be carried by each cubic inch of piston displacement." He added, more accessibly to the average reader, "That's why Ford cars are 'always going' wherever and whenever you see them—through sand and mud, through slush, snow, and water, up hills across roadless plains."

In the meantime, Spider Huff was figuring out what might be the single most revolutionary component of the Model T. Almost all the cars of the time carried batteries, and these were costly, feeble, and in near-constant need of replacement. But you couldn't do without them, for they gave the spark of fire that ignited the gas in the cylinders.

Huff was going in another direction. For three-quarters of a century engineers had known that when a coil of wire passed close by a magnet, it picked up a charge of electricity. Ford and Huff thought about this. The car's flywheel spun all the time the engine was running: Why not stud it with magnets—sixteen was the number the two men settled on—and face it against a circle of sixteen stationary wire coils? As the flywheel whirled past these, the magnets embedded in it would spit electricity into the coils, and the car would generate its own power to fire the engine. And all of this could be contained in Wills's oil bath.

Always, through every technical decision, Ford was searching for beauty in his machine. Once the car was covered with its superstructure, which had to accommodate the driver and up to five passengers, it might not be an object to inspire aesthetic regard. But the chassis—its proportion, its confidence, its forthrightness—most certainly is.

The first factory-built Model T was finished on September 24. Henry Ford got into it and set off for what he described as a hunting trip up to northern Wisconsin. Jimmy Smith was along to do much of the driving. Smith was nervous about the magneto, and brought a storage battery just in case it didn't do its job. After about eight hours, while they were heading to Chicago, the storage battery tipped over and spilled acid all over the floor of the car. Ford made Smith throw it away. They pushed on, and without the help of the battery made it to Chicago over bad roads at an average speed of more than twenty miles an hour, then headed to Milwaukee, up to Iron Mountain, back through Milwaukee, and got home to Detroit on October 2. The Model T came in looking pretty ratty, caked as it was with a thick impasto of Michigan mud. But it had gone 1,357 miles and suffered nothing worse than a single flat tire.

Time to put it on the market, for $850. Couzens's dealers were close to rapturous. Some actually hid the early brochures so they could get rid of their stock of Model Ss before the messiah arrived. A Detroit representative wrote, "We have rubbed our eyes several times to make sure we were not dreaming," and one in Pennsylvania declared that the Model T "is without doubt the greatest creation in automobiles ever placed before a people."

The road lay shining ahead. Half of America seemed ready to buy this car. If, that is, Henry Ford was allowed to sell it.

CHAPTER 10

The Man Who Owned Every Car in America

Selden files a patent on all gas-powered automobiles and sues their makers; the court finds for him; most carmakers give in; Ford won't pay "graft money"; a second trial; "One of the greatest things Mr. Ford did . . ."

So many stories about Henry Ford that sound apocryphal may not be.

It is quite possible that while he was in the freight yard in his shirtsleeves sending off his first Model As under Couzens's stern gaze, a messenger really did pick his way across the tracks to give the men the news that the sixteen-year-long fuse George Selden lit in 1879 had just burned down to the main charge.

On October 23, 1903, Selden filed suit against the Ford Motor Company for infringement on the patent he claimed gave him authority over every gas-powered automobile in America. Selden seems truly to have believed this even though he'd never built an automobile based on his patent, but he didn't have enough money to hire lawyers to act on it. Now, though, he came with a powerful partner, for he had filed his suit in alliance with the Electric Vehicle Company.

As the name suggests, the Electric Vehicle Company was not enthusiastic about the internal combustion engine. When Hiram Maxim gave up trying to build a gas-powered car on his own and accepted the job Colonel Albert Pope offered him in his Hartford factory in 1895, he worked on both gasoline and electric cars, though always favoring the former. This put him somewhat at odds with George H. Day, who was in charge of automotive development for Pope, and who thought gas buggies far too noisy and oily.

Colonel Pope was doing nicely selling both kinds of cars in April 1899 when the financier William C. Whitney came up from New York to Hartford to have a look at his shop.

Whitney liked electric cars, too, and already had a fleet of taxicabs gliding almost noiselessly around Manhattan, built by the Electric Vehicle Company. Now he wanted more cabs—a lot more—and, backed by solid investors, he proposed that the Pope automobile efforts merge with the Electric Vehicle Company. Colonel Pope was delighted: The new company would be capitalized at $3 million.

Before he closed the deal, though, Whitney thought he'd better check and see if there were any lurking patents that might cause problems down the road. Pope had a diligent man in charge of patent matters, and he tracked down Selden.

When Maxim—who by this time knew as much about cars as anyone alive—saw the patent, "I snorted my derision. I pointed out that the engine shown in the patent was utterly impractical and a joke. . . . The claims were so broad that they were ridiculous."

Whitney didn't think so; he gave the fortunate Selden ten thousand dollars for the rights to his patent and offered him 5 percent of any royalties it might generate. In June the Electric Vehicle Company's lawyers started sending a letter out to American carmakers: "Our clients inform us that you are manufacturing and advertising for sale vehicles which embody the invention of the Selden patent. . . . We notify you of this infringement, and request that you desist from the same and make suitable compensation to the owner thereof."

These demands drew the responses that could have been expected—either hostile or nonexistent—and the Electric Vehicle Company began to sue.

Alexander Winton was the main target. The patent holders figured that if they could get a judgment against the best-known automaker in the country, the smaller-fry would fall into line.

Winton, by nature a fighter, let his company's treasurer speak for him: "The Selden patent is preposterous, and should never have been granted. . . . It does not have a leg to stand on." Winton joined in a loose confederation of other carmakers that stood against the claim. The confederation would turn out to be too loose.

In September 1900 Winton's attorney filed a writ of demurrer. This instrument held that although the alleged facts in a complaint may be true, they do not add up to a legal cause for action, and thus the defendant is free to ignore it (today this is known as a motion to dismiss). The Selden car, Winton's lawyer argued, was no invention at all: The substitution of a gas engine for the steam ones that inventors had been mounting on their road vehicles for nearly a century was nothing more than common sense.

Judge Alfred C. Coxe disagreed. "The patentee's contributions to the art should not be considered from a narrow point of view," said Coxe in an impressively eloquent ruling issued that November: "His work should not be examined through an inverted telescope; the horizon of invention should not be contracted to the periphery of a sixpence." Selden "must be regarded as the first to construct a road-locomotive provided with a liquid hydrocarbon gas-engine of the compression type."

The weakest part of the ruling is the word "construct," as Selden had never constructed any road-locomotive, hydrocarbon or otherwise. Beyond that, despite the more than one hundred changes the would-be inventor had appended to his patent during its interminable gestation, the car it described was like nothing on the road in 1900. But in what was still the dawn of a fast-flowing technological revolution, courts tended to look kindly on sweeping claims for basic patents. Everything was moving so swiftly, and flinging off new and complex puzzlements, that judges were reluctant to summarily dismiss an idea a couple of decades old just because the pace of the dawning century might make it seem archaic.

Nor did Judge Coxe's ruling ratify the validity of the patent; it only meant there was no quick way for Winton to resist it, so the case would have to be tried in the courts.

Not that this brought Winton much comfort, for at the time patent struggles were the most complex and time-consuming of all litigation. There would be few sharp, brisk courtroom exchanges, even though there was a great deal of testimony. That testimony had to be gathered by attorneys in the field, painstakingly transcribed and with no judge presiding to stifle irrelevancies or hurry things along. Winton knew that his defense could take years.

Moreover, the patent holders were making plenty of noise about Coxe's decision, promoting it as a complete victory. The companies opposing the patent were lackadaisical in defending their position, and when two small operators, Ranlet Automobile and Automotive Forecarriage, facing the legal fees inevitable in challenging what had swiftly grown to be an $18 million consortium, folded and accepted the patent, the entire industry began to get nervous.

Winton persevered. He hired a leading New York City patent law firm and sent associates across the country and to Europe to gather evidence refuting Selden. In February 1901 the lawyers filed their answer to Coxe: thirty-two separate defenses unfurled across 1,400 pages and backed by 126 patents—American, British, French—awarded beginning in 1794.

The Selden interests brought the case to trial. The trial lasted two years, during which Winton's confederation fell apart, and he found himself alone responsible for the legal fees. In the autumn of 1902 Winton discovered that some of his old allies had applied for Selden licenses. He approached the Electric Vehicle Company and asked about terms. They were generous. The EVC badly wanted Winton, and immediately waived any royalties accrued before a settlement while offering to deduct all the expenses of his suit from his future payments.

What would those payments be? This was determined by a group of automakers that would form the organization of companies that had agreed to honor the patent. Ten of them were based in Detroit. They were prepared to deal with Selden, but chafing from the coercion, and not warm to the Electric Vehicle Company's demand for a 5 percent royalty on every car sold. They established a miniature organization of their own, and each contributed twenty-five hundred dollars to it before sending five representatives off to New York in March 1903 to take in the auto show at Madison Square Garden and, more important, to negotiate with William Whitney.

The financier invited them to what he meant to feel like an informal meeting at his Fifth Avenue mansion. Whitney was a famously gracious host, but he had made a tactical blunder here. Frederick L. Smith, the treasurer of the Olds Motor Works, wrote, "Neither the urbanity and courtesy of Mr. Whitney nor his evident sincerity and straightforwardness could offset the bad effect of proposing to shear us sheep in a New York drawing room. Straightaway we became rams, mules, lions, if you like, charging bulls, with $25,000 real money."

The committee put its negotiations in the hands of Elihu Cutler, a pragmatic New Englander who owned the Knox Motor Company in Springfield, Massachusetts. Cutler took a simple approach to the proceedings. He had written his terms on the back of a frayed blue envelope and whenever Whitney or one of his colleagues raised a point, he would pull it out and read aloud:

"First.—We will pay one and one-fourth per cent royalty, three-fourths of one per cent to the Electric Vehicle Co., one-half of one per cent into an association of our own.

"Second.—This association shall say who shall or shall not be sued under the patent.

"Third.—It shall say who shall be licensed and who shall not be licensed under the patent."

Cutler's recitation never varied and it never ceased. In time, the
EVC fell beneath his relentless pecking, Winton agreed that Selden's
patent was valid, and the wrangling ended with its sometime opponents delighted by the brand-new organization they had founded: the
Association of Licensed Automobile Manufacturers.

The ALAM was born plump with good intentions, among them
keeping slipshod and shoddy automakers from tarnishing the reputation of the industry it now controlled.

—————〰〰〰〰〰—————

Like many of the ALAM members themselves, Ford thought Selden's
claims ludicrous. He was not by nature a man to fall in easily with
plans formed by others, and this particular situation must have infuriated him. But he had a car company to launch on a paid-in capital of
twenty-eight thousand dollars, and he knew that litigation could lap
that up in a matter of months.

In the summer of 1903 he went to Fred L. Smith, who was president of the new organization. Looking back on the meeting across a
quarter century, Smith said, "Henry Ford called on me on a morning
long ago and wanted to know if, in case application were made, mem-
bership in the association would be granted then. Not as the exalted
president of A.L.A.M., but as one man to another, I told him I did not
think that an application from the Ford Motor Co. at that particular
moment would be considered favorably . . . I remember telling Henry
Ford that his outfit was really nothing but an 'assemblage plant'—
poison to the A.L.A.M. and that when they had their own plant and
became a factor in the industry, they would be welcome, because,
among other reasons, the type of car they were making was not being
turned out by any of the A.L.A.M. members."

This "one man to another" talk would have grated on Ford for several reasons. First, Smith was applying to Ford the same suave ingra-
tiations that had so rankled Smith when he had been on the receiving
end of them from Whitney. Then there was the scorn of the "assem-

blage plant," although most of the ALAM members built their cars that way, and not one of them was wholly independent of outside suppliers. The delicate reference to the fact that the type of car Ford was making "was not being turned out by any of the A.L.A.M. members" meant that it was too cheap.

The ALAM didn't like cheap automobiles. The organization favored the heavy, expensive cars that Malcomson was eager to build. Most of the makers that had gathered under the Selden patent produced cars that sold for three to six thousand dollars. The weeks-old association had already become as haughty as any ancient guild that made breastplates or tableware for the nobility.

Still, Ford went to another meeting with the ALAM, most likely at the urging of John Gray, who lived in a state of perpetual worry about the automobile business, and the usually sanguine John Anderson, whom the ALAM had succeeded in frightening.

The Ford shareholders met for lunch with ALAM representatives at the Russell House, which was—or said it was—"the most complete and elegant hostelry in Michigan." Smith once again tried to be emollient, even though he had the uneasy feeling of being in a slightly false position. During the meal John Gray talked about what the Ford Motor Company hoped to accomplish, and wondered why its aims did not suit the ALAM. Smith recalled, "Mr. Gray put their case so fairly and simply that I had a guilty feeling of 'sassing' my elders and betters when I, in turn, tried to state the A.L.A.M. policies and purposes . . . I was conscious of cutting a rather sorry figure before a group of friendly men who put me personally in the wrong by dealing with me officially."

The friendliness did not outlast the lunch. When Smith had finished making his case, and sat down, James Couzens said, "Selden can take his patent and go to hell with it."

Smith looked unhappily around the room. Ford, his chair tilted back against the wall, had silently been taking in the proceedings. Now he spoke.

"Couzens has answered you."

"You men are foolish," said Smith. "The Selden crowd can put you out of business—and will."

Ford clacked his chair's front legs back to the floor and stood. "Let them try it," he said, ending the lunch and the negotiations.

—————————wwwwwwww—————————

The ALAM began taking out newspaper ads warning readers that if they bought a Ford car, they were buying a lawsuit, too.

Couzens replied with a defiant letter to the *Cycle and Automobile Trade Journal* saying in part, "So far as our plan of action is concerned for the future it is extremely simple. We intend to manufacture and sell all the gasoline automobiles of the type we are constructing that we can. We regard the claims made by the Selden patent as covering the monopoly of such machines as entirely unwarranted and without foundation in fact. We do not, therefore, propose to respect any such claims."

This was meant to provoke, and it did. The ALAM sued Ford.

Ford and Couzens hired the best patent lawyer in Detroit, Ralzemond A. Parker. A sixty-year-old Civil War veteran—he had fought at Antietam—Parker was on the verge of retiring. But he had early gotten interested in automobiles and thoroughly understood them, he thought the Selden patent absurd, and he admired Ford's opposition to it. So he took a job that turned out to consume him for years.

Soon after Ford retained Parker, the Detroit newspapers carried a "NOTICE To Dealers, Importers, Agents and Users of Gasoline Automobiles. We will protect you under any prosecution for alleged infringements of patents." The advertisement named Parker, and quoted him: "The Selden Patent is not a broad one, and if it was, it is anticipated [that is, people had the idea before Selden did]. It does not cover any practicable machine, no practicable machine can be built from it, and never was."

The copy goes on to make the strong but false claim that "our Mr. Ford made the first Gasoline Automobile in Detroit and the third in the United States," then swerves back to the truth: "Our Mr. Ford also built the famous '999' Gasoline Automobile, which was driven by Barney Oldfield in New York on Saturday a mile in 55 4-5 seconds on a circular track, which is the world's record. Mr. Ford, driving his own machine, beat Mr. Winton at Grosse Pointe track in 1901. We have always been winners."

The fight continued in the papers, with Ford more and more using a word that had appeared in Couzens's opening sally: "monopoly." In an era that had become deeply suspicious of "trusts," Ford was drawing on a widespread public antagonism that was shared by—and fed by—President Theodore Roosevelt.

By 1905 the Ford company was referring to the ALAM simply as "the Trust" in its ads. One of them shows a man (inexplicably wearing a gleaming opera hat) standing, his hand on a Ford, looking with calm disdain at a scarecrow who is tottering toward him blowing a tin horn.

"Watch for Him Whenever the Automobile Show is in Town, that pretty, straw stuffed Bogie Man—the official mouthpiece of the Trust—is equipped with a new supply of wind, straw, and springs—1905 model." The ad concludes by assuring "purchasers of 'Ford' cars . . . as before, that we will protect them absolutely.

"So don't let the Trust, by vigorous agitations of its straw man's arms, scare you into paying $1,000 to $2,000 more than you need for an automobile."

Parker was traveling the country, taking down evidence in the same way his Winton predecessors had done back when they were still on Ford's side: an examiner or notary public on hand to ensure an accurate record, but no judge to stanch the flow of testimony, which eventually came to a stupefying fourteen thousand pages containing five million words.

More tangible evidence was being offered. The Electric Vehicle Company underwrote the construction of Selden's car, a quarter century after its conception, to demonstrate that it would run. Some citizens of Rochester, where it was built, said they had seen it perform, but when it was introduced into the case as Exhibit 89, Parker, who was not at all pleased that no one on the defense had been told of the exhibit's existence, said, "Personally I don't believe that Exhibit 89 . . . ever ran ten rods in Rochester."

Meanwhile, Charles Sorensen got an assignment that must have surprised him. "Mr. Parker tracked down a description in a French technical magazine of a vehicle driven in 1862 by a gas engine made by a Belgian, Jean Lenoir. It was decided to build an engine according to Lenoir's specifications; if it worked, it might upset Selden's claim. From drawings in the Ford drafting room, I made patterns, produced the castings, and brought them into the plant. Mr. Ford delegated Fred Allison [one of the company's electrical experts] to build the engine and set it up on a Ford chassis. This took a year and a half and many tests before the contraption ran."

Parker had requested, and been granted, a public test of the Selden car, which bore the date 1877 emphatically painted on its side. It didn't do well: After hours of being fussed over, it ran 1,309 feet. Finally, in September 1907, it was tormented into covering 3,450 feet of Manhattan pavement.

Ford's exercise in automotive archaeology did far better. The company had retained Charles Duryea, as ancient and knowledgeable an automobile veteran as the young industry possessed, to serve as a witness. Riding in the Ford-built Lenoir from the Ford office at Fifty-Fourth and Broadway up around Columbus Circle and back, Duryea reported that "the vehicle started with certainty when wanted, ran when wanted to the limit of its ability, which I should say was as high as 12 miles an hour on some occasions when the streets were good, stopped, started, slowed up, accelerated, reversed and otherwise handled in a satisfactory and practical manner."

In the end, neither of the brand-new antiques had a decisive effect on the case, but their highly public trials fascinated first the New Yorkers who witnessed them and then their countrymen who read about them. The reports showed that this strident newcomer, the automobile, already had a venerable past and thus possibly a greater future than many imagined, and that an issue was being decided that would shape that future.

As the dispute wore on, the public also became more and more aware of Henry Ford. A photograph of his Piquette Avenue plant taken in 1906 shows a sign running the length of the building that reads, "HOME OF THE CELEBRATED FORD AUTOMOBILES." The adjective is misleading: The cars and their maker were known, but hardly celebrated. The company's founder had gained attention with his racing, and his Model A was selling well enough to allow him to defy the ALAM—before long he would be paying six dollars per car to defend his case—but his was just another company in the general ruck of automakers. As he held out against a $70 million consortium, however, more and more Americans began to see in him a brave incarnation of the antimonopolist spirit of the times.

Ford took shrewd advantage of this moment when his business instincts were in perfect harmony with his beliefs. "We possess just enough of that instinct of American freedom," he said, "to cause us to rebel against oppression or unfair competition.

"It goes against the grain of Americanism to be coerced, or bluffed, or sandbagged; and men who will not fight in such circumstances do not, in my estimation, possess the highest degree of self-respect or even honesty—for I protest it is dishonest to bow to expediency in such a case, and thereby not only become contributors of graft money, but subject the entire automobile industry and buying constituency to a tax that is unjust and uncalled for."

The ALAM was equally determined. It sent "patent sleuths" out onto the streets checking automobiles to see whether they carried the proof of having paid the demanded levies, which was a three-inch-wide brass plaque stamped with an image of Selden's theoretical car.

The agents could be thorough. When a young New Yorker named William J. Moore bought an unlicensed Swiss-made Martini, the ALAM found out and sued him. He failed to appear in court, and had an injunction issued against him. This scared him enough to drive him underground after he persuaded the New York Martini dealer to announce that his customer had gone to Texas and died there. Moore stayed in the East under an assumed name, but the ALAM's men tracked him to Albany, where they got a federal marshal to hand him an injunction while he was trying to steady his nerves at the bar of the Ten Eyck Hotel.

Parker kept taking his testimonies, and he was good at it. He looked a little like General William Tecumseh Sherman; photographs of him give the same sense of a tight-skinned face charged with tenacity. Here he is dismantling Hugh C. Gibson, an engineer hired as an expert witness by the ALAM. The issue is the "flame ignition" Selden specified in his patent, which had been universally superseded by electrical ignition (even in Exhibit 89). Parker asked Gibson to explain it.

A. I have no knowledge in my present capacity of flame ignition.

Q. What do you mean by "in my present capacity"?

A. I mean that as an ordinary individual without special knowledge I have no knowledge of pure flame ignition.

Q. Have you any knowledge of "purely flame ignition" as applied to that engine [the one put into Exhibit 89]?

A. As an ordinary individual I do not, nor could I possibly.

Q. What do you know as an expert?

A. I cannot tell what I know as an expert.

Q. You mean you can't or won't?

A. I mean I can't as I say.

Q. Why can't you?

A. I don't know.

Formidable interrogator though he was, Parker could make no headway with Selden himself. The inventor sat facing his questioner, his cravat held in place with a pin crafted in the shape of his car, its wheel hubs and headlamps sparkling with diamonds, full of calm certainty about being the father of the automobile. Yet Selden offered sly evasions if questioned on specifics. When, for instance, Parker asked, "Have you given the public any information whatever in your patent as to which ratio of speed of the crankshaft relative to that of the propelling wheels they must have in order to secure the new and useful results which you have specified . . . ?" Selden replied, "As my invention is a pioneer in the art, my understanding is that my patent on it under existing decisions is to be liberally construed."

Pressed on one detail after another, Selden would instead speak at length of his lonely struggles as a young inventor, or about the ever-growing importance of his invention. When Parker asked him to "answer yes or no," Selden replied with unruffled hauteur: "You have tried several times to dictate my answer to me, and so far as I know you have not yet succeeded, and I really doubt whether you will."

There was no cordiality whatever in these exchanges. At one point Parker asked, "Did you intend to tell the truth?" and Selden replied, "Your question is an insult, sir, and I refuse to answer it."

Parker kept coming at Selden, but he never made a dent.

The case went to trial in the spring of 1909 before the Circuit Court of the Southern District of New York, in the old Post Office Building at the southern end of City Hall Park. Although years had passed since Parker began working on it, he had written Ford, "I wish the case could be delayed a little . . . [and not come] before Judge Hough. Now Hough is said to be cranky and I *know* he is *not* a patent Judge."

That was true, but Judge Charles Merrill Hough took the case anyway. Although Hough was energetic and diligent, and familiar with the fundamentals of patent law, he knew nothing about automobiles or their history. He tried to be fair, but Parker, so effective in taking testimonies, made the mistake of overpreparing. He had spent years absorbing all that testimony, and he had an unfortunate tendency to tell all that he had learned. He bored and irritated Judge Hough. The Selden lawyers were crisp and precise in their arguments.

Hough went off to a dismal summer of reading through the

immense record. On September 15 he delivered his opinion. He acknowledged that Selden had contributed virtually nothing to the development of the automobile, but said that his "patent represents to me a great idea, conceived in 1879, which lay absolutely fallow until 1895, and then concealed in a file wrapper, and is now demanding tribute from later independent inventors . . . who more promptly and far more successfully reduced their ideas to practice.

"But the patent speaks from the date of its issue, and unless Selden did something unlawful during his sixteen years' wrangle with Examiners . . . he is within the law, and his rights are the same as those of the promptest applicant."

Judge Hough found for Selden.

What the magazine *Motor World* called "by far the most momentous and vital decision ever affecting the automobile industry" held that by law no car could be built in, imported to, or driven in America without the permission of the ALAM.

Alexander Winton, his own resistance to Selden's claims far behind him, said with satisfaction, "Nothing now remains but to exact from all trespassers a share of that income they have enjoyed for years without letters patent."

Ford thought plenty remained. The day of the decision he sent a telegram to a fellow carmaker in Indianapolis: "Selden suit decision has no effect on Ford policy—we will fight to the finish."

He would be fighting an increasingly solitary battle. Within a month of Judge Hough's decision eight independent carmakers came into the ALAM fold, and the organization was suing the holdouts. On October 19, William C. Durant, head of the year-old General Motors, surrendered.

The defections troubled Ford, of course, but by now his stand had made him a national figure. The *Detroit Free Press* ran an editorial under the heading, "Ford, the Fighter," and, in case the reader might have found that too vague, opened with the line, "Ford, the fighter, salute!"

The public stuck by Ford. He wrote that when "some of my more enthusiastic opponents . . . gave it out privately that there would be criminal as well as civil suits and that a man buying a Ford car might as well be buying a ticket to jail," he pledged that his company would indemnify every new owner with a bond. "We thought the bond would give assurance to the buyers—that they needed confidence. They did not. We sold more than eighteen thousand cars—nearly double the output of the previous year—and I think about fifty buyers asked for bonds—perhaps it was less than that."

On November 22, 1910, the contestants were back again in the Post Office Building. Parker had told Ford that clearly he wasn't the one to carry on this fight in the courtroom, and recommended a well regarded New York patent attorney named Edmund Wetmore, who came aboard with an equally capable colleague, Lawrence Gifford. They argued the appeal before three seasoned judges, the youngest of whom, the forty-five-year-old Walter Chadwick Noyes, was already known for his grasp of patent litigation.

Wetmore and Gifford made almost the same case Parker had, but far more succinctly. The judges retired with the testimony, and given the quantity of it Henry Ford and everyone else involved thought they'd take months to come to a decision. They took six weeks.

On January 9, 1911, Judge Noyes read the decision. "Every element in the claim was old, and the combination itself was not new." So much for Selden's insistence that he alone had thought up the automobile. Therefore, the case came down to the engine Selden had named, a two-cycle Brayton. The court upheld the patent where a two-stroke engine was concerned, but of all the cars in America, only the Ohio-built Elmore was still using one. "We can see," Noyes concluded, "that had [Selden] appreciated the superiority of the [four-cycle] Otto engine and adopted that type for his combination, his patent would cover the modern automobile. He did not do so . . . and we cannot, by placing any forced construction upon the patent or by straining the doctrine of equivalents, make another choice for him at the expense of these defendants, who neither legally nor morally owe him anything."

———∿∿∿∿∿∿∿∿———

During the next few hours Ford received a thousand telegrams, one from his old friend Charles King: "Hurrah for Henry Ford." Hurrah for Henry Ford was the general response. The *Detroit Journal* echoed scores of other editorials when it wrote, "It would have been considerably to Mr. Ford's personal advantage, in dollars and cents, had he compromised with or capitulated to the Selden patent holder years ago. But for more than seven years now he has fought on, almost alone, against huge odds—for a principle. He believed that his own rights were imperiled and the rights of every American citizen who is entitled to the rewards of his enterprise, industry, and brains."

Although Charles Sorensen had many sour and equivocal things to say about his boss in the memoir he published in the mid-1950s, he was still as much on Ford's side against the ALAM as he had been while he was carving the patterns for the Lenoir car put up against Exhibit 89. "The Ford fight against the Selden patent is a milestone in the history of the automobile industry. I believe it is one of the greatest things Mr. Ford did not only for Ford Motor Company but for everybody in the auto-making business. All of us around him took only minor parts in this long-drawn-out case. He carried full responsibility for success or failure on his own shoulders with little or no encouragement from members of his board."

Henry Ford himself was reticent about his victory. "Whatever I'd say now might sound like boasting. I think the decision speaks for itself."

The day after it came down, he and Edsel drove over to Royal Oak, where Parker lived, to congratulate him and wish him well at the outset of the retirement he had postponed for the better part of a decade. Parker lived to enjoy it until 1925.

Selden was unshaken. "Morally the victory is mine," he said on his deathbed in 1922.

The ALAM dissolved, leaving behind it a few valuable legacies, among them the reform of the patent laws that had so protracted the long case, and a patent-sharing arrangement among carmakers that prevented perpetual litigation, and that exists in the industry to this day. Henry Ford, who never joined any trade association, nonetheless shared his patents with the industry all his life.

Alfred E. Reeves, the ALAM's last president and surely one of the least sore losers in history, said, "Henry Ford is the greatest man in the automobile world; the Ford plant is the greatest automobile plant in the world; the Ford organization is the greatest automobile organization in the world."

In that victorious year of 1911, the organization sold 34,528 Model Ts.

The Dearborn, Michigan, farmhouse where
Henry Ford was born in 1863 as it looked
one wintry day three years after he revisited
it in 1919 and decided to save it.

In 1886: This is the twenty-three-year-old Clara Bryant
first saw when she met him at a dance.

Ford stands at the far right in the engine room of the Detroit Edison
Illuminating Company. It is 1894, and he still understands those big,
immaculately maintained steam engines far better than the electric
generators they drive.

Clara and the infant Edsel. Henry took the snapshot in their Bagley Avenue home in 1894, and . . .

. . . Clara took this picture of her husband and son in their backyard two years later.

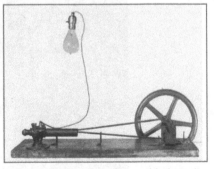

The substantial "woodshed" behind Ford's house, where he conducted his experiments with internal combustion. The door on the right has been widened—with an ax in the middle of the night—to let his first car out for his first drive.

An early offering from the woodshed: Ford's first gasoline engine. He had put it together from scavenged pieces of scrap metal, and on a busy Christmas Eve in 1893 fastened it to the kitchen sink so Clara could help him with a trial run.

The interior of the Bagley Avenue woodshed as Ford re-created it in Greenfield Village. The Quadricycle stands at the rear, up on blocks.

Ford sits at the wheel of his first race car in 1901, while his indomitable colleague Spider Huff mans the perilous post of the "riding mechanic." Scientific American magazine said this was the first car truly to look American.

The enormous 999: Ford was a bit scared of it, but Barney Oldfield, who is holding the brutal steering mechanism, wasn't scared of anything, and his racing successes helped make Ford's name.

The 1903 Model A, the Ford Motor Company's first car, proved its mettle in the San Francisco earthquake.

Ford turns a cartwheel during a trip to Atlantic City in 1905. He is forty-three now and a success. Clara sits behind him, and Edsel is digging in the sand at her side.

Ford and his indispensable partner James Couzens, the former looking wary, the latter characteristically grim, with a good two feet of chilly air between them, in about 1910.

By 1913 the company was turning out finished Model Ts in Oklahoma City.

Workers fit wheels to hubs at Highland Park in the mid-1920s.

The machine shop—with finished crankshafts—at Highland Park appalled at least one journalist, who wrote that the racket it made was like that of ". . . a million monkeys quarreling, a million lions roaring, a million pigs dying, a million elephants smashing through a forest of sheet iron . . . [and] a million sinners groaning as they are dragged off to hell."

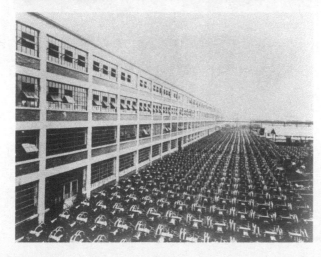

A thousand Model T chassis, here marshaled outside the plant, represented the production of a single nine-hour shift at Highland Park in 1913.

Fair Lane, the Ford estate. Charles Sorensen said it gave him "the creeps" to visit there.

Henry and Clara bird-watching, he more intently than she, in 1914.

Ford with Evangeline Dahlinger. His confidante for more than three decades, she kept him up-to-date on what was happening in Greenfield Village and in return received such gifts as a Tudor manor house, a summer place on Lake Huron, a herd of cattle, and a Curtiss flying boat.

One of the none-too-festive executive lunches, in 1933: Edsel sits to his father's right, Sorensen to his left (by the window), and Peter Martin to Sorensen's left.

Edsel and his father take a final ride just before the end of the Model T's two-decade run.

The Rouge was the largest industrial plant on earth. The docks in the foreground took in 850,000 tons of ore and 2.5 million tons of coal each season.

The "signed photograph" Edsel requested in return for sending Franklin Roosevelt a new Model A in 1929.

Ford has a word with Thomas Edison in 1925; the inventor was very nearly deaf.

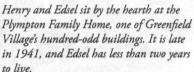

Henry and Edsel sit by the hearth at the Plympton Family Home, one of Greenfield Village's hundred-odd buildings. It is late in 1941, and Edsel has less than two years to live.

B-24 Liberator bombers come down the assembly line at Willow Run, Sorensen's last achievement at the Ford Motor Company and, he thought, his greatest.

Henry Ford sits beside Clara at the tiller of his Quadricycle in June 1946 on the fiftieth anniversary of its inaugural run. The car is on a quiet street in Greenfield Village; beyond the farmhouses and their picket fences, a remade world clamors along the thoroughfare its inventor built.

CHAPTER 11

The Model T Takes Over

New York to Seattle on thin ice; learning to drive the Model T; birth of a dealer; the farmer and the car; caring for your Model T; the perils of starting it; "Funny Stories About the Ford"; five thousand accessories; remaking the nation in a decade: "I'll go without food before I'll go without my car."

Ralzemond Parker had begun his futile argument before Judge Hough on June 1, 1909.

During recesses that morning everyone in the court went over to the grimy windows of the Post Office Building to watch what was going on a few stories below.

A continent away, the Alaska-Yukon-Pacific Exposition, celebrating the development of the Northwest from the almost frivolously close vantage point of the gold rush that had started twelve years earlier, opened that day in Seattle. Robert Guggenheim, who had a mining fortune and liked cars and was still in his thirties, thought a coast-to-coast automobile race would be a good way to publicize the fair, and he sponsored one.

171

No car had yet driven from the East Coast to Seattle, and most of the three-hundred-odd automakers active in America that year didn't want to publicly test their products in mountainous country where roads were always poor, and often nonexistent. Moreover, the ALAM opposed the race, which further discouraged many manufacturers, but made Henry Ford the more eager to take part.

In the end, just five cars got to the starting line; two of them—awarded the designations No. 1 and No. 2—were Model Ts. The other three were far heavier and more powerful: a six-cylinder, 48-horsepower 3,500-pound Acme; a 50-horsepower Itala—the only foreign entrant—weighing 2 tons; and the 45-horsepower Shawmut, which was half a ton heavier than the Itala.

Despite the thin field, Guggenheim's race attracted all the publicity he could have hoped for. In the White House, that June 1, President William Howard Taft opened the fair by putting his forefinger to a gold telegraph key. At the moment of the presidential spark, Mayor George B. McClellan fired a pistol (like the telegraph key, gold plated), and the cars left City Hall Park, bound for Seattle. Henry Ford had gone down from the courtroom to wish his drivers well. After he got back, a member of the defense counsel turned from the window to call in mock astonishment, "Your Honor, there is something that puzzled me. I don't see a Selden car. I see a Ford car, two Ford cars, but I see no Selden car!" This amused even Judge Hough.

It hardly seems credible that these goings-on in lower Manhattan should change the life of a Washington State farm boy, but that's how the Model T went about its business.

Roscoe Sheller lived in the Yakima Valley town of Sunnyside, incorporated six years earlier with 314 residents. He had recently gotten his first job, which was doing everything in Charles Amundson's hardware store that Charles Amundson didn't want to do: sweeping, plumbing, some tinsmithing, keeping the books.

Guggenheim's racers were going to be coming up the Yakima Valley along the wagon road that followed the newly built high-tension line, and everyone in town knew it. Publicity had been growing since the cars left Boise, Idaho, with a Ford nine hours ahead of the costly heavyweights.

After word came that Ford No. 2 had crossed the Columbia River the evening before and was now in the valley, townspeople, skeptical but interested, began to make their way down to the foot of Sixth Street to mill about under the new power line. Roscoe Sheller didn't ask his boss for permission to leave the hardware store, fearing it would be denied, but he joined his neighbors anyway.

The crowd was still gathering, Sheller wrote, "when dust was sighted far down the pole line. Whatever stirred it was driving faster than a wagon, or even a spirited team and buggy."

"Here she comes!" And Bert Scott and Jimmy Smith jolted into Sunnyside, their car pumping indignant gouts of steam from its radiator. Scott, at the wheel, climbed down and asked, "Can we have water?" He and Smith pulled off their goggles, leaving pale ovals in faces otherwise, Sheller remembered, "plastered with many-hued mud. . . . They appeared like an eerie something from another world, which to us they were."

Sheller looked at their car, and saw it nearly as Henry Ford had first envisioned it, for it was "a skeleton," he said, stripped almost to the bare chassis. This Model T had shed nearly a third of its normal weight, and was down to a little over nine hundred pounds. The battered hood, flailed by the road detritus of twelve states, had a blocky numeral "2" painted on its side.

Number 1, driven by Frank Kulick, had been enjoying a nine-hour lead out of Boise before a local had led it astray with confusing instructions. The other cars were either hours or days behind.

The water came, and Smith and Scott drank before No. 2 did, simultaneously gulping it down and washing their faces. The small platform behind the Model T's two seats was stacked with tied-down tires in various states of distress. Smith leaned over and pulled from this rubber nest a can of motor oil. As the crowd pressed closer he poured it into the engine.

"Sure takes a lot of oil," said a bold young boy out in front. Smith glanced at him. "You would too, if you'd been through what this car has."

"A horse wouldn't." The little reactionary got a laugh from the crowd.

During this back-and-forth, Scott pulled on heavy driving gloves and gingerly unscrewed the radiator cap. He gave it a final turn at arm's length, and stepped back as "belching steam and boiling water blew the cap from Scott's hand, showered Scott and christened front-row spectators with an 'I-was-there' souvenir, about which they might boast to unborn grandchildren."

The driver retrieved the cap and fed a thin stream of water into the radiator, which alternately protested with spitting fury and sighed with relief. Before the bucket was empty the machine had calmed down.

"Say, mister," the boy asked the driver, "is oil and water what makes her go?"

"It helps, kid." Scott got back in his seat. "Ready, Smitty?"

"Ready," said Smith. While Scott manipulated a couple of levers on the steering wheel, his partner went to the front of the car, took hold of a crank beneath the importunate radiator, and gave it a jerk. The still-warm engine instantly came to life—a busy threshing sound. The car was already moving when Smith dodged around the right front wheel and vaulted into his seat.

The Sunnyside townspeople watched until No. 2 was out of sight. Only a couple of hundred miles stood between it and Seattle, but they ran across the Cascades and even now, in late June, the mountains might still be deep in snow.

Sheller returned to the hardware store consumed with thoughts of No. 2, and of someday owning a car himself.

His boss was there. "Late, aren't you? Been down to see the racer?"

Sheller said yes, sir, he had, certain his sixty-dollar-a-month salary was about to evaporate.

Mr. Amundson went over to the window. "Why waste your time on that tin pipedream, when there's something *really* nice to see right here?"

"What do you mean?"

"Look there—across the street."

"*Whew!* Who—who—who is *she?*"

"Don't know her name. She's the new clerk at Moore's drug store."

Her name was Iva Benjamin, and a year later the hardware store clerk married her. All in all, it had been quite a day for Roscoe Sheller.

—wwwwwww—

Smith and Scott did find snow in the Cascades, deep but frozen so hard on top that No. 2 could make its way along the crust for miles. But when the sun got high in the sky the fickle paving weakened and broke, dropping their Model T hub-deep in immobilizing powder. The two men struck out in search of help, and soon came upon the familiar cursing and clanging of a track gang at work. The railroaders obligingly freed the automobilists from their final obstacle.

Smith and Scott were on their way down the last western slope of their journey, ninety miles from Seattle, when they came upon the boss waiting for them, in a Model T touring car, with his Denver and Seattle branch managers.

On June 23 they drove into the Seattle fairgrounds to the cheering of fifteen thousand spectators. As No. 2 passed through the gates, Guggenheim thumbed his stopwatch. Smith and Scott had covered 4,106 miles in twenty-two days and fifty-five minutes. A record, of course, since no other car had ever made that particular trip before.

The Shawmut got there seventeen hours later, and Frank Kulick in No. 1, unlucky ever since he'd left Boise, nonetheless finished third, on June 25. The Acme came in days after Kulick. The Itala arrived in a freight car: Its team had given up in Cheyenne.

Robert Guggenheim awarded the prize with a speech that could not have pleased Henry Ford more had he and Couzens drafted it themselves: "Mr. Ford's theory that a light-weight car, highly powered for its weight, can go places where heavier cars cannot go, and can beat heavier cars, costing five and six times a much, on the steep hills or bad roads, has been proved. I believe Mr. Ford has the solution to the popular automobile."

Ford left an identical Model T in Seattle to absorb the admiration of the fairgoers, and, having given the car a complete overhaul and Scott and Smith five days of rest and sightseeing, sent No. 2 on a leisurely six-thousand-mile trip back to Detroit by way of Los Angeles. The victors stopped at Ford dealerships on the way, while all along their route newspaper advertisements drove home their missionary message: "A duplicate of the winner with a five-passenger touring car body costs you $850. No other car was entered that cost less than five times as much. The winner was a stock car. Any Model T could do as well. It's the one reliable car that does not require a $10,000 income to buy, a $5,000 bank account to run and a college course in engineering to keep in order. Better order now if you want August delivery."

After five fruitful months of this campaign, the judges of the race discovered that Henry Ford had offered his drivers more than moral support. The Ford Motor Company's unrivaled network of dealerships had everywhere been on hand to help them. Somewhere along the punishing route, Ford mechanics replaced No. 2's entire engine, a violation of Guggenheim's rules so egregious that the judges took the prize away from the Ford and awarded it instead to the Shawmut.

As the high-spirited Wall Street buccaneer James Fisk had remarked a generation earlier about one of his exploits, "Nothing is lost save honor." People were no longer interested in details of the race, but they remembered the rich harvest of publicity that it had brought in. They remembered the Model T. The Shawmut had already gone to eternity's garage, where the poor old two-stroke Elmore would soon join it.

—————~~~~~~~~~~—————

Roscoe Sheller remembered the Model T; in fact, he thought about it every day. Automobiles became something of an obsession with him in

1912, when his father died and left him the family farm. Sheller turned out not to like farming any better than Henry Ford had: "Why should I nestle my head in the hairy flank of a squeamish, sad-eyed bovine twice every day, and yank away at her dangling appendages, to her profound disgust—and mine, when a coming motor-age could use my help?"

The coming motor age had little interest in Roscoe Sheller, though: no work at Aub Webber's Studebaker agency, nor at Speck and Roland, which had just started selling Buicks.

One day the squeamish cow summoned enough spirit to give her milker a powerful kick behind the ear, and followed it with a second that emptied the pail on him where he lay.

Sheller was leaning against the barn wall collecting himself when his friend Bob Barnett stepped inside.

"Hello, Farmer, I—" He spotted Sheller. "Haw-haw-haw," was his immediate reaction, followed by some sketchy expressions of concern.

Sheller fingered the growing bump on his head and Barnett said, "Maybe I've brought you the medicine you need."

He'd come to offer his friend a job: "I've just been made manager of a branch Ford agency Fred Chandler is opening in Sunnyside. I'll be needing a helper, and of course I immediately thought of you."

Sheller raised the reasonable objection that he didn't know how to drive.

"I'll teach you in a little while," Barnett said. "Nothing to it."

The job paid sixty dollars a month, which Sheller had been earning at the hardware store three years earlier. He had to start Monday. He jumped at the chance.

Barnett showed up at the farm in a Model T at six-thirty Monday morning, and Sheller began the initiation so many millions of Americans would be undergoing year after year for decades to come. His tutor slid across the seat so Sheller could get behind the wheel. The first thing the novice discovered was that the car had no door on the driver's side. His momentary confusion might not have been as amusing to Barnett as his friend getting kicked in the head by a milk-cow, but it drew several haw-haws.

Sheller squirmed over the sill, dropped onto the shuddering seat—the car was running—and looked down at the floor to see three pedals. Perhaps it was to his advantage that Sheller had never driven a car before, as not one of them was an accelerator. If he had a lot to learn, at least he had nothing to unlearn.

He put his hands on the wheel and looked over to his instructor, who said, "Now rest your left foot—*left* foot, I said—on the left pedal. Hold it exactly where it is now, while you shove the hand lever as far ahead as it will go. Understand?"

The lever, next to the nonexistent door, looked like an emergency brake, and in fact was called one, although it was almost useless for stopping the car, nor could it reliably hold it on a grade. The brake's real job was to take the car out of gear: once it was set, the Model T was in neutral.

Barnett told Sheller to "give her a little gas, like this." He pushed a small lever on the steering column, just behind the wheel. That was the throttle. "The motor *buzz-z-z-ed*, fenders quivered in fevered excitement and rattled a noisy, 'Let's go!'"

Sheller pushed the hand lever but forgot all about keeping his left foot on the pedal. The car stuttered forward a few feet and died.

Barnett climbed out, told his student to set the brake and then not touch anything, and spun the crank. The car started, and Barnett jumped back in, reaching across Sheller to fiddle with the throttle lever and its counterpart on the other side of the steering column, which regulated the spark. The engine relaxed into the businesslike grumble that every Model T owner sought. "See what happens when you do things right?" Barnett asked, but the novice was confused. When Barnett told him to push that left pedal down slowly and feed in a little gas gradually, Sheller remembered, "I was generous with both."

The car took off with a jerk that made Barnett scream, "Hell's fire!" Sheller lifted his foot from the pedal as if it had scalded him. This put the Model T into high, and "we plowed down the lane, hopping from rut to rut, like a panicked jack rabbit." Faced with a sharp turn, Sheller shouted a hopeless, anachronistic, and wholly sincere "Whoa!"

Barnett seized the wheel, cut off the gas, and stamped on the right-most pedal, which was the actual brake. Then, cursing, he sent Sheller out to crank the car back into life.

During the course of what had come to seem an eternal morning, Sheller learned that after pushing the far-left pedal to the floor and releasing the brake he had the Model T in low. At about ten miles an hour he was to lift his foot, and the transmission would slip into high gear, which could take the car up to forty miles an hour if the road permitted. When he wanted to back up, Sheller had to push the left pedal halfway in, putting the car in neutral, adjust the throttle with his right hand, and, with his right foot, step on the middle pedal, which was stamped with an R for "reverse." The band collaring the forward speed drum would loosen while the one on the reverse grabbed hold. As Sheller's tutorial amply demonstrated, Henry Ford's planetary transmission could take an awful pounding and still continue to function.

Sheller ran off the road, flung himself through impossible turns, alternately enraged and terrified Barnett—and ended the day a competent driver.

That fall Barnett sold enough Model Ts to keep Mr. Eidelberry at the bank at bay, and then the winter of 1915 came down hard. Car buyers disappeared with the first frosts, but the Ford men kept their shop open.

Early one December morning Sheller glanced at the Carter's Little Liver Pills advertising thermometer "that had hung for years beside the post office entrance" and saw it "cuddled its red fluid low in the glass, as though striving for what warmth it might find there." The seasons had scoured away the instrument's numerals, but everyone knew that when that red dropped below the *v* in "Liver" it was destroyingly cold.

Sheller opened the garage, fired up the stoves, and then set about following Barnett's standing orders to start a Model T as soon as he got there and drive it out front. People had to see that this workhorse stood ready to help no matter what the weather.

Sheller strained at the crank, but Spider Huff's ingenious magneto was useless if the engine wouldn't turn in the first place, and this morning the freezing oil had coagulated about the planetary transmission and glued its gears into a solid lump. Sheller couldn't budge the crank with his right arm, and even when he jumped on its handle his two hundred pounds merely got it to give him a creeping ride floorward.

Hoping to melt the oil, he pushed the car over to a stove, which turned out to be hot enough to blister the paint on the nearest fender. Sheller knew he'd catch hell for that, but when he next took hold of the crank the oil had relaxed, and he was able to start the engine and drive the Model T through the big door to stand on the street proclaiming its hardihood.

Barnett arrived in the office minutes later and immediately berated him for bringing the car out on such a cold day. Sheller muttered about orders; Barnett said, "Get it back in here—*now!*"

Sheller went outdoors, reached through the side curtains to set spark and throttle, and tried the crank. Nothing doing. Once again he stood on it, "hoping to wear a channel through the congealed oil."

Despite the freezing morning, a small crowd gathered to watch Sheller cope with his dilemma. Apparently taking pity on him, Sunnyside's blacksmith, a man named Morrow, came forward. "Let me twist 'er tail."

The blacksmith was almost invariably the strongest man in any turn-of-the-century community. Morrow was able to move the crank without standing on it, but he couldn't get a snort of life from the engine. After the smith had the crank loosened enough for an average human to turn it, Barnett emerged from his office and said with Olympian disingenuousness, "'Smatter boys? Can't start her, eh?" He made some adjustments to the spark and throttle, then took hold of the crank. Despite Morrow's having drilled a path for him, the Model T stood mute.

After a while Barnett stood and said, "You guys have flooded the carburetor." He opened the hood, poked ostentatiously at some fixtures beneath it, and turned back to his audience with an I-thought-as-much "Humph."

He went back to the crank, and gave it a confident spin, then a less confident one, and then kept churning it while his hands grew raw and his vanity bled.

John Steinbeck would write that the Model T was always a shrewd judge of its driver's patience: It would tease you every chance it got, but never more than you could take; and it always came through for you in the end.

Not this time.

At last Barnett stood up, red-faced with effort and fury, and shouted at Sheller, "Go write Chandler a letter. Tell him that I'll not crank MY life away for him, Henry Ford, or any damn man on this earth! Tell him that I'm through!" He strode magnificently off toward the frigid horizon. Morrow helped Sheller push the Model T back inside.

Seated in Barnett's abruptly vacated manager's chair, Sheller immediately began to write a dignified letter to the Ford agent in North Yakima.

> *Dear Mr. Chandler,*
>
> *Mr. R. N. Barnett, your Sunnyside Branch Manager, has resigned, effective today, and has directed me to so inform you.*
>
> *I hereby make formal application for the position formerly held by Mr. Barnett. . . .*

The letter was going out by the night mail, which left on the first morning train, but that evening, talking things over with his wife, Sheller realized that he'd better go up with it. After all, he'd never even met Mr. Chandler.

So he rode on the same train as his letter, and got to Chandler first. He found the agent to be "a kindly man, well-fed and jovial." Chandler was surprised by Barnett's sudden defection, but evidently not too troubled by it. Sheller told him how badly he needed the job: He'd sold off all his farm equipment and rented out the farm itself to come work with Barnett. He had, he admitted, yet to sell a car, but Mr. Chandler knew that.

Chandler didn't exactly offer Sheller the job, but said he could try it on for a month and see how it fit. Emboldened, Sheller asked if he could have a car.

Chandler pointed out that he had one down in Sunnyside already, the recalcitrant Model T that had driven—or, rather, not driven—Barnett into another line of work. The way the agency worked then was that once Sheller sold a car, he would take the train up to North Yakima, forty miles away, and pick up another one.

Sheller argued that bringing a car back that morning would save the cost of him having to come back up on the train a few days later.

"We sell no cars in the winter," Chandler said. "What makes you think *you* can?"

"Maybe I can't, but I'm going to try harder than I've tried anything before."

Chandler led him down into the garage and told the crew there to get a new Model T ready. Sheller thought he saw him wink at the shop foreman as he called out, "Put the side curtains on good and tight. We want to take good care of our new *branch manager*."

Sheller drove home in a stew of elation and terror. He had a spanking new Model T. He was a branch manager of the Ford Motor Company. And if he didn't sell that new T in an impossible season, he most likely wouldn't be any kind of manager after thirty days.

He reached Sunnyside in the middle of the afternoon, to receive surprising news from an assistant who had been watching the garage: "There's a man in the office, been waiting to see you. Couldn't find anything else to read, so I gave him a Model T instruction book."

Sheller hurried in to find a farmer in a heavy sweater and a denim jacket—a dairy farmer, given the amount of dried milk on his overalls.

"I kinda figured I'd look over one of them thar autos," the man said, and asked if Sheller would teach him to drive.

"Nothing to it," the branch manager replied as airily as Bob Barnett had to him a few months earlier.

While Sheller showed him the Model T, the farmer said he'd been reading the book, and it looked easy. The car, its engine still warm, started with the merest twitch of the crank. Sheller got it out on the road, nervously issued instructions, and turned the wheel over. The dairyman drove it effortlessly, said "whoa" only once and immediately laughed at himself, and happily observed that it all went "just like it said in the book." After a while, he added, "I think I got 'er now. Let's go back."

When they got to the garage, the farmer asked, "You fill 'er with gas if I buy 'er?"

Already the salesman, Sheller said, "For you, I will."

"I'll drive 'er up to the pump. You fill 'er up, and we'll go in and settle up."

In the office that had been Sheller's for a little more than a day, the farmer reached under his milk-stiff overalls "and produced a wallet from somewhere in his several layers of pants." He paid for the car with a mixture of folding money and gold pieces, then drove it off into the winter dusk that Sheller rightly saw as the dawn of his career.

———◦◦◦◦◦◦◦———

That transaction in the Yakima Valley echoed ones that were taking place in the Hudson River Valley, in the Sacramento Valley, the Valley of the Tennessee, in towns like Sunnyside, in towns like Des Moines, in towns that weren't anything like other towns: New York, Chicago, New Orleans.

At just about the time Roscoe Sheller was joyfully showing his wife the money from his first sale, the company he represented had made, in December 1915, its millionth Model T.

That Sheller's customer was a farmer was representative, too: 64 percent of those Model Ts had been sold to a rural market. Henry Ford had won over the motorcar's most stubborn enemy. Just a few years earlier, Woodrow Wilson, then president of Princeton University, said automobiles "are a picture of the arrogance of wealth, with all its independence and carelessness," and that "nothing has spread socialistic feeling more."

This sounds pretty high-strung, but those brass-bound juggernauts did foment a good deal of rural anger during their forays from the city, particularly when they killed a chicken or hurt a cow or, occasionally, a person. "I'm a Southerner and know how to shoot," Wilson said. "Would you blame me if I did so under such circumstances?" Some farmers did go that far at first, and others laid snares in the roads, hoping to break a spring or perhaps an axle.

Such occasional violence notwithstanding, the farmer's hatred of automobiles in particular and machinery in general was far from innate. Farmers had been using steam engines to saw wood as early as 1807, and it was not on the streets of Detroit but on a country road that Henry Ford first saw the self-propelled steam traction engine majestically crawling toward its day's work. Gasoline also reached the farm before the automobile did. Stationary internal combustion engines, some putting out as much as sixteen horsepower, were grinding grain and shredding corn in American fields from the 1870s on.

In any event, Henry Ford quenched whatever hostility remained by making his car cheap enough for any modestly successful farmer to buy—"Even You Can Afford a Ford," said his billboards—and insisting that he had developed the Model T largely to lessen the toil of farming life.

The car did. The owner could, for instance, jack up his Model T and belt one of the driving wheels to a buzz saw, or use it to lift a hog from the scalding tub or corn into a silo. And when the car wasn't running a thresher, it could take the farmer and his family out beyond the boundaries of their everyday lives. It was these excursions, and their consequences, that made the Model T the single most important automobile ever, and possibly the most significant force in twentieth-century America.

The Model T is no longer any sort of force in our lives, but it refuses to look placid or quaint, to acquire that gloss of appeal that time puts on so many ugly things. The high, unlovely body and pugnacious snout still flaunt the boxy antique's power to change a world.

It was the first car for millions of Americans, and every one of those new owners found it was about as demanding as their first baby. We who live in a world where an automobile might require some trifling maintenance every twenty thousand miles or so can scarcely imagine how much tending a car needed a century ago. The wealthy then didn't hire chauffeurs merely to decorate their homes with another servant, but because keeping a motorcar in running condition was a full-time job.

The Model T was simple enough to allow an amateur to learn fairly quickly how to care for it, but the owner had a great deal to do.

Take the matter of lubrication. The manual for 1909—the car's first full year of manufacture—featured a page captioned, "Where to Oil the Model T." Everywhere, and all the time, it must have seemed to the oiler. Going aft from the radiator, you began with, "Hub, Grease every 500 miles." Nestling against the hub was the "Spindle Belt. Oil every hundred miles." A few inches away the "Steering Ball Socket" also wanted to be oiled every one hundred miles, while a little further inward from it, under the hood, the commutator had to have oil every two hundred miles, but would accept Vaseline instead. Then came the unforgiving "Fan Hub, Grease Cup": "Every fifty miles."

So it proceeded to the "Rear Spring Hanger" and its neighbor the "Hub Brake Cam"—200 miles each. The list ended with the general suggestion that "a drop or two of oil should occasionally be applied to all small connections and joints throughout the car."

One chore needed doing every morning: "Lubricate Engine and Transmission by daily Replenishments through breather tube. Oil level in crank case should be carried slightly above lower pet cock."

That was how you checked your oil: Crawl beneath the engine and twist open the higher of two little valves. If oil drips out the car has too much, and needs draining off. Now to the lower valve. If it bleeds oil, all is well. If it doesn't, add more oil, but not, of course, enough to submerge the upper valve.

So, too, with the gasoline. There was no fuel gauge, and when the supply needed checking the owner lifted up the front seat cushion to reveal the elongated drum of the gas tank. The Ford Company published a cross section of the tank with the number of gallons on one side and the number of inches they occupied in the tank on the other. The drawing came with a chummy directive: "Here's a little diagram that will tell you easily and accurately exactly how much gasoline is in the tank of your touring car. How many times can you remember, when it would have come in handy to have known just how many gallons you had. A little care in marking on a stick the figures on the accompanying table will provide a means of always knowing your exact supply." You dipped the stick in the tank, and checked how many inches came up damp. Ford owners didn't have to make their own gauges for long, though: Every kind of automobile advertiser began producing the rulers, stamping them with the appropriate self-celebrations, and supplied them free for decades.

That was not all with the fuel. "Always strain through a chamois skin to prevent water and other foreign matter from getting in the carburetor." The carburetor: The Model T had no fuel pump to feed it, because the under-seat gas tank was set high enough for gravity to do the job, just as it had been on the Quadricycle. This worked fairly well, except on steep hills, when as the car nosed upward the gas sloshed toward the back of the tank, away from the port that fed the engine, and the carburetor ran dry. Ford owners learned to compensate by backing up steep grades.

They had to learn a great deal more about the car's foibles, and in time there were so many Model Ts on the road that this knowledge became a national shared wisdom, some of it pure superstition (good idea to drop a ball of camphor in the tank every now and again), but much of it crucial.

The dangers of starting the car took only a few years to become universally known. You always held the crank in the hollow of your hand and *never* put your thumb around it, because if the engine kicked back, the crank could break your arm. Before this wisdom was fully disseminated, there was a regular plague of bandaged right wrists across the country.

Even without imperiling an arm, starting the Model T was a chancy business. The motor pioneer Bellamy Partridge was able to give a vivid description years after he'd last done it. "Tickle the carburetor, hold the choke wire [a thin metal loop that poked out from the radiator] at exactly the right spot—a hair's breadth either way would spoil the combustion. Draw a long breath and hold it—this was supposed to protect you in the case of backfire. Then give a sudden yank on the starting crank. This had to be done just so. It wasn't a push—it was rather a flip or a flirt. You had to take the engine by surprise, make a quick delivery, and then step back out of reach. Cranking was something that had to be learned by long practice, for it was a fine art like a sinker or a knuckle ball. Some people never could learn it."

E. B. White took the same wily approach to starting his Model T: After giving the crank "two or three nonchalant upward lifts" and "whistling as though thinking about something else," he "would saunter back to the driver's cabin, turn the ignition on, return to the crank, and this time, catching it on a downstroke, give it a quick spin."

Other menaces still lay in ambush once the engine was firing. "Often, if the emergency brake hadn't been pulled all the way back, the car advanced on you . . . and you would hold it back by leaning your weight against it. I can still feel my old Ford nuzzling me at the curb, as though looking for an apple in my pocket."

In their cautious, devious courting of their car's approval, both men clearly felt it a sentient being that required psychological as well as mechanical attention. Most other Ford owners did, too, and, with the possible exception of warships and warplanes, no machine has ever been more personalized.

The proliferating Model T got christened early in its life. Lizzie had been a generic horse's name for earlier generations (as Rover was a dog's), and the car inherited it. But that turned out to be, as it were, the surname. Chris Sinsabaugh, a newspaperman who began his career reporting on the bicycle industry and moved over, along with much of the industry itself, to automobiles about the time Ford started making them, wrote that although "many wondered how the T got its famous nickname," he had never been able to find out. "One story [I] heard was that once upon a time a Ford dealer in San Antonio, who had been complaining about ill-fitting doors, wrote the factory that if the bodies were shipped without doors, a can-opener might be included in the tool kit and each dealer could cut his own doors and make them fit. Hence 'Tin Lizzie.'"

Never mind the strenuously touted vanadium steel; that "tin" would stick to the Model T for the rest of its long life.

A frugal housewife saved her empty tin cans, and one day on impulse sent them to the Ford Motor Company. A week later she got a letter from Ford saying they had repaired her car and were returning it along with seven leftover cans.

People told that joke to one another for two generations. They swapped hundreds and hundreds of others like it, too, and the surest indicator of how quickly and firmly the Model T battened itself onto the American psyche is the immense literature of jokes it produced. This was an actual literature, in that it flourished in scores of books, ranging from dime pamphlets to substantial hardcovers: *Funabout Fords; Ford Jokes and Stories; Original Ford Joke Book: If It Hurts You to Laugh Don't Buy One; A Book of Ford Jokes; More Funabout Fords. . . .*

The automobile joke is as old as the automobile. Bellamy Partridge remembered that the Duryea brothers played a part in its genesis when, a year after their triumph in the snows of Chicago, they made a poor showing at a race in Narragansett, Rhode Island. As their car repeatedly stalled, the exasperated spectators began to call out, "Get a horse!"

In 1950, the radio comedian Henry Morgan, asked to choose the most popular jokes of the last fifty years, believed "Get a horse!" was "the one that lasted longest, was told the most, and made the greatest impact on mankind." Morgan said that "the phrase made every man a comedian." He added that "it wasn't hard to remember."

In the spring of 1936 Dr. Ralph Hutchinson, president of Washington and Jefferson College in Pennsylvania, invited the seventy-four-year-old Henry Ford to visit the campus. As they were smoothly heading there in a Lincoln limousine, President Hutchinson said,

"I happened to notice an old Model T Ford of the vintage of about 1915." It had long since shed its fenders, and two college students were straining at the crank to get it going. They knew it would start eventually, and so did the ruin of a car. It was just teasing them. President Hutchinson pointed to the roadside scene, and Henry Ford rolled down the window, leaned out, and yelled in the highest good humor, "Get a horse!"

Still, the majority of all the automobile jokes ever conceived bounced along with the Model T.

Few commodities age as quickly as humor, and not many Ford jokes would strike anyone as funny today. But they are eloquent of the feelings of the Model T owner: a mixture of self-mockery and pride. Many centered on how inexpensive the car was, and its relative smallness. Ring Lardner amalgamated a bushel of these into a surprisingly tiresome story he wrote in 1915 for the second volume of *Funny Stories About the Ford*. Phil, in a letter to his friend Dave, recounts buying his Model T "for $150.00 dollars and the car was . . . in good repares. The man was going to move out of town and I suppose he didn't want to stick it in his sutecase for the fear that he would get some grease on his other shirt. . . . It was supper time when I got her home but Nell says to hell with supper and I would half to take her out for a ride and while we was out we happened to think all of a sudden that we didn't have no garridge to keep a car in it and we couldn't leave it out on the st. all night for the fear that some stew [drunk] might trip over it and sew us for dammidges and Nell says she would sleep on the lunge in the living room and I could take the car in with me." He brings the Model T up to bed, gives it a bath in the sink, and loses it down the drain. And so forth.

After tin and size, the jokes light on the Model T's loose-knit joints:

Q: Why is a Ford like a millionaire baby?
A: Because it gets a new rattle every day.

An owner explains that his car doesn't need a speedometer because "it's easy to gauge your speed. When you go ten miles an hour, your lamps rattle; when you get up to twenty miles an hour, the fenders rattle; at twenty-five miles the windshield begins to rattle; and when you go faster than that your bones rattle."

And then there was the car's cheapness. A Ford dealer comes up with the promotional idea of giving a new Model T to the first person who manages to assemble four dimes with the mintmarks F, O, R, and D. Not long after he publicizes the contest, a man comes in and hands him the dimes.

"You've done it!" the dealer says. "Look around the showroom and take your pick." After twenty minutes the man returns.

"Well?"

"If it's all the same to you, could I have my forty cents back?"

The folklorist B. A. Botkin thought the jokes largely a defensive measure on the Ford owner's part: Make fun of yourself first, and you defuse anyone else who might be planning to. A great many of the jokes, though, turn the car's supposed weaknesses into strengths, as with the one about the two brothers, George and Fred, who each inherit two thousand dollars. George spends the entire legacy on a fine, big six-cylinder limousine. Fred buys a Model T for five hundred dollars.

Driving home, George is surprised to be passed by Fred, who is there waiting when he arrives.

Nettled, George asks "what caused that terrible rattling noise" he heard as Fred's car passed him.

"Oh," Fred replies, "that was the fifteen hundred dollars in my pocket."

If the jokes ever stung the occasional Model T owner, they were only a source of pleasure to the Model T's maker. Henry Ford so obviously relished them that some of his colleagues thought he was underwriting the joke books. He wasn't, but he always made a show of buying them and passing them about. Ford saw every joke as an advertisement, free as the air and living sometimes for years. Their swarming ubiquity was one of the reasons he decided, in 1917, to cease advertising altogether.

He may even have invented a Model T joke, though he said it was a true story. He was out on a trip testing one of his cars on the Upper Peninsula when he rounded a bend and came upon a man standing beside a new Model T scowling helplessly at its engine. Ford pulled and stepped on all the things necessary to bring his car to a halt, walked over, and asked what the trouble was. The frustrated owner had no idea. Ford asked for his toolbox, and in a few minutes had the car ticking over and ready to go anywhere.

The owner took two dollars from his pocket and offered them to Ford, who declined. When the man persevered, Ford thanked him, but said he had all the money he needed.

The man laughed. "The hell you do! You drive a Ford."

But when it came time to tell Woodrow Wilson—who had bought a Model T in 1914 and was now president of the United States— a joke, Ford chose one that made a different point about the car. A farmer drafting his will stipulated that he must be buried in his Model T. When his lawyer asked why, he said, "Because I ain't been in a hole yet it couldn't get me out of."

That was always tacit in the jokes. The Model T might flap and rattle and get lost in your bathtub, but it did its job: It kept on going.

Bellamy Partridge told of anxiously nursing his Packard through a mudhole near his home, and then went on to recount a story that has the architecture of a Ford joke, but isn't one: "That mud hole, by the way, was destined to become famous. So many cars were bogged down there that Andy Brackett used to keep a team of horses close at hand most of the time to tow out the unfortunates. For a large car he charged three dollars. A medium-sized car he would pull out for two. He made a special price for a Ford, though this concession was academic, since Fords rarely were stuck there."

The car's dependability was the only luxury it offered. When it first appeared, the Ford copywriters asserted, "No car under $2000 offers more, and no car over $2000 offers more except in trimmings."

This was pushing things some. Today, for instance, few people would consider a heater "trimming," but the Model T didn't have one.

Such lacks, however, could be rectified by the products of hundreds of companies that rose and prospered solely through making accessories for the Model T. In the case of the heater you could buy a tin shield that got clamped to the exhaust manifold and diverted some of the heat it generated through the floorboards. "Not a bad fix," one owner remembered. "It would warm the car up to about the temperature of a barn."

The accessories—eventually there were five thousand of them—ranged from "Top Prop Nut to replace nuts lost because of vibration . . . well made of steel, finely enameled black, 3c" to embellishments that transformed the car: "Make a Full-Fledged Speedster of your Ford. . . . Here is a real nifty, classy, up to the minute Speedster body that would do credit to any car. We have correctly named it the Cyclone because it glides so easily, noiselessly and swiftly through the air on any Model T Ford chassis." The Cyclone body cost $68.75 in lead priming paint, $78.75 in glossy red, yellow, or black. There were speedometers and valve grinders, and a host of mechanical starters, all of dubious utility, any number of brackets and clamps and ball joints to reduce rattling, and a spidery assemblage of levers that "permits manipulating the throttle with foot," which E. B. White thought "madness" because "the Model T, just as she stood, had a choice of three foot pedals to push, and there were plenty of moments when both feet were occupied in the routine performance of duty and when the only way to speed up the engine was the hand throttle."

One aftermarket product that lasted, however, was the "Hind-View Auto-Reflector," which went on sale in August 1911, just three months after Ray Harroun had mounted the first rearview mirror on the bright yellow Marmon Wasp he drove to victory in the Indianapolis 500.

For the unusual Model T owner who preferred the appearance of the car to its innards, Hinkley Motors stood ready to replace the works—engine, transmission, and all: the transmission for $132, the engine for $184. "All this at only a little more than the cost of a major overhaul, and without chassis alterations of any kind. Not even a hole to drill! And a Ford which, after the installation, is stronger than ever before."

Just as the owner was expected to install his own heater or starter or better headlights if he wanted them, so was it up to him to maintain his car. A midwesterner named Albert Stephenson, who had a succession of Ts in the 1920s—"like so many others, I drove only second- or third-hand models"—remembered that "the whole car was simple, accessible, and tolerant. . . . On a cold morning a quick jerk or two at the choke rod on the dash would cure a harsh and persistent coughing spell. In the evening you could tighten the bands, look at the timer, or clean the plugs. A weekend would do nicely to reline the bands or grind the valves and clean the carbon or maybe tighten the rods. A four-day vacation was plenty to overhaul the engine or the rear end. If any of these jobs was a bit beyond your experience, you had merely to ask your neighbor, who not only knew but would come over and help." The ramifications of this were far-reaching and frequently unexpected. In the Second World War, for example, German tanks were often superior to their American counterparts. But this advantage was canceled by how quickly a disabled Sherman could get itself repaired and back into action. The Germans were baffled and dismayed to find that among his other accomplishments, Henry Ford had created a whole generation of mechanics.

But the Model T's most profound impact was succinctly expressed in the *Ford Times,* a company magazine born just a few months before the car in 1908. Originally a house organ "published solely to afford a means for the interchange of ideas among all dealers and employees of the Ford Motor Company," who were frequently and forcefully enjoined to contribute articles, it was full of selling tips and pictures that could be imported into ads ("No. 106—two column cut of Coupe for newspaper advertising") and such insider news as employee bowling scores. Before long, though, it had grown into a richly produced monthly aimed not only at dealers but also at Ford owners and potential buyers. Within a decade of its founding it had a circulation of nine hundred thousand, and its popularity reflects the vigor of the product it promoted.

In 1915 *Ford Times* declared, "Best of all," the Model T "has remodeled the social life of the country."

In a decade, the Model T broke the age-old isolation of the farm. The recipients of this new freedom appreciated their benefactor, trusted him, called him by his first name. "You know, Henry," wrote a Georgia farmwife in 1918, "your car lifted us out of the mud. It brought joy to our lives. We loved every rattle in its bones."

In 1926 an Alabaman expressed the same feelings in more high-flown terms: "We of the South affectionately acclaim you, instead of Lincoln, as the Great Liberator. Lincoln has freed his thousands, you have freed your ten thousands. The rutted roads on mountain sides and water sogged wheel tracks on lower lands have been smoothed, that the wheels of Fords may pass. The sagged barbed wire gates of barren cotton patches and blighted corn fields have been thrown open that brainblinded and soulblinded recluses might rise joyously into the world with their families in Fords."

The Model T soon became as much an urban being as a rural one. When Robert and Helen Lynd published their famous sociological study of the effects of the young century on a typical small city in the 1920s—it was Muncie, Indiana, which they called "Middletown"—they met a lifelong resident who said, "Why on earth do you have to study what's changing this country? I can tell you what's happening in just four letters: A-U-T-O!"

The machine had already taken a hold on American society that it has not relaxed yet. The Lynds found that many Muncie residents were mortgaging their houses to buy an automobile, and the trend alarmed almost everyone who wasn't a part of it. The recently established custom of the Sunday drive was a "threat against the church," while a labor organizer complained that "as long as men have enough money to buy a secondhand Ford and tires and gasoline, they'll be out on the road and paying no attention to union meetings."

The Lynds found that the automobile had been "spreading the 'vacation' habit. The custom of having each summer a respite, usually of two weeks, from getting-a-living activities, with pay unabated, is increasingly common."

A mother of nine children, reflecting on this radical new gift that combined mobility with privacy, said, "We'd rather do without clothes than give up the car. We used to go to my sister's for a visit, but by the time we got the children shoed and dressed there wasn't any money left for carfare. Now no matter how they look, we just poke 'em in the car and take 'em along."

Another mother went further: "I'll go without food before I'll see us give up the car."

The Lynds were looking at the general impact of the automobile, but when they came to make an inventory of the cars in Muncie, they found that of the 6,221 registered in 1923, 2,578 were Fords, with Chevrolet running a distant second at 590.

Years after he'd ceased to wrestle with one, John Steinbeck recalled the Model T with the same fond precision E. B. White did. Olfactory memories are sometimes the strongest, and he mentioned how his car smelled—"a lovely odor . . . of oil-soaked wood and sunbaked paint, of gasoline, of exhaust gases and ozone from the coil box"—even before saying what it meant to him: "I think I loved that car more than any I have ever had. It understood me. It had an intelligence not exactly malicious, but it did love a practical joke. It knew, for instance, exactly how long it could keep me spinning the crank and cursing it before I would start kicking its radiator in. It ran perfectly when I was in blue jeans, but let me put on my best suit and white shirt, and maybe a girl beside me, and that car invariably broke down in the greasiest possible manner."

Steinbeck went on to discuss the car's larger significance, basically agreeing with the Ford Motor Company's assessment, but expressing it in terms the *Ford Times* would be unlikely to have countenanced: "Someone should write an erudite essay on the moral, physical and esthetic effect of the Model T Ford on the American Nation. Two generations of Americans knew more about the Ford coil than the clitoris, about the planetary system of gears than the solar system of stars. With the Model T, part of the concept of private property disappeared. Pliers ceased to be privately owned and a tire pump belonged to the last man who had picked it up. Most of the babies of the period were conceived in Model T Fords and not a few were born in them. The theory of the Anglo Saxon home became so warped that it never quite recovered."

CHAPTER 12

Terrible Efficiency

The Crystal Palace; taking the work to the worker; speeding up; the twentieth century's only industrial revolution; the workers hate it.

Of course the Model T could never have made such an impression had it not been deployed in vast numbers, and at a price folks like Roscoe Sheller's dairy farmer could afford. That Ford developed a way to do this is, more than the car itself, the measure of his genius.

Several automakers were turning out a hundred cars a day during the Model T's early years, which demonstrates impressive planning and organization, but as Allan Nevins points out, there is a fundamental difference between "quantity production" and true "mass production." It was by inventing the latter that Henry Ford invented the modern age.

First, though, he needed a place to invent it in. The success of the Model N had badly strained the Piquette Avenue plant. In 1906, months before the first Model T was built, Ford bought sixty acres of land in Highland Park, a small suburb six miles north of downtown Detroit.

He hired Albert Kahn to design his new factory. The architect was still in his thirties, but he had already built a plant for Packard that impressed Ford with its advanced reinforced concrete design and broad stretches of glass. Ford wanted something bigger, and he got it: the largest building in Michigan and the largest automobile factory in the world. Four stories high and 865 feet long—equivalent to an eighty-six-story skyscraper lying on its side—its concrete corners fortified with steel supporting rods beneath a shell of decorative brick framed fifty thousand square feet of glass. That was three-quarters of the building's walls, and on fair days the workers would stand in a lake of sunlight so bright that some took to calling the place the Crystal Palace. In a few months Kahn had put up next to this prodigy a machine shop nearly as large, with an all-glass roof. The two buildings were connected by a craneway to carry materials from one to the other. Eight hundred and sixty feet long and nearly sixty high, it was itself a corridor of glass. The Highland Park factory set Kahn on his way to being the foremost industrial architect in America.

Ford operations moved from Piquette Avenue at the end of 1909, "without," the *Ford Times* pertly reported, "a brass band, a ball, a clambake, or even a speech from the mayor." The house organ had a right to its complacency. On the last day of 1909 all the new Ford cars were shipped from Piquette Avenue. On New Year's Day of 1910, most of them rolled out of Highland Park.

This extraordinarily smooth transition was largely the work of Sorensen and his immediate boss, a French Canadian named Peter Martin whom Nevins describes as "burly" and, somewhat more surprisingly, "stodgy." Martin was the plant's superintendent, although he never held that title.

Henry Ford abhorred titles. Sorensen remembered that in the spring of 1908 Ford summoned him and Martin—who was universally known as Ed—to his office. It was a brief meeting. Ford said, "You, Ed, will be plant superintendent and you, Charlie, will be assistant superintendent. Just go out there and run the place. I know you can do it. But there's one thing I want to add: work together as one. I don't ever want to hear that you can't work together. And don't worry about titles."

Martin and Sorensen received their promotions because Walter Flanders had just quit.

Flanders had blown through the company like a line squall. A Vermonter who had managed to educate himself about machine tools so effectively that by the time Ford hired him in 1906 he understood plant design perhaps better than anyone else in the country, he was everything his new boss was not: loquacious, brash, noisy (Sorensen said he had "a voice that could be heard in a drop forge plant"), domineering, and something of a libertine, at least by Henry Ford's standards. He immediately made himself so popular in the company with both the workers and the board that Sorensen thought Ford was a little scared of him: "He was aware of Flanders's ability yet feared the man might take his place. There was a streak of jealousy here."

To be sure, Flanders sounded as if he already owned the company when he stipulated what his duties would be: to hire and fire anyone he chose, and "to manage the different manufacturing departments of your companies, [and] reorganize same, on what, in my judgment, is the most economical basis of manufacture for producing commercial products at the minimal cost."

Whatever Ford might have thought of this summary, it alarmed Couzens, who wrote his boss, "I am afraid he will want the earth if he gets started on a proposition like this. The terms and salary [seventy-five hundred dollars a year] I think are all right, but he wants [needs] to be confined to the manufacturing end in the shop and have nothing to do with policy or designing or finances or sales." Couzens concluded with a request that surely reflects earlier aggravations: "Please don't leave this letter around on your desk or show it to anyone."

Flanders didn't try to fire Couzens and he didn't try to take over the company. Instead, he set about establishing principles that would drive American manufacturing all through the new century.

He immediately began rearranging the machine tools in the factory. Previously, as in the Dodge brothers' operation, as in nearly every plant in the country, they were grouped together: here a colony of drill presses, there a dozen lathes. This made sense if a factory had to do many different jobs, but Flanders understood that the Ford works would be doing only one, and it would be done far more efficiently if the machines stood along the path the work took. That is, if a part needed to be heated between being milled and being drilled, Flanders put an oven between the milling machine and the drill.

He went on to study the stocks of materials that fed the newly rationalized sequence of machine tools and pared them down. Keep only a ten-day supply on hand, he ordered; let the suppliers carry the inventory at their expense and not the Ford Motor Company's.

Flanders also stressed the necessity of interchangeable parts. Every axle housing and cylinder head must match every other one as closely as possible right down to the atomic level. Having to file or hammer a part to make it fit would slow production, create bottlenecks, and extinguish profits.

Henry Ford already believed this, as had generations of mechanics before him. American manufacturers had long been striving for perfect interchangeability of the elements in their product, first in firearms, then sewing machines, and most recently bicycles. But the accuracy of machine tools could not wholly be trusted until the early twentieth century, when increasing technological sophistication began to let them meet the demands of the automotive industry.

Finally, Flanders pressed for single-purpose tools. The repetitive manufacture of a single car part did not require a trained mechanic. Flanders ordered what he called "farmer tools," ones far from simple, but so easy to operate that anyone just in from the country could learn how in a couple of hours.

Henry Ford was again in agreement with his production manager, and the company would never stint in buying the newest and best machine tools.

Then, less than two years after his arrival, Flanders was gone, lured away by a fat offer from the Wayne Automobile Company and taking some valued employees with him.

Henry Ford may have felt intimidated by Flanders, but he was so angry to see him leave that his response shook the hard-minded Couzens.

"If you say the word," Ford told him, "I will have his head knocked off."

"What do you mean?"

"Oh, I have a couple of fellows who will beat him up."

"Oh, no. We will stand this without *that*."

Couzens left the office brooding. After a while he came to think what others would in the years ahead: "Mr. Ford was not one man, but two."

Ford didn't follow up on his threat, but he kept sulking about Flanders's defection. "Hereafter," he told Sorensen, "anybody who goes along with us must come up from the bottom and work right through the organization."

Despite the blow he dealt Henry Ford's amour propre, Flanders had more than justified the fifteen thousand dollars he earned during his brief tenure. Sorensen, who was never free with a compliment, wrote, "Ford, a quiet, sensitive person, got a few gray hairs at this stage, but he learned a great deal from Flanders and so did I." He went further: Flanders "headed us toward mass production."

Ford would take some time to get there, but the Highland Park factory proved itself immediately. A few months after the company had moved into its new home it was completing more than 100 cars a day, and in April alone it put out 3,728. Henry Ford had made the job easier by decreeing the year before that this magnificent new plant would be building just one car: the Model T. And so it would for the better part of twenty years. The manufacturing year closed that September with 19,000 new Model Ts on the road. The next year Ford made 34,500, and the year after that, 1911–12, 78,440.

Henry Ford sought economy in the speed of production, and wherever else he could find it. In the beginning, the plan had been to cast the crankcase, which covered the bottom of the engine and contained the oil bath in which it had to run. Casting was expensive, and the result would be too heavy.

While Ford mechanics were puzzling through this, an owner of the John R. Keim stamping mill in Buffalo came to see Ford. Rather than melt and pour and work metal, Keim's big presses took in a piece of sheet steel and punched it into shape, like a notary public's seal embossing a piece of paper. The representative brought Ford only a shiny black telephone stand the mills were then pounding out, but Ford got the idea, and sent Sorensen and Wills to Buffalo to have a look at the operation.

Sorensen was tickled by the assignment. He remembered, as a boy, visiting the Keim works. "At the time they made bicycle crank hangers and pedals. With other young bicycle enthusiasts, I used to go to the back of the plant where there was a scrap pile of rejected ball bearings. I had quite a boxful of these bearings, which I kept around our home."

When Sorensen and Wills entered the factory, they were taken to a press busily showing its capacity to make a larger stamping than a telephone stand. The machine was doing just fine, but apparently the job required a lot of lubrication, because from beneath it, slick and black as a seal with heavy oil, "came a supervisor who had been handling the press-work. . . . The man from the pit, a tall lanky fellow, was covered with grease from head to foot. And that was my first, but not my last, sight of my fellow Dane, William H. Knudsen."

No instant friendship grew from this fortuitous reunion of countrymen. "I must correct extravagant stories told about him when he left Ford," Sorensen wrote of Knudsen forty years later. "He had nothing to do with major producing or its planning at Highland Park. Few of the basic staff seemed able to get along with him."

Here is a scent of the same alarm—and jealousy—Henry Ford must have felt about Walter Flanders. In fact, Knudsen would get along with every level of the Ford staff, and become one of the greatest car men of his century. But at the moment this oil-basted, eager stranger only wanted Wills and Sorensen to take the stampings he'd just made to Detroit and see how their boss liked them.

He didn't, much. Henry Ford felt there was something a little sleazy, a bit hasty and coarse, about stampings. Castings appealed more to the engineer in him. Galamb pushed for the stampings. When you could get away with it, bending metal was cheaper than pouring it.

Ford would not compromise on his vanadium steel, but he knew that to keep down the price of his car he would have to use the stampings. He took what comfort he could from teasing Galamb—"Hungarian stimpings," he would say, making fun of Galamb's accent, and started calling him "shit-iron Joe"—but he accepted the stampings and, in 1911, when his victory over the Selden patent suit opened the way, he bought the factory that made them.

For a while the Buffalo plant kept the flow of supplies coming to Detroit. Then, just before Labor Day in 1912, Keim factory hands, angry at what they were being paid for some piecework that had nothing to do with Ford, walked off the job on a wildcat strike.

Knudsen, now the plant's general superintendent, called Detroit with the news. "That suits me," said Ford. "If the men don't want to work, get some flat cars and move the presses and machinery to Highland Park."

A troubled Knudsen went to talk with the strikers. I know this man, he told them; he isn't kidding. Best to back off for the moment.

They jeered Knudsen, and three days later the Keim stamping machines were dispensing transmission covers in the Crystal Palace.

That was fast work, but all the work at Highland Park was fast now. Ford and Sorensen and Martin were shifting Detroit's heaviest machinery around as casually as checkers players move their pieces. Labeled with brass tags to show where they belonged (affixing these was one of the teenaged Edsel's first jobs in the factory), each new machine would shoulder aside a slightly less effective one, even if the predecessor was only a few months old. No effort, no expense, was too great if it would speed up the work by the smallest increment. "Whenever I approached Mr. Ford on the possibility of new types of machine tools, he never hesitated for a moment," said Sorensen. "'Don't wait, Charlie,' he would say. 'Let's get these things right away.' He was wonderful in that respect: he never started out being skeptical and then saying 'I told you so' when things went wrong."

The great tools themselves became increasingly specialized. For instance, in its journey from metal cube to Model T engine, a casting would be snatched by something that looked as if it might have been designed to power an ocean liner. As the machine briefly embraced the block, forty-five drills pierced the engine-to-be on every side. The machine was invaluable to the Ford shop, and worthless outside it, because the sole thing it could do was put holes in a Model T engine.

The prepared engine block would be hurried on to its next station, but it would have to pause there. Everything moved quickly, like the second hand on a pocket watch of those days, but, as with the second hand, the motion was made up of incessant brief interruptions.

In the engine assembly room workers stood elbow to elbow at long tables, each one fitting parts kept readily at hand. The men were quick. Nevertheless, each man was working on just one engine at a time.

The engines, and all the other components of the car, came together in the chassis assembly, where groups of workers moved from car to car, fifty cars in a batch, each group with its own task, while handcarts wheeled up and down the line delivering assembled units as large as completed dashboards, steering wheels and all.

In the 1912–13 year the highly refined process yielded 181,951 cars. A finished chassis left the factory floor every forty seconds. This was quantity production at its most impressive. Still, it was at heart static. As Henry Ford put it, "The first step in [mass production] came when we began taking the work to the men instead of the men to the work."

Charles Sorensen says he invented the moving production line at the Piquette Avenue plant, in 1908: *"The idea occurred to me that assembly would be easier, simpler, and faster if we moved the chassis along, beginning at one end of the plant with a frame and adding the axles and wheels; then moving it past the stockroom, instead of moving the stockroom to it* [italics Sorensen's].*"*

On Sundays when the plant was quiet, Sorensen had helpers put clusters of parts along the length of the factory. They tied a rope to a car frame mounted on skids and tugged it past workers who fitted on parts. By the time it had reached the far wall, Sorensen said, they had "put together the first car, I am sure, that was ever built on an assembly line."

He had Ford, Wills, and Martin watch the demonstration. All three were skeptical. Martin didn't think it was possible to build a car on the move. Wills, according to Sorensen, said flatly that any such attempt would "ruin the company." Ford alone encouraged Sorensen to keep trying.

There could be no further progress, though, until the flow of work and materials at Highland Park had been put into rational operation. "The entire plant," Sorensen said, "had to be functioning before the Ford mass production and assembly system could be completely worked out into one great synchronized operation. . . . It was that complete synchronization which accounted for the difference between an ordinary assembly line and a mass production one."

When that happened, the nascent creative power of the new factory brought on mass production like a battle: swift, violent, and so hard to follow that even now it is not clear how the victory—and it was the great industrial victory of the twentieth century—came about. The Ford Motor Company maintains superb archives, but during the incandescent months that gave birth to the new system, nobody had time to keep track of what was happening.

The change likely started, appropriately enough, with Spider Huff's revolutionary flywheel magneto, in April 1913. On the first day of the month, the men who put it together came to work to find themselves standing not at their usual wooden tables, but in front of a long waist-high pipe-metal frame that held a row of magneto shells. The day before, each worker would have entirely assembled the magneto in front of him—sixteen bolts, sixteen of the enlivening V-shaped magnets, and so forth. This morning they were told to put on a single part, or loosely set a couple of bolts, and then push the flywheel a yard along the line to the next worker, who also would contribute only a part or two.

These twenty-nine men, working alone the week before, had been completing a magneto every twenty minutes. In company they began turning one out every thirteen minutes and ten seconds. They complained that all the bending over hurt their backs. The next morning they found the line had been raised eight inches. Some of them were faster than others. Soon a chain conveyor moved the flywheels along at a uniform speed. Within a year fifteen men were putting out 1,335 finished flywheels during their eight-hour shift. The time required to make a magneto had dropped from twenty minutes to five.

Ford wrote, "It must not be imagined, however, that all this worked out as quickly as it sounds. The speed of the moving work had to be carefully tried out; in the flywheel magneto we first had a speed of sixty inches per minute. That was too fast. Then we tried eighteen inches a minute. That was too slow. Finally we settled on forty-four inches per minute. The idea is that a man must not be hurried in his work—he must have every second necessary but not a single unnecessary second."

In fact, all this *did* work out almost as quickly as it sounds. The new system immediately flung itself at engine assembly, and once that line was up and running the time dropped from 594 minutes per engine to 226.

If Sorensen might have exaggerated his 1908 breakthrough, he now had a far more public chance to tie a rope to a chassis and winch the car past the workstations while six men attached the components. As crude as the demonstration might have been, its results were extraordinary. The Ford Motor Company was spending twelve and a half man-hours putting together a chassis. When the experimental chassis finished its 250-foot journey, it had required—taking into account all the time that went into the making of the parts it now incorporated—less than six hours to complete.

"In the chassis assembling," Ford wrote, "are forty-five separate operations or stations. The first men fasten four mud-guard brackets to the chassis frame; the motor arrives on the tenth operation and so on. . . . Some men do only one or two small operations, others do more. The man who places a part does not fasten it—the part may not be fully in place until after several operations later. The man who puts on a nut does not tighten it."

Throughout Highland Park new chutes reached down from one floor to another to let gravity do the labor of moving metal from station to station. Everything that could be hitched to a conveyor was. More and more workers found themselves standing on the same small patch of flooring during their entire shift. Ford said, "The undirected worker spends more of his time walking about for materials and tools than he does in working; he gets small pay because pedestrianism is not a highly paid line."

By December highly directed workers were taking two hours and thirty-eight minutes to build a chassis; by the next April, ninety-three minutes. Before the Model T was done, a finished automobile, chassis, body, and all, would be coming off the line, shining and ready for its buyer, every ten seconds.

Those hectic, under-recorded months at Highland Park had witnessed the beginnings of the only true industrial revolution of the twentieth century—an undiluted triumph for all who took part in it.

The only trouble was that Henry Ford's workers hated their new stationary life in the Crystal Palace, and they wouldn't stay there.

———————

In 1914, shortly after the system of moving assembly lines was complete—or, at least fully operational: Continuous experimentation and improvement meant it would never be "complete" while Highland Park lived—a journalist named Julian Street stopped by to have a look at the factory. A New Yorker, Street was traveling across the country to write a book of impressions he called *Abroad at Home*. Few of the impressions were more vivid than those Highland Park dinned into him. "Of course there was order in that place, of course there was system—relentless system—terrible 'efficiency'—but to my mind . . . the whole room, with its interminable aisles, its whirling shafts and wheels, its forest of roof-supporting posts and flapping, flying, leather belting, its endless rows of writhing machinery, its shrieking, hammering, and clatter, its smell of oil, its autumn haze of smoke, its savage-looking foreign population—to my mind it expressed but one thing, and that thing was delirium.

"Fancy a jungle of wheels and belts and weird iron forms—of men, machinery and movement—add to it every kind of sound you can imagine: the sound of a million squirrels chirking, a million monkeys quarreling, a million lions roaring, a million pigs dying, a million elephants smashing through a forest of sheet iron, a million boys whistling on their fingers, a million others coughing with the whooping cough, a million sinners groaning as they are dragged to hell— imagine all of this happening at the very edge of Niagara Falls, with the everlasting roar of the cataract as a perpetual background, and you may acquire a vague conception of that place."

Street was free to leave this Moloch's funhouse, but the men tending all that noise and motion were not. Or at least they weren't until they got sick enough of it to stop taking Henry Ford's paycheck which, at $2.34 an hour as the minimum daily wage, was as good as or better than those being offered by his competitors.

But the work at Highland Park was different, and it told on the men who did it. Many of them felt a massive, mute condescension in the very existence of Flanders's "farmer tools," some of which, Henry Ford said, "could be attended by a child of three."

There was good reason to have such tools: "The rank and file of men come to us unskilled; they learn their jobs in a few hours or a few days. If they do not learn in that time, they will never be any use to us. These men are, many of them, foreigners, and all that is required before they are taken on is that they should be potentially able to do enough work to pay the overhead charges on the floor space they occupy."

A great many of them were the "savage-looking" foreigners that, along with everything else, alarmed Julian Street about Highland Park. By 1914, with all the assembly lines running, 70 percent of Ford's workers were foreign born: a fifth of them Polish, 16 percent Russian, smaller groups from a score of countries. Arabs were particularly valued. They'd gotten the word they were welcome at Highland Park, came with their families, and picked up the farmer tools and were glad to have them, while their wives and children ran little stores that sold coffee and pastry and sandwiches, socks and gloves and boots, to company workers during their breaks. A descendant of one wrote, "Ford Motor Company is part of our lives. Henry Ford hired all the minorities, and of course they worked so hard. . . . And I think the Arab immigrants, as hard as they worked, they were grateful for the jobs that they had."

Just as Arabs knew who was hiring, so did American blacks. Far from being part of a newly arrived immigrant group, most of their ancestors had been in America long before William Ford came over. But they were immigrants in the northern world of heavy industry. They knew that you couldn't count on getting work at any of the plants, but that your best bets were Packard and the Ford Motor Company. If they were often assigned the heaviest jobs, like those in the foundry, these were real, paying jobs nonetheless. By 1917 the Ford Motor Company had become the industry's leading employer of African Americans, many of them on the highly paid assembly lines, and some in supervising positions with the authority—nearly unique in that place and time—to fire white workers.

So: Muslims working the lines, and African Americans, Serbs and Maltese, Mexicans, a surprising number of Japanese who had heard the Ford factory whistles ten thousand miles away. As Julian Street made his wary way past the foreigners, he would have heard scraps of Finnish slung back and forth between men who had learned the trick of talking to one another underneath the clamor of the machinery, and some high-spirited Arabic banter (until a foreman made his inevitable effort to shut down conversation on the line), the occasional French oath, and what might have been Malay speech.

But he would have heard no Yiddish at all.

———

However steady and spectacular the work, there were those who shared Street's view of it. A good deal of disaffection came from the workers who (and how strangely long ago it seemed now) had been with Ford when the Piquette Avenue plant was finding its legs. These men didn't like the farmer tools, and they didn't see themselves as fortunate three-year-olds. They were, many of them, skilled mechanics who could with the tilt of an ear diagnose whatever was ailing a steam engine, and fix it before the farmhands knew there'd been an interruption in the harvesting.

Now they were being asked to put three nuts on three bolts—but don't tighten them!—and then three more, and then three more, forever.

Henry Ford understood. "Repetitive labor—the doing of the same kind of thing over and over again and always in the same kind of way—is a terrifying prospect to a certain kind of mind. It is terrifying to me."

But then he goes on to say that bankers and businessmen also have jobs that are "nearly all routine," too. Here he veers off into fantasy. Bankers and businessmen rarely walked off their jobs in disgust after five days. Just when the efficiencies of the moving assembly line had proved themselves at the end of 1913, the Ford managers discovered that they were having to hire 963 workers to be assured 100 of them would stay with their jobs long enough to learn them.

In *U.S.A.*, his great, jagged epic about America between the turn of the century and the Depression, John Dos Passos wrote, "Good roads had followed the narrow ruts made in the mud by the Model T. The great automotive boom was on. At Ford's production was improving all the time; less waste, more spotters, strawbosses, stoolpigeons (fifteen minutes for lunch, three minutes to go to the toilet, the . . . speedup everywhere, reachunder, adjustwasher, screwdown bolt, shove in cotterpin, reachunder, adjustwasher, screwdown bolt, reachunderadjustscrewdownreachunderadjust, until every ounce of life was sucked off into production and at night the workmen went home gray shaking husks)."

Many never returned. When, at the close of that same annus mirabilis of 1913, Henry Ford wanted to reward men who had been with him for at least three years, he had his board of directors vote them a 10 percent bonus. There were some fifteen thousand employees in the plant that winter. Six hundred forty of them had stayed long enough to qualify for the bonus.

CHAPTER 13

The Five-Dollar Day

Couzens and his conscience; "It's a good round number"; Ford bids against himself; "every worker a potential customer"; Ford at his zenith.

The authorship of the solution for stabilizing the Ford Motor Company's wavering, volatile workforce is still disputed. Sorensen, who was there, doesn't go so far as to claim it, but he is eager to make sure James Couzens gets no credit.

What happened may very well be Couzens's work, though, even if it is not an idea one would have expected from a man who, as Sorensen said, "could squeeze a penny until it hurt." But Couzens had been going through changes.

In 1913 the Ford Motor Company paid its twelve shareholders $11.2 million in dividends. Nobody could have worked harder and more grimly than Couzens to make a lot of money, but no one as intelligent as Couzens could ever have expected to become so rich in the single life span we are allotted for moneymaking. As he started into his forties, he found to his surprise that his wealth didn't sit well with him.

The men in the factory noticed no change in Couzens. Showing an acquaintance around the plant one evening, he came upon a diligent clerk at his post long after dark. "See that gentleman over there?" he asked the visitor in the clerk's hearing. "The only man in the organization who can't get his work done in the daytime!"

When old friends from Chatham dropped by the factory for a surprise visit and said, "Hello, Jim," he greeted them with "They call me Mister Couzens here."

Beneath the cold truculence, though, things were shifting. When his daughter Marguerite read about the big dividend in the newspaper, she came to her father happily and said, "Whew, that's a lot of money we have."

"But it doesn't belong to us," Couzens replied. "It's a trust. It's a responsibility, and a tough one."

For a while his job helped: "I am never happier than when I am working at top notch, and the only reason I let down at all is to be able to work at top notch the majority of the year." Then, it didn't.

"You know," he said, "there comes a time when the fun of making money is all gone. Say what you will, every man deep in his heart just acknowledges that. . . . The battle is won; the goal is achieved; it is time for something else."

Until the nature of that something else made itself clear to him, "I seemed to have no interest in life for a while," and thinking about his money made him feel "a kind of nausea."

Henry Ford was changing, too. Late in 1913 Elbert Hubbard, writer, philosopher, promoter of the Arts and Crafts Movement, and author of the preposterously successful parable "A Message to Garcia," published an essay about Ford that lay at the opposite end of the spectrum from the Tin Lizzie jokes. Here, he said, was the carmaker as he had come to be known "in all the places where the theme is Henry Ford. You hear it in barber shops, barrooms, ad-clubs, Sunday Schools, sewing circles. . . .

He is a man of few words—simple, plain, unaffected, democratic, direct. He uses no tobacco, no strong drink, and no strong language. Moderation is his watchword. He is temperate in all things, except in the manufacture of automobiles. . . .

Into his car Ford has put the truth, integrity, simplicity, sanity and commonsense which he himself possesses. . . . Henry Ford is not a highbrow, not a theorist, not a professional reformer—he is a worker and an executive. Also he is a teacher and a learner. . . . He has the work habit, the health habit, the play habit, and the study habit.

Whatever pleasure this tribute may have given its subject disappeared when Hubbard sent him a bill for eight hundred dollars, but Hubbard had expressed the general view of Henry Ford at the time: straightforward, modest, downright as the frontier ax in the old McGuffey's Readers. And much of it is true. But just as his company's unprecedented success was working on Couzens, so, too, was it on Ford. He was drawing away from his most valuable partner. When a British Ford dealer wrote Couzens to ask how the boss was doing, he got this response: "I have not been able to visit with Mr. Ford very much . . . but I hope and believe he had a most excellent time this summer."

Ford had been chafing to assume more of Couzens's role on the business side, once saying to an acquaintance, "I own fifty-eight percent of the stock, and I can do with the company what I like, can't I?" He began to go around Couzens on business matters, overruling him in minor ways without letting him know it was going to happen, seemingly just to bait his general manager, but perhaps also to experiment with how best to assert himself.

One day Ford asked for something from the stores, and was annoyed when the employee who brought it also handed him a printed form. What's this? Ford wanted to know.

A receipt, said the employee.

Where did it come from?

Mr. Couzens.

Ah. Ford asked to be given all the copies of that particular form. He carried them out into the factory yard, threw them to the ground, poured gasoline on them, and set them afire.

Ford was overruling Couzens in more significant ways, but this time not merely to humiliate him. When Couzens approached his boss with sales strategies or a new advertising campaign, Ford would veto them. By the midteens Ford had just one sales strategy, and that was to keep lowering the price of the car. Do that, he said, and the marketing would take care of itself.

The Ford Motor Company usually announced the new prices on the first day of August and October. On October 1, 1910, the Model T dropped from $950 to $780. A year later it was $690, and a year after that, $600. So it went throughout the decade: August 1, 1913, $550; August 1, 1914, $490; August 1, 1915, $440; August 1, 1916, $360. Until, on December 2, 1924, it reached its all-time low of $290.

This complete inversion of monopoly capitalism (if you are the sole source of a universally demanded good, you should *raise* the price) baffled observers throughout the car's career.

In 1909 the company made a profit of $220.11 on each car. Once the moving assembly line was at work, the profit fell to $99.34. That was fine with Henry Ford: "Every time I reduce the charge for our car by one dollar," he said, "I get a thousand new buyers."

Ford was right. His policy was drawing more customers than any artful sales campaign could have. And the torrent of money that came with them gave Couzens and Ford one great final occasion of being in perfect accord.

Even as big an operation as the Ford Motor Company was seasonal in those days, and usually slack times came right around Christmas. Then the plant would let off workers and send them home to wait, hoping their jobs would resume in a few weeks.

So it was with Christmas 1913, when Couzens stood at his office window watching workmen shuffling homeward in the frigid early dusk from what, for all they knew, might be their final shift ever. He thought, this famously hard man, "We had been driving our men at top speed for a year and here we were turning them out to spend the Christmas holidays with no pay. The company had piled up a huge profit from the labor of these men; the stockholders were rolling in wealth, but all the workers themselves got was a bare living wage."

The thought stayed with him. "All winter I sat in my office on the second floor of the Ford building and every time I looked out the windows I saw a sea of faces looking up. These men were shivering in the cold with their coat collars turned up."

That same troubling winter Couzens was reading a magazine "of socialist tendencies" when he came upon a passage in which the editor answered a reader's question that must have been put to him many times before: Why, "if it believed in socialism, the magazine did not practice what it preached in its own affairs." The editor replied that no one man or organization could alone deflect the flow of history—in order for there to be any real progress, change had to be universal, to somehow overtake everyone and everything at the same time. "That," said Couzens, "was an asinine answer."

Later he talked to B. C. Forbes, the leading business journalist of the day, who reported, "An idea flashed through his head. Why shouldn't the Ford Motor Company take a decided lead in paying the highest wages to its workers, thus enabling them to enjoy better living conditions?"

The next morning Couzens went to his boss and said that the company's minimum wage should be five dollars. "It's a good round number," he explained.

So it was. It was also a round number that was more than twice the average industrial worker's paycheck.

Couzens said the startled Ford was initially against it. "We pay as much as anyone pays."

His vice president—for Couzens had recently secured that title from his title-averse employer—replied with a gesture that, if accurately recalled, is impressively cinematic. Pointing out the window to the shivering job seekers below, he said, "But we're responsible for those men, because we don't pay them enough to live on. . . . We should give our people wages that permit them to save against the time we have no work for them."

Ford went to Peter Martin, who predictably found the idea ludicrous, and returned to tell Couzens, "Martin says he is ready to pay three dollars a day. That five dollars a day will cause trouble. That other firms—"

Couzens interrupted. "I know what Martin thinks. He thinks if we pay five dollars a day it will cause a general disturbance in the labor market. That we will be flooded with requests for jobs. What if it does? What if we are? We'll get the pick of the workmen and you know as well as I do that a good workman is worth five dollars a day."

"Well, I'll go back and talk with Martin."

Leave Martin alone, Couzens said. "If we talk of anything for more than forty-eight hours we never do it."

Whether he spoke with Martin or not, Ford returned with a counterproposal of $3.50.

"No," said Couzens, continuing to conduct the negotiation as if it were his company and not Ford's. "Five or nothing."

Ford raised the bid against his profit margin. "Then make it four."

"Five or nothing," Couzens persisted, and added, "A straight five-dollar wage will be the greatest advertisement any automobile concern ever had."

Ford, who had come to understand the advantages of advertising as well as anyone, once told a colleague that this final argument persuaded him.

Ford had other memories of the decision, though. He said it began on a day—also that Christmastime of 1913—when he and Edsel were walking through the factory and came upon two workers, full of fury and desperation, savagely fighting. Disgusted that his son should have seen this, Ford wondered what forces might make two of his workers turn from their tools in favor of trying to kill each other.

Soon after, he told a colleague, "There are thousands of men out there in the shop who are not living as they should. Their homes are crowded and unsanitary. . . . They fill up their homes with roomers and boarders in order to help swell the income. It's all wrong—all wrong. It's especially bad for the children. . . .

"Now, these people are not living in this manner as a matter of choice. Give them a decent income and they will live decently—will be glad to do so. What they need is the opportunity to do better, and someone to take a little personal interest in them—someone who will show that he has faith in them."

Yet Ford also insisted, once he had launched what he called "a kind of profit-sharing plan," that "there was no charity in any way involved. That was not generally understood. Many employers thought we were just making the announcement because we were prosperous and wanted advertising and they condemned us because we were upsetting standards—violating the custom of paying a man the smallest amount he would take. There is nothing to such standards and customs. They have to be wiped out. Some day they will be. Otherwise, we cannot abolish poverty. . . . We wanted to pay these wages so that business would be on a lasting foundation. We were not distributing anything—we were building for the future. A low wage business is always insecure."

In thinking this, Ford was reaching toward a conviction that may not fully have jelled in him by 1914, but that Sorensen crisply articulated years later. "Mr. Ford was saying that one ought to be one's own best customer; that unless an industry keeps wages high and prices low, it limits the number of its customers and destroys itself. Thus the wage earner is as important as a consumer as he is as a producer; and that enlarged buying power by paying high wages and selling at low prices is behind the prosperity of this country."

The innovation, Couzens and the Ford accountants figured, would cost $10 million the first year out.

On January 5, 1914, the company convened a press conference, but not much of one. Just three local newspapers were invited to James Couzens's office to hear the biggest piece of news that had ever come out of Detroit. Henry Ford stood by a window, restlessly glancing between it and the handful of reporters while Couzens explained the plan, and passed out a two-page typed press release "whose crude rhetorical flourishes," Nevins points out, "were not without justification."

It began, "The Ford Motor Company, the greatest and most successful automobile manufacturing company in the world, will, on January 12, inaugurate the greatest revolution in the matter of rewards for its workers ever known in the industrial world.

"At one stroke it will reduce the hours of labor from nine to eight, and add to every man's pay a share of the profits of the house. The smallest amount to be received by any man 22 years old and upwards will be $5.00 per day. The minimum wage is now $2.34 per day of nine hours."

"'If we are obliged,' said Mr. Ford, 'to lay off men for want of sufficient work at any season, we propose to so plan our year's work that the lay-off shall be in the harvest-time . . . not in the winter. . . . We shall make it our business to get in touch with the farmers and to induce our employees to answer calls for Harvest help.'" (Ford backed up what he said about the virtues of farming all his life: A few years later, when the company was having a harder time than it had expected making tractors, Sorensen complained to his boss that they were losing fifty-five dollars on every one they sold. "Well, I'm glad of it," Ford said. "If we can give a farmer $55 with every tractor that's just what I want.")

Couzens got into the text with his continuing indignation about the insufficiently socialistic magazine editor: "We do not agree with those employers who declare, as did a recent writer in a magazine, in excusing himself for not practicing what he preached, that the movement toward the bettering of society must be universal. We think that one concern can start and create an example for others. And that is our chief object."

The owner had the final word in the release: "'We believe,' said Mr. Ford, 'in making 20,000 men prosperous and contented rather than follow the plan of making a few slave drivers in our establishment multi-millionaires.'"

Ford and Couzens and the other company managers knew they

had taken a big step, but despite that bumptious press release, they may not quite have realized how big.

Their audience did, though. The *Detroit News* was an afternoon paper, and got the story into print that same day.

By sunrise the next morning a crowd was standing outside the Highland Park gates in ten-degree weather—"unemployed men," wrote the *Detroit Free Press,* "and men whose jobs suddenly had grown distasteful; rough-handed, white-collared men, eager to trade book-keepers' stools for manual labor in the gasoline Golconda where even sweepers get $5 a day." There were ten thousand of them. The short-ened hours and the extra shift required hiring perhaps five thousand new hands. The company quickly posted signs that said "No hiring," but people across the country were already scraping together rail fare.

In Pittsburgh, Pennsylvania, the news reached the unhappy home of a fifteen-year-old named Frank Marquart. "My father hated his job as a common laborer in the chain mill and he hated me for not finding a steady job, and life became a living hell for me." Then came January, and his father "excitedly waving the *Pittsburgh Press* and shouting . . . 'I'm going to quit my job tomorrow and Frank and me will go to Detroit. We'll both get jobs at Ford's—why, we'll be making 10 dol-lars a day, think of it, 10 dollars a day!'"

Frank's mother asked how they could be sure of a job, and the father's enthusiasm changed at once to rage. "'How the hell can we ever get ahead if you always pull back like that,' he demanded, half in German and half in English."

So father and son went, like so many others right then, on a trip they couldn't afford, first to a Detroit boardinghouse, then to a succes-sion of streetcars that brought them finally to Highland Park.

"There were thousands of job seekers jam-packed in front of the gates. It was a bitterly cold morning and I had no overcoat, only a red sweater under a thin jacket." The temperature still stood below ten degrees, and the crowd kept building. "Suddenly a shout went up—a shout that became a roaring chant: 'Open the employment office, open the employment office!'"

A man—who must have wished at that moment he had almost any other job in the company—shouted through a megaphone, "We are not hiring any more today; there's no use sticking around; we're not hiring today."

The crowd pushed forward. "You sonsabitches, keeping us here all this time and then telling us you ain't hiring, you bastards!"

Frank, teeth chattering, told his father he thought they should leave, "and he shouted at me in German that he didn't bring me to Detroit so I could loaf like a bum." Voices started calling, "Crash the goddam gates!"

The man with the megaphone yelled something about fire hoses. "Someone near us shouted, 'Aw, that's bullshit, they wouldn't dare do a thing like that.' He had hardly finished the sentence when the water came, the icy water that froze as soon as it landed on our clothing."

The people in front drew back while those behind still pushed forward, and soon there were brief whirlpools of fistfighting as the crowd fragmented into discouraged individuals who'd had enough for one day.

Frank said his father had been lucky: "The water did not soak through his overcoat as it soaked through my jacket and sweater. By the time we were able to board a Woodward Avenue streetcar I was shivering from head to foot."

On the streetcar, his father told him that Henry Ford was a Jew "and that what we suffered that morning was the result of 'a dirty Jew trick.'"

Frank said that Ford didn't sound like a Jewish name, and his father told him not to be stupid: "Don't you know that Jews change their names for business reasons!"

That melee embarrassed the company, but it would have given bleak satisfaction to some who had been as surprised by Ford's announcement as had all the would-be employees. Sorensen was one of the first to hear the complaints. "Alvan Macauley, president of the Packard Motor Car Company, got me on the telephone that night at my home. 'What are you fellows trying to do?' he demanded. 'We got the news about your

$5 day while we were having a board meeting. It was so astonishing that we broke up the meeting. We all felt "What is the use; we can't compete with an organization like the Ford Motor Company.""

Sorensen remembered his emollient reply as, "Of course, Mr. Macauley, you don't have to follow our example unless you want to. Perhaps you have an advantage over us if you don't pay as much wages as we do."

"That would be fine," Macauley snapped, as people always do when they think something is not remotely fine. "But how are we going to avoid paying these wages once you start paying them here in Detroit?"

A good question. *The* question. And the answer was that of course Packard would have to match Ford's wages, and in time such wholly unrelated businesses as Nabisco and Armour meatpacking and Kellogg's would, too, and the entire economic climate of America would change.

The *Wall Street Journal* wrote that "to inject ten millions into a company's factory, and to double the minimum wage, without regard to length of service, is to apply Biblical or spiritual principles in the field where they do not belong. . . . Henry Ford . . . has in his social endeavor committed blunders, if not crimes. They may return to plague him and the industry he represents, as well as organized society." The *New York Times* agreed, calling the five-dollar day "distinctly Utopian and dead against all experience." The president of Pittsburgh Plate Glass foresaw "the ruin of all business in this country," but took some solace in his certainty that "Ford himself will surely find that he cannot afford to pay $5 a day."

He could, as it turned out. The turmoil at the gates of Highland Park subsided after the company made clear it would be hiring only those who had lived in Detroit for at least six months, and the complaints in the press dried up, and all that remained was a continuing tide of goodwill that flowed in from everywhere. Thomas Edison cabled the *New York World,* "Some time ago Mr. Ford reduced the price of his wonderful touring car to the extent of fifty dollars. The user of the car received the entire benefit. Now he has practically reduced it another fifty dollars, but this time the men who make them get the benefit. Mr. Ford's machinery is specialized and highly efficient. This is what permits these results. This is open to all in nearly every line of business. Let the public throw bouquets at the inventors, and in time we will all be happy."

Ford's employees were already happy. Within two weeks of the announcement Detroit's marriage license clerk had issued fifty licenses to Ford workers. A factory hand named Woljeck Manijklisjiski told a reporter, "My boy don't sell no more papers. My girl don't work in the house of another and see her mother but once in the week no more. Again we are a family." A machine shop subforeman said, "The big worry that leads a lot of fellows to the suicide route, and a lot more to the booze route, is just a lot of little worries added together mostly, and that's exactly what the big boost in pay is going to do away with in the Ford Plant."

Rabbi Leo Franklin of Detroit's Temple Beth-El said, "This is a big advance toward the day when the workingman and the employer shall cease to be sworn enemies, and will be friends and brothers."

Rabbi Franklin went on to point out that "if the workingman is to get the maximum raise, he must in return give the best of which he is capable." Ford's workingmen seemed to agree. One said, "Mr. Ford pay me two-fifty, he get 250 pieces. Mr. Ford now pay me five dollars a day, he get 500 pieces. I pay him back."

The radical John Reed, no pushover where the interests of powerful capitalists were concerned, agreed (in a way) with the *Wall Street Journal*, when he wrote, "This new Ford plan is turning into something dangerously like a real experiment in democracy, and from it may spring a real menace to capitalism." In Ford, Reed saw "that most dangerous of revolutionists—a man who translates platitudes into action."

In his book *The Public Image of Henry Ford*, which sounds as if it might be some sort of sociological study, but is in fact a lively, engaging, and thorough biography of the man as seen through the eyes of an increasingly fascinated nation, David L. Lewis quotes the French intellectual Father R. L. Bruckberger speaking in 1959: "How I wish I could find words to impress the reader with the importance of the decision of the five-dollar day! Let me speak plainly; I consider that what Henry Ford accomplished [in] 1914 contributed far more to the emancipation of workers than the October Revolution of 1917.... He took the worker out of the class of the 'wage-earning proletariat' to which . . . Marx had relegated him and . . . made every worker a potential customer."

No man drilling engine blocks in Macauley's factory would ever be able to buy a Packard out of his earnings. But now the prudent Ford worker could in time purchase a Ford. The business historian and management sage Peter Drucker wrote in 1974, "Ford's action transformed American industrial society. It established the American workingman as fundamentally middle-class."

That was the destination toward which all those assembly lines had been moving, the final logic of mass production: mass consumption; the middle class; the modern age.

A newspaper reporter named Garet Garrett was in the composing room of the *New York Times* when the boss, Adolph Ochs, came in with his "arms held a little out, as if he were bearing a load on his chest, and his eyes were wide and staring. . . . When he spoke it was hardly above a whisper, saying: 'He's crazy, isn't he? Don't you think he's gone crazy?'"

Garrett knew what he was talking about; everyone in the room knew what he was talking about. The reporter spoke right up, saying, "It might be well to have a look. I'll go out and see."

The next morning he was being shaved by a Detroit hotel barber who told him, "Our Mr. Ford has gone crazy. Did you know?"

Garrett spent the next two days with Henry Ford. "He made it seem quite simple. He said: if a sweeper's heart is in his job he can save us five dollars a day by picking up small tools instead of throwing them out."

The reporter became friendly with Ford, and also with Samuel

Crowther, who had helped (to say the least) Ford write his autobiography. Of this collaboration, Garrett remembered, "They wrote several books together, with Ford speaking in the first person as *I* or *we*, and the ideas were entirely his own, but as he conceived them they were wordless revelations or sudden flashes of insight. It was Crowther's part to clothe them with reason and argument and house them in the proper premises."

It was Garrett and not Crowther, though, who reported what Ford said when the newsman asked him how he got his ideas. "There was something like a saucer on the desk in front of him. He flipped it upside down and kept tapping the bottom with his fingers as he said: 'You know atmospheric pressure is hitting there at fifteen pounds per square inch. You can't see it and you can't feel it. Yet you know it is happening. It's that way with ideas. The air is full of them. They are knocking you on the head. You don't have to think about it too much. . . . You can go about your business thinking and talking of other things, and suddenly the idea you want will come through. It was there all the time."

Garrett saw it happen once. Ford started talking about money to him and Cameron: how it was essentially meaningless (Ford used the term "holy water"), yet of course necessary as a sign. "The bankers had so bitched it up, with their speculations and manipulations, that now nobody could understand it. If only—"

This went on for a solid hour, until William Cameron, Ford's spokesman, put a stop to it to by saying lunch was ready. As they went toward the dining room, he murmured to Garrett, "Do you wonder how so much chaff can come out of what you know to be a really fine mill?"

At lunch Ford started all over, on the same topic but from a slightly different beginning. "Then suddenly his tall body stiffened: the expression of his face, which had been very lively, changed to that [of] a sleepwalker, and he said to no one in particular—to himself, really: 'A-h-h! I'm not thinking about that at all.'"

An idea had come to him, and without saying another word he stood up from the table and left the dining room.

"That happens often," Cameron told Garrett. "We may not see him again for a week."

―――――〰〰〰〰〰――――

Ford behaved the same way in his Highland Park office. It had been built on the scale of the rest of the factory, but he didn't like spending time in it any more than he had in his humbler offices, and he didn't like meetings at all. Sometimes in the middle—or at the beginning—of one, he'd spring up as if he had to go to the bathroom, or mumble that he'd forgotten to check on something, always giving the impression he'd be right back. He never came back.

The office, although often silent with its railroad-station vacancies of empty air, was nonetheless just what one would expect of the world's foremost automotive executive—the dark wood walls with the austere authority of cut stone, the several glossy desktops, the heavy, richly leathered furniture. It might have been made for the director of the Cunard Line or the Mellon Bank, save for a scale model of the car that had paid for the reverent space and that kept all the heroic clockwork beyond the windows turning its unceasing revolutions.

But, if you will, imagine a meeting in this rarely visited place sometime in the spring of 1914. The five-dollar day has made its sensational impact, and, with the exception of the financial press and the heads of competing auto companies, has been nationally accepted as a near-saintly act, one that in a single stroke has wiped away the bitter legacy of all the battles—many of them literal battles, with guns and blood—between worker and owner during the last half century.

Why the meeting? Maybe just to catch a collective breath and assess all that has happened so quickly since the assembly lines started moving. Whatever the cause, Henry Ford won't stay at it long. James Couzens will be there. There is a cooling between the two men, but both have promoted the five-dollar day, and it has more than fulfilled their hopes for it. Sorensen will surely be in the room, big and still and handsome (the manager of Ford's British operations refers to him as "Adonis"), incubating behind his flat blue glare envy about this and

that, but enormously capable. He will be with Ford longer than anybody but Clara.

There is a chance that Edsel Ford might be there. He'd started by
attending Detroit public schools and then, after the success of the
Model N, went to the excellent Detroit University School, which prepared him for college. His father didn't want him to go to college.
Now he is helping keep inventory, fastening those brass tags to the
machine tools. He had looked forward to college, but he is fascinated
by the automobile business, and is getting a grasp of it that impresses
the once skeptical superiors to whom he's been assigned. Next June
he will drive a Model T across the country, he and his fellow driver
sharing all the work, Edsel as competent at tightening the bands and
grinding the valves as any Ford company mechanic. He and his father
have few serious differences.

Joe Galamb? Again, maybe he's there, accepting with practiced
good humor Ford's teasing about his "Hungarian stimpings." Wills
is certainly in the room. Recently married and pleased with the way
the work is going, he's nonetheless thinking that any other company
meeting on a similar occasion (although actually there have been no
similar occasions in the history of American industry) would have
offered champagne, or at least a few swallows of wine.

Drinks won't be served. But perhaps Ford, glancing out the window as he had while Couzens read the initial announcement of the
five-dollar day, will look back into the room and speak to his small
audience. He can't talk to large groups, but he is good with ones of
four or five.

Slim, gray-eyed (or blue or green; no two interviewers could agree
on his eye color), gray-suited, he might say what he did during an
initial test of the Model T: "I think we've got something here." Sometimes these days he mocks Couzens, but perhaps he doesn't now. Perhaps he says that he and Couzens have done this between them (even
though that will irritate Sorensen), and that it has worked out pretty
damn well.

And perhaps Couzens will briefly offer his once-a-year, break-the-
Erie-ice smile.

I hope something like this happened, that there was a moment of summation when everyone understood what they had accomplished, and how they'd done it together, and made something honorable and new.

Because next year Couzens will be gone, and Ford's jealousies and the jocose anger that inspired those pranks, that made him publicly set fire to Couzens's receipts, will grow more destructive, and although he is soon to be the richest and most famous man in America, things will never be so good for him again.

———∿∿∿∿∿∿———

All seemed well, and better than well, for quite a while. Right after the five-dollar-day announcement Couzens took his family out West for a vacation, leaving Ford alone to sop up the praise. One Michigan newspaper ran as a headline, "God Bless Henry Ford and the Ford Motor Company," while the *New York World* called him "an inspired millionaire." He had been acclaimed for his racing successes and more for the Selden suit. Yet when Julian Street, preparing for his visit to the plant, wanted to check Ford's age, "I took up my *Who's Who in America* one evening with a view to finding out. But all I did find out was that his name is not contained therein. . . . (There is a Henry Ford in my *Who's Who,* but he is a professor at Princeton and writes for the *Atlantic Monthly.*)"

His car had carried his name everywhere, and people thought, as Elbert Hubbard suggested, that he probably shared its virtues: simplicity, honesty, no meretricious frills. But Ford remained the name of an automobile rather than of a man. That changed in a day. For the first time, Henry Ford was more famous than his car.

Long before his partnership with Malcomson he'd chafed under the obligation of answering to people, and this resistance hardened in the heat of public admiration. So, too, did a conviction he expressed in 1922. "None of our men are 'experts.' We have unfortunately found it necessary to get rid of a man as soon as he thinks himself an expert— because no one ever considers himself an expert if he really knows his job. . . . The moment one gets into an 'expert' state of mind a great number of things become impossible."

This was a way of saying that Henry Ford knew as much as anybody about anything. "Success had given him . . . a feeling that was almost infallible," wrote Nevins, and went on to quote a company executive who half believed it. Ford had given him an absurd order. "It's a fool thing, an impossible thing, but he has accomplished so many impossible things that I have learned to defer judgment and await the outcome. Take the Ford engine, for example; according to all the laws of mechanics the damned thing ought not to run, but it does."

Ford said, "I refuse to recognize there are impossibilities."

———————

One of the first effects of the five-dollar day that Henry Ford had not anticipated was being driven out of his home.

After the long succession of rentals, and with the Model T about to swarm the roads, Clara and Henry Ford had built a house on Edison Avenue. The street's name probably weighed in Ford's choice of the location, but it was a pleasant, leafy, prosperous neighborhood. The couple put up a good-looking brick Italianate house that, while solidly at the high end of "comfortable," was far from opulent.

A Steinway grand replaced the player piano from Bagley Avenue days, along with a Victrola, which cost an impressive two hundred dollars (forty five-dollar days). Clara worked happily in her best garden yet and tried to persuade her husband that she could not crank a Model T, even though he insisted it was easy. Clara stood firm, and her husband gave in and bought her, for three times the price of a Model T, a Detroit Electric, a plush little rolling parlor that carried her through the neighborhood in a whirring hush.

The three Fords liked their new home, but Edison Avenue was a public street, and once the five-dollar-day meteor struck the city, they were never alone. At dawn, at dusk, men stood on the lawn and in Clara's garden, hoping personally to ask Henry Ford for a job.

The couple discussed moving to Grosse Pointe, but Detroit's aristocracy were building their homes there, and Henry wanted nothing to do with them. He had bought hundreds of acres around Dearborn—he was always buying land—and he and Clara decided they would be happiest here among old friends.

They were not, however, going to live like those old friends. Ford had approached Frank Lloyd Wright in 1909 to commission a house, but Wright was distracted by one of his marital imbroglios, and recommended the Chicago firm of Van Holst and Fyte. Ford asked for a house that would cost $250,000. By the time it got under way the project had become so extravagant that he fired the architects and shut down work in February 1914.

Clara found another Van—W. H. Van Tine, a Pittsburgh builder and architect—who went right to work and quickly ran the cost of the house up to $1 million. Possibly because Van Tine was Clara's choice, Ford stood still for this.

He remembered his grandfather Patrick talking about the street he had lived on in County Cork. It led to the fairgrounds, and journeys along it were sweetened by birdsong. Patrick taught Henry the birdcalls.

The street was called Fair Lane, and that was the name the Fords gave to their new home. There was plenty of birdsong, for Henry had peppered his holdings with hundreds of birdhouses, and a "bird hotel" with seventy-six electrically heated compartments, an edifice that required a full-time employee to keep it properly cleaned and stocked with suet. But the house itself does not suggest the convivial sunniness of a country fair. Built of Indiana limestone, it contained fifty-six rooms, and dark walnut paneling and darker carved oak and three-foot-thick walls ensured that many of them were gloomy. Clara had some of the paneling painted in lighter hues, but that didn't really help, and she and Henry spent as much time as they could on the sunporch. "The Fords never seemed quite at home at Fair Lane," Sorensen said. "It used to give me the creeps to go there."

———~~~~~~~~———

The Fords evidently enjoyed the outside of the house more than the inside. There Henry could keep an eye on his birds (the naturalist John Burroughs, whom he had befriended, said he saw more birds at Fair Lane than anywhere else in the country), and Clara could oversee, with real horticultural knowledge, the five pungent acres of her roses, where twenty gardeners tended ten thousand plants.

Of the whole project, Ford was most interested in the power plant. Its two big turbines, driven by water from the Rouge River, turned twin generators that fed Fair Lane with 110 kilowatts of direct current. Thomas Edison came to Detroit in October 1914 to dedicate the powerhouse, which stood four stories high, and cost $244,000, just $6,000 less than the original estimate for the house itself. The machinery is still there, and it is one of the estate's most attractive features.

Yet perhaps Fair Lane is more emblematic of Henry Ford at this time, or a prophecy of what he would become. The walls are oppressive and suggest battlements; the house scowls and looks in on itself.

CHAPTER 14

Simple Purposes

Telling workers how to live; ugly enough to be a minister; war; Ford on the American soldier: "Lazy, crazy, or just out of a job"; Couzens quits; "GREAT WAR TO END CHRISTMAS DAY: FORD TO STOP IT"; from "peace angel to Vulcan."

An early stirring of Fair Lane's owner's messianism might be seen in his company's Sociological Department.

Ford company workers discovered that achieving their five-dollar day required more than a half year's residence in Detroit. Henry Ford was worried the sudden wealth would send its recipients into drink, gambling, domestic violence, and every other sort of dissipation. To qualify for his doubled salary, the worker had to be thrifty and continent. He had to keep his home neat and his children healthy, and, if he were below the age of twenty-two, to be married.

The job of ensuring such behavior went to John Lee, another executive who had come to the Ford Motor Company with the Keim mills. He was in charge of what today goes under the pallid name of "human resources," and he was one of the very few of Ford's high lieutenants who was universally liked.

Lee put out a booklet called *Helpful Hints and Advice to Employees*, which opened by declaring a "sole and simple" purpose that was far from simple. It was "to better the financial and moral standing of each employee and those of his household; to instill men with courage and a desire for health, happiness, and prosperity. To give father and mother sufficient for present and future; to provide for families in sickness, in health and in old age and to take away fear and worry. To make a well rounded life and not a mere struggle for existence to men and their families, and to implant in the heart of every individual the wholesome desire to Help the Other Fellow, whenever he comes across your path, to the extent of your ability."

This irreproachable aim was advanced by investigators who brought their questionnaires to the home of every Ford employee (although not Sorensen's, who from the start thought the endeavor a time-wasting distraction). The agents weren't mere busybodies. They'd been trained to offer useful advice on hygiene and on how to manage household finances. Behind them stood the Ford legal department, whose lawyers would help, free, with everything from buying a house to becoming an American citizen. Should an employee get sick or be injured, the company maintained a full-time staff of ten doctors and a hundred nurses.

The agents, initially recruited from among Ford's white-collar workers, soon grew to a force two hundred strong. Its members had to assess some thirteen thousand people, and do it quickly. Naturally they met resistance, from newly arrived Russians, for instance, whose memories of the czar's secret police were all too fresh, and from the occasional descendant of an original settler whose family had been in Detroit for generations and who didn't care to have some company hireling tell him how to live like a decent American.

For the most part, though, the interviewees took the intrusion into their lives philosophically. A few nosy questions that opened the door to the highest-paying job in the industry were easier to bear than being doused with fire hoses in the dead of a Detroit winter and having no job at all.

William Knudsen, who by now was busy sowing branch assembly plants across the nation, opposed the plan as strongly as did Sorensen, but for different reasons. He told his biographer that "as he saw it, the men were entitled to the money and, having earned it, it was theirs to spend without answering the snooping questions of investigators."

Knudsen was greatly amused to learn about a boardinghouse close to the factory on Manchester Avenue where eleven young Ford workmen lived. None of them was married, but whenever an agent stopped by, the man he was visiting would borrow the generous-spirited landlady and present her as his wife. Fortunately, said Knudsen, the social workers never called on all eleven at the same time.

One stipulation of the new mandate was that a Ford worker needed permission from a Ford executive if he wanted to get his own automobile. Knudsen was in Lee's office when an employee came in and said, "Mr. Lee, I would like to buy a car."

"Got any money?"

"I have seven hundred dollars."

"Do you have a family?"

"Yes, a wife and four children."

"Is the furniture paid for?"

"Yes."

"Have you any insurance?"

"Yes."

"All right, you can buy a car."

"Thanks, Mr. Lee." On his way out the door the man turned and said, "Oh, by the way, Mr. Lee, my wife is going to have another baby. I'm going to buy a Buick."

The occasional worker was openly defiant. When asked if he had any savings, one man told the investigator that he had invested his earnings "in houses and lots." When the skeptical agent pressed him for details, the man explained he'd meant "whorehouses and lots of whiskey."

On the other hand, there was Joe, who had come from a peasant life in Russia with his wife and six children.

F. W. Andrews, one of the Ford investigators (they were later to be given the less provocative title of "advisors"), told his story. "Life was an uphill struggle for Joe since landing in America," Andrews wrote. But he was willing to work, and work hard, digging sewers and farming, making his way to Detroit where "for five long months he tramped in the 'Army of the Unemployed'—always handicapped by his meager knowledge of the English language, and unable to find anything to do." Joe's wife "worked with the washtub and the scrubbing brush when such work could be found."

Joe landed a job at Ford, and that's when Andrews entered his life, to find him living in "an old, tumbled down, one and a half story frame house." Joe and his family were in "one half of the attic consisting of three rooms, which were so low that a person of medium height could not stand erect—a filthy, foul-smelling home." It contained "two dirty beds . . . a ragged filthy rug, a rickety table, and two bottomless chairs (the children standing up at the table to eat)." The family owed money to their landlord, to the butcher, to the grocer. The eldest daughter had gone to a charity hospital the week before. Andrews said the remainder of the family "were half clad, pale, and hungry looking."

Andrews at once got the pay office to issue Joe's wages daily instead of every two weeks. He secured a fifty-dollar loan, and such was the Sociological Department's seriousness of purpose then that Andrews, not Joe, borrowed the money. Andrews paid the butcher and the landlord, rented a cottage, and filled it with cheap but sound new furniture, new clothes, and, he said, "a liberal supply of soap."

Then the messianic moment. Andrews "had their dirty, old, junk furniture loaded on a dray and under cover of night moved them to their new home. This load of rubbish was heaped on a pile in the backyard, and a torch was applied and it went up in smoke.

"There upon the ashes of what had been their earthly possessions, this Russian peasant and his wife, with tears streaming down their faces, expressed their gratitude to Henry Ford, the FORD MOTOR COMPANY, and all those who had been instrumental in bringing about this marvelous change in their lives."

Were those tears only of gratitude as Joe watched this strange pyre of his family's old life?

Today the Sociological Department might seem the essence of suffocating paternalism, and many felt it so even at the time. Certainly no other big industrial operation had anything like it. But with its medical and legal services, and the English language school it ran for the company's thousands of immigrant workers, the department appears to have done more good than harm. In 1914 the average Ford worker had $207.10 in savings. For those who stuck with the company during the next five years, the average had risen to $2,171.14.

The reformer Ida Tarbell went to Highland Park planning to expose the oppressive Ford system. Instead she wrote, "I don't care what you call it—philanthropy, paternalism, autocracy—the results which are being obtained are worth all you can set against them, and the errors in the plan will provoke their own remedies."

The Sociological Department also brought into Henry Ford's life a man who turned out to be his keenest observer.

Samuel Marquis, three years younger than Ford, was born in Ohio in 1866. The descendant of several generations of Episcopal divines, he liked to tell his friends, "They say that when I was born, my aunt looked at me and said to my mother, 'This is the homeliest baby I ever saw,' to which my mother replied, 'All right, then, he shall be the minister.'"

And so he was, but not before twice being expelled from his ecclesiastical studies at Allegheny College in Pennsylvania during spells of severe buffeting by religious doubts. He overcame them, got a bachelor of divinity degree in 1893, married the next year, and had four children. He was sanguine, sturdy, direct, energetic, and full of Progressive-era zeal that made him believe he should use his faith to improve social conditions. In the spring of 1906 he was made dean of St. Paul's Cathedral in Detroit.

He applied himself so strenuously to his new job that by 1915 he had become one of the city's most popular preachers, but had also driven himself to the verge of collapse. His doctor ordered him to take a year off and recuperate, but Marquis said, "A change in work would be more beneficial to me than being idle," and he volunteered to help John Lee at the Ford Sociological Department. Lee was glad to get him, and Henry Ford was, too, because Marquis and the carmaker had become friends.

Marquis and his wife had called on Ford shortly after he moved to Edison Avenue. They were seeking, as so many Ford visitors did, money. Ford usually hated this, and was good at putting them off.

When Julian Street, having run the gauntlet of the factory, managed to get an interview with its owner, he concluded the meeting by asking, "Mr. Ford, I should think that when a man is very rich he might hardly know, sometimes, whether people are really his friends or whether they are cultivating him because of his money. Isn't that so?"

Mr. Ford's dry grin spread across his face. He replied with a question:

"When people come after *you* because they want to get something out of you, don't you get their number?"

"I think I do," I answered.

"Well, so do I," said Mr. Ford.

Marquis wanted to get something out of Ford for his church, but he proved a most engaging and direct supplicant. A writer for the *Detroit Journal* said, "His activities are perpetual, save as he sleeps. He is in deadly earnest, he hits from the shoulder," yet there was "no clerical contagion of gloom for him." He liked to tell a funny story as much as he liked to hear one. What Marquis said about John Lee could equally have served as a description of Samuel Marquis: "He is a man of ideas and ideals. He has a keen sense of justice and a sympathy with men in trouble that leads to an understanding of their problems. He has an unbounded faith in man, particularly with the 'down and out,' without which no man can do constructive work. Under his guidance the department put a soul into the company."

Marquis's beliefs and qualities appealed to Ford, who soon was calling him Mark (Mark, like everyone but Mrs. Ford and Edsel, called

Henry "Mr. Ford"). It didn't hurt the friendship that Clara took to the couple, too, and was a strong supporter of the Episcopal Church.

If Henry Ford had any religion at all, it was likely Episcopal, although he once said that he was born an Episcopalian but hadn't worked at it since. As his fame continued to grow he was often cited in pulpits as a Christian exemplar. A Methodist magazine said that he prayed daily for guidance, and the *Christian Herald* wrote that he kept the Scriptures in every room of his house for swift and easy reference. After this, a reporter asked him if he attended church regularly. Ford said, "No, the last time I went somebody stole my car."

For years he believed, or said he believed, in reincarnation. Back in 1901 the McKinley assassination had shocked Ford and Oliver Barthel into having a metaphysical discussion. Barthel gave Ford a book that he said had deeply influenced him. Written by Orlando Smith, a Mississippi cotton planter and Confederate officer with a strong spiritual bent who went on to become a newspaper owner, it was called *A Short View of Great Questions* (the student will be pleasantly surprised to find that it really *is* short) and argued for reincarnation and the transmigration of souls.

One can see why the philosophy might appeal to Ford. He hated any waste of energy, and what could be a greater waste of it than accumulating knowledge and experience over an entire lifetime only for it all to be extinguished at the end, leaving blank-minded babies having to start over again? Ford provided a compact rationale for his belief: "When the automobile was new and one of them came down the road, a chicken would run straight for home—and usually be killed. But today when a car comes along, a chicken will run for the nearest side of the road. That chicken has been hit in the ass in a previous life."

Ford was also strongly influenced by what one of his biographers rather shockingly calls "the simplicities" of Ralph Waldo Emerson. Ford had Emerson's dictum "cut your own wood and it warms you twice" hewn into one of Fair Lane's oak rafters. In his copy of Emerson's essays he put a mark next to "We love characters in proportion as they are impulsive and spontaneous" and wrote "good" beside "only in our easy, simple, spontaneous action are we strong."

Marquis said that Ford "is not an orthodox believer according to the standards of any church that I happen to know. His religious ideas, as he stated them, are somewhat vague. But there is in him something bigger than his ideas, something of a practical nature that is far better than his theories."

The minister was to learn a great deal more about Ford during their years together, but first and last he puzzled over the difficulty of actually visualizing the man. We can share his frustration today, for in any collection of Henry Ford photographs the subject looks different in every one.

"A still picture of Henry Ford is impossible," Marquis wrote, "for the simple reason that there is something in him that is never still. . . . In his presence no one is entirely at his ease. . . . You come to feel certain of but one thing, and this is that with any work he has to do the unexpected is bound to happen. . . ."

> The outward man reveals what is within. The ever-changing expression of his face, the constant play upon it of lights and shadows reflecting his rapidly changing thoughts and moods are the subject of remark on the part of those who see Mr. Ford daily.
>
> Photographers complain that he is "hard to get." There are snapshots of him a-plenty. Each looks as he looks at times. But no one of them reveals him as he is. No satisfactory photograph of him, so far as I know, has ever been taken.
>
> . . . In spite of a long and fairly intimate acquaintance with him, I have not one mental picture . . . of which I can say "This is as he is, or as I know him." There are in him lights so high and shadows so deep that I cannot get the whole of him in proper focus at the same time.

(Burnet Hershey, a reporter who met Ford a few months later, was harsher about this duality: "There is a fascinating little illusory trick which may be played with one of Ford's portrait-photographs. If one side of Ford's face is covered, a benign, gently humorous expression dominates. When the other side is covered, the look is transformed into one of deadly, malevolent calculation. This ambiguous effect is created by Ford's hollow, heavy eyes, the pale eyes one would associate with a visionary or a killer.")

Samuel Marquis's study of Ford's lights and shadows began with a course as intense as it was unwelcome when he was dragooned into an extraordinary project. Henry Ford was going over to Europe to put a stop to the First World War.

The war would make Ford for the first time feel the claws of a hostile press. But its earliest and most damaging cost to him was James Couzens.

Relations between the two men had kept eroding. When the outset of the conflict ignited bank runs across the country, Ford told Couzens he wanted to withdraw his money from the Highland State Bank, a subsidiary of the Ford Motor Company that Couzens had founded in 1909 and of which he was president. Couzens told Ford his money was safe there, and he should leave it be. Ford said he would. Then, without notifying Couzens, he ordered it transferred. Couzens sent him a telegram on August 5:

> IN THESE STRENUOUS TIMES MEN INVARIABLY
> SHOW THE KIND OF STUFF THEY ARE MADE
> OF. WE ARE MAKING ARRANGEMENTS TO
> TRANSFER YOUR MONEY TO THE DIME BANK.
> JAMES COUZENS

The insolence of the message led no further because three days later Couzens's elder son, Homer, driving alongside a lake, overturned the Model T his parents had given him a few months earlier for his fourteenth birthday. The car trapped the boy beneath the surface, and he drowned.

Couzens started out with his family on a motor trip, but soon realized this wouldn't help any of them. As always, he needed hard work, and he went back to his office and worked as hard as he ever had in his life.

Henry Ford kept piercing this shield against grief. War was another kind of waste to Ford, and a particularly bad one. He said—and it made headlines because of who he had become—"To my mind, the word 'murderer' should be embroidered in red letters across the breast of every soldier." The only people who benefited from war were "the militarists and the money lenders."

Couzens was no militarist. He had given five thousand dollars to a "League to Enforce Peace." But he was a Canadian, his countrymen were fighting to hold the Western Front, and Ford's talk about murderers grated on him. When, in the spring of 1915, a U-boat sank the British liner *Lusitania,* killing 1,200 people, 128 of them American, Ford said that the dead (his celebrator Elbert Hubbard among them) had only themselves to blame. They'd been warned. Later he told *Metropolitan* magazine, "I think nations are silly and flags are silly too." Then, in a nod to his own nation's fighting men, he added, "In this country most soldiers are lazy, crazy, or just out of a job."

That October, Charles Brownell, who managed publicity for Ford, made a routine stop at Couzens's office to show him the proofs of the next issue of the *Ford Times.* Couzens leafed through them perfunctorily until he came to an article, signed by his boss, once again denouncing any American effort to prepare for war.

"You can't publish this."

Brownell told him that Mr. Ford had approved it.

Couzens didn't care. "This is the company paper. He cannot use the *Ford Times* for his personal views. I will go and talk to Mr. Ford tomorrow."

The brief discussion started out amicably with some chat about a vacation in California that Ford was planning with Edison. Then Couzens said he'd postponed publication of the company paper because of the antiwar article. Ford "just went off the handle," according to Couzens. "I was shocked, aghast."

"You cannot stop anything here!"

"Well then, I will quit."

Ford, his fury immediately dissipated, told Couzens to think it over.

"No. I have decided."

"All right, if you have decided."

The rest of the talk was quiet, both men perhaps remembering the summer night, now more than a decade gone, when Ford had said the two of them were together against "those fellows."

Couzens went back to his office, wrote out a letter of resignation, and left, briefly displaying a flash of anger to a colleague: "I decided that I had enough of his God damned persecution."

Couzens did not go to another car company, and he never gave the coal business a backward glance. He became mayor of Detroit, and then a Republican senator from Illinois for fourteen years, losing his seat in 1936 only because the hidden flow of liberalism deep in the stony chasms of his spirit put him on the side of FDR's New Deal.

Ford said he was glad to have Couzens gone. Sorensen didn't believe it. "One morning in 1915, Mr. Ford came to my office. 'Mr. Couzens has quit,' he told me. 'I've just left him. Charlie, he was one of the hardest men I ever had to work with, but I wish I had one just like him to take his place.'

"He never got that wish."

———~~~~~~~~———

Henry Ford was sincere in his feelings about the war. He told the *Detroit Free Press,* "I will do everything in my power to prevent murderous, wasteful war in America and in the whole world . . . I would teach the child at its mother's knee what a horrible, wasteful, and unavailing thing it is. In the home and in the schools of the world I would see the child taught to feel the uselessness of war; that war is a thing unnecessary; that preparations for war can only end in war."

He could do more than talk to a child. He had already changed the habits of his nation. Now he would end the war.

Garet Garrett wrote, "When men say anything is possible if you don't know any better they express a kind of contempt for history, experience and expert opinion. . . . They are bound to go on to the thought that if anything is possible, so anything may be true, with the cynical notation that what people generally believe is probably wrong. With that, they expose themselves to every cracked wind that blows."

The cracked wind came from a woman named Rosika Schwimmer, who persuaded Ford to be her partner in what Garrett called "the weirdest single episode of his life."

Schwimmer, a radical Hungarian Jew, had been traveling America speaking with astringent wit first for woman suffrage and then for peace in Europe. She shared with Henry Ford energy, a genius for self-promotion, and the confidence that if people—in this case ranging from the kaiser to Lord Kitchener—would only listen to her, she could set the burning world aright.

Such were her powers of persuasion that she made Ford believe he could, too. She was able to proselytize him first at Highland Park, and then, later, over lunch at Fair Lane with Louis Lochner, a fellow pacifist. You are a man to whom anything is possible, she told Ford. You can stop this war. As Garrett put it, she said, "In the chancelleries of Europe, on both sides, they were praying for someone to show them how. He believed it."

Clara didn't, and begged her husband not to follow Schwimmer and Lochner to New York, where the two were going to make further plans. Her husband, feeling the same call of destiny that had led him to the Model T, did go to New York, and at a lunch there on November 21, 1915, heard Lochner say it would be a great thing to hire a ship and fill it with a cargo of persuasive pacifists who, working from neutral countries, would draw the leaders of the warring ones into "continuous mediation."

This was a discussion that could have lasted for months, but the Ford of Highland Park, who would order up a new machine tool in a minute, left the restaurant and hired a passenger ship from the Scandinavian-American line, the *Oscar II.*

Then he went to Washington to call on Woodrow Wilson. The

president was not eager to see Ford, but he didn't want to appear hostile to a famous American who hoped to bring peace to the world. So the two men met, and Ford got the chance to tell the joke about the farmer who asked to be buried in his Model T, and Wilson responded with a limerick—he loved limericks—and after that the meeting went much the way the final one with Couzens had.

Wilson said his position prevented him from getting involved in this peace effort. Ford offered him the use of the *Oscar II*, a remarkable piece of effrontery given that if Wilson wished to sail to Europe he could do so aboard a battleship in company with as many destroyers and cruisers as he thought proper. Ford pushed right ahead. "If you don't act, I will."

Leaving the presidential office he said Wilson was "a small man." He went back to New York and convened a press conference for the next morning, November 24.

Oswald Garrison Villard, the pacifist owner and editor of the *New York Evening Post,* had founded the American Anti-Imperialist League after the war with Spain and was already worried that America might be drawn into the European conflict. A few hours before the press conference, he wrote, "I was summoned from the breakfast table to the telephone to hear that Henry Ford, the automobile manufacturer . . . wished me to come at once to the Biltmore Hotel as he had something of the greatest importance to tell me." Villard had never met Ford, but he was a newspaperman, and by now everything Ford did was news. He went and was introduced to Ford, who told him "the astounding news that . . . Mr. Ford had chartered the steamer *Oscar II* to bring about the end of the war by rousing the neutral nations to a joint offer of mediation. Mr. Ford at once asked me to go along and explained that he had summoned me in order to aid him in presenting the news to the press."

Villard was "almost speechless." He thought that "as a means of advertising the idea that the war should and could be stopped by reason and arbitration . . . the chartering of the ship a master stroke." But everything depended on how well the expedition had been planned, starting with the initial press conference.

"I asked if any statement had been prepared and typed to be given out. There was none. I warned him that the press would be largely hostile."

Ford said he wasn't worried about that. "Oh, I always get on very well with the boys. All you need is a slogan." Then he supplied one: "We'll get the boys out of the trenches and home by Christmas. What do you think of that?"

"I thought privately that it was crazy. When I got my breath I replied: 'Mr. Ford, there are said to be at least ten million men in the trenches. You have chartered one of the slowest steamers on the Atlantic and she is not to sail until December 4. If you succeed in stopping the war the day you arrive, which will probably be December 16, it would be physically impossible to march or transport those men home by Christmas.'"

"Oh," said Ford, "I hadn't thought of that."

He thought about it then, for a moment, and came up with a modification: "Well, we'll make it, 'we'll get the boys out of the trenches by Christmas.'"

Villard regarded him bleakly. "It would be possible, if you obtained an armistice over the holidays, to have them sitting on the tops of the trenches by Christmas."

"It disheartened me no end," wrote Villard, "for I knew it laid the enterprise open to ridicule; it was already evident to me that he had no clear conception of what it was all about, what the war conditions were, or what he was undertaking."

Once ten o'clock came around and the reporters assembled, Villard saw that Ford's "brashness in regard to the press vanished. It was evident that he dreaded this interview. He pushed me into the parlor ahead of him and there ensued a scene so extraordinary that I have no parallel in my experience."

Ford opened the conference with, "Well, boys, we've got the ship."

"What ship, Mr. Ford?"

"Why, the *Oscar II.*"

"Well, what about her? What are you going to do with her?"

"We're going to stop the war."

"Stop the *war*?"

"Yes, we're going to have the boys out of the trenches by Christmas."

"My, how are you going to do that?"

"Well, we're going to Holland and all the neutral nations."

"And then what?"

To Villard's horror, the reply to this last was, "Well, Mr. Villard will tell you all the rest."

Villard said, "No, Mr. Ford, I cannot do that"—"of course I knew nothing," he wrote later—"but I can explain that the idea is to seek a delegation of important Americans to induce the neutral nations to join together to offer mediation to the nations at war."

After some more questions to Ford, and then to Schwimmer and Lochner, the reporters, said Villard, "fled to their offices to ridicule the whole proposal. The *Evening Post* was almost the only newspaper to treat the peace voyage seriously and respectfully."

The *New York Tribune* ran a straight-faced headline: "Great War to End Christmas Day: Ford to Stop It."

The *Louisville Courier Journal* was more direct in its scorn. "It is worse than ineffable folly for pestiferous busybodies in this country like Henry Ford . . . to nag the president to make an ass of himself by mediating on behalf of a peace that is impossible."

Several cartoons showed Mars reclining against the wall of a trench laughing at what the god of war thought was "the best Ford joke yet."

"Prominent People to Go with Ford," ran one headline. They didn't. They sent best wishes, and some even came to the pier. But Jane Addams of Hull House, and Ida Tarbell, and John Wanamaker, a longtime Ford supporter, Helen Keller, William Jennings Bryan, Luther Burbank, Robert LaFollette, William Dean Howells, Louis Brandeis, William Howard Taft, Rabbi Stephen Wise, even Edison begged off.

When the *Oscar II* sailed on December 5 from New York Harbor, she had aboard the lieutenant governor of North Carolina, the magazine editor S. S. McClure, Berton Braley "The Hobo Poet" (a curious choice, in that his poems rejoiced in the war: "Out there I'm in the thick of a man's sized fight / An' it's one I'm thankful for!"), several militant vegetarians, some free-love advocates, Theodore Hostetter, a patent-office examiner who was representing the Washington Sunday School Association, a number of sincere academics, Governor Louis Hanna of North Dakota, who explained his presence by saying he owed a visit to relatives in Sweden, and more than fifty newspaper reporters.

Samuel Marquis was there, too, at Clara's urging. Initially drawn to Schwimmer, she had come to believe her an egomaniacal spendthrift and she wanted the reluctant Marquis to look after her husband.

The minister "spent most of the night before the expedition trying to prevail upon [Ford] to abandon it. It was no use. His reply to me was, 'It is right, is it not, to try to stop war?' To this I could only answer 'Yes.' 'Well,' he would go on, 'You have told me that what is right cannot fail.' And the answer to that, that right things attempted the wrong way had no assurance of success, had no effect. He was following what he calls a 'hunch,' and when he gets a 'hunch' he generally goes through with it, be it right or wrong."

A plan of sorts had evolved since the press conference. The *Oscar II* would sail to Norway, and the peace delegates would travel from Oslo through neutral Sweden, Denmark, and Holland, giving lectures all along the route.

No December Atlantic crossing is pleasant, and this one took thirteen days during which the peace delegates fell to quarreling with one another and the reporters drank (although there was a prohibitionist faction aboard, the *Oscar II* maintained a fully stocked bar where the most expensive drink cost fourteen cents). Rosika Schwimmer always carried a bag, which she claimed contained crucial documents from many heads of state, but she would neither show them nor discuss their contents. She became increasingly reclusive, but Ford made himself continually available. "I questioned his judgment at the time," said Marquis, "but not his motives." Many of the reporters began to feel that way. "I came to make fun of the whole thing," one of them said, "but my editor is going to have the surprise of his life. I tell you I believe in Henry Ford and I'm going to say so even if I lose my job for it."

The press at home was not so forbearing. The *New York World* wrote, "Henry Ford says he would give all his fortune to end the war. So would many another man. But it is something that money will not do." The *Sacramento Bee* published a drawing of the Angel of Peace vomiting over the rail of the *Oscar II*.

Some ten thousand Americans in a carnival mood had come to wave and shout as the *Oscar II* sailed. There were no welcoming crowds when it arrived in Norway, a country near enough to the fighting to feel its furnace breath.

By the time the ship docked, the temperature stood at twelve degrees below zero. Ford was down with a bad cold, and went to ground in the Grand Hotel, which, despite its name, offered drab, chilly quarters. At the steady urging of Marquis, he agreed to call it a day.

"Guess I had better go home to mother," he said to Lochner. "I told her I'd be back soon. You've got the thing started now and can get along without me."

Marquis helped smuggle him out of the dank hotel and they boarded a steamer that docked in Brooklyn on January 2. Not even Henry Ford had got home by Christmas.

———————

There were compensations awaiting him on his return from the disappointing crusade. While he was away the one millionth Model T had come off the line and snorted forth to its destiny. And the fate of its successors would surely be buoyed by the press Ford was getting now. After the initial burst of mockery, the editorial tone of the papers had become warmer. The *New York American* echoed many of its rivals when it regretted having "caricatured, lampooned, ridiculed, and vituperated" Ford. That had been wrong: "Henry Ford Deserves

Respect, Not Ridicule." "No matter if he failed, he at least TRIED. Had every citizen in the United States, including the President and his Cabinet and the members of Congress, put forth one-tenth the individual effort that Henry Ford put forth, THE BOYS WOULD HAVE BEEN OUT OF THE TRENCHES BY CHRISTMAS." G. K. Chesterton, the British novelist, journalist, and almost everything else, wrote, "Now anyone who knows anything about America knows exactly what the Peace Ship would be like. It was a national combination of imagination and ignorance, which has at least some of the breath of innocence."

Ford said of his adventure, "I wanted to see peace. I at least tried to bring it about. Most men did not even try."

The Peace Ship's more blatant hangers-on came home not long after Ford, but he kept picking up the tab for the core of his delegates until, in February 1917, America severed diplomatic ties with Germany.

When that happened, Allan Nevins remarked, "The transformation of Henry Ford from peace angel to Vulcan took less than a week." He said that "in the event of a declaration of war [I] will place our factory at the disposal of the United States government and will operate without one cent of profit."

When America entered the war two months later, Ford said he was still a pacifist, but now he was that uncommon being, "a fighting pacifist."

At first he was full of febrile ideas, all of which the newspapers embraced. The correspondents may not have had much faith in the Peace Ship, but they were wholly credulous about Ford's abilities where mass production was concerned.

He was going to build 1,000 submarines a day, each of them to carry a crew of one. The captain—if that's the right word—would bring his vessel alongside an enemy warship and destroy it with a "pill-bomb." When the U.S. Navy proved able to resist this tactic (Franklin Roosevelt, the assistant secretary of the navy, said that the carmaker, "until he saw a chance for publicity free of charge, thought a submarine was something to eat"), Ford proposed mass-producing 150,000 airplanes a year, then promised to build 1,000 two-man tanks daily. The army went for these last, and ordered 15,000 of them, although the war was over before any made it across the Atlantic.

In the end, though, Ford got some real defense work done: 39,000 Model T ambulances and cars and trucks (a year earlier the U.S. Army had fewer than 80 motor vehicles), 7,000 tractors sold at cost to a U-boat-blockaded Britain badly needing to grow food, and 75 of the fine Liberty airplane engines a day. William Knudsen, back in Detroit after setting up his branch assembly plants, drew on his increasingly distant memories of the bicycle industry to form bicycle-like tubing from vanadium steel that greatly improved the performance of the Liberties.

Knudsen soon got a more unusual assignment. The U-boats that had made Britain so eager to have those tractors were constantly threatening the sea routes that kept supplies of everything from guns to grain moving across the Atlantic. The navy wasn't interested in toy submarines and pill-bombs, but it urgently wanted a horde of cheap, quickly built two-hundred-foot antisubmarine vessels, and every shipyard on the East Coast was fully occupied.

Knudsen found out about this, got hold of the designs for the ships, and took them to Henry Ford, who said he could do this job.

Knudsen went to Washington and calmly and steadily diverted what was at first a stream of politely expressed ridicule into reluctant acknowledgment that this man knew what he was talking about. That was quite a conversion of opinion, for Knudsen was saying that real warships could be built like Model Ts, on assembly lines.

The navy, with no other plausible option, gave the Ford Motor Company the contract.

Knudsen put up a building a third of a mile long—like Highland Park, made of reinforced concrete—with three production lines, each of them capable of carrying seven ships slowly toward the building's mouth, which opened on the same Rouge River that flowed past Fair Lane.

A *Washington Post* editorial had said, "The crying need of this hour is an eagle that will scour the seas and pounce upon and destroy every submarine that dares to leave German or Belgian shores," so the vessels would be known as Eagle boats. Knudsen got his plant up in five months, and the first of the Eagles was floating in the Rouge on July 10, 1918, just eight months after the concrete of its hatchery had been poured. Then things slowed down. By Armistice Day, November 11, the company apparently had only 7 Eagles heading for the Atlantic. Knudsen says the number was 14, with 46 to follow close behind. The company had 112 on order, and completed 46.

Ford wanted the Eagles produced by his mass-production methods, and, like the Model T, you can see the results in them. Slab-sided for easier construction, they have the squarish look of a child's drawing of a boat. Ford was wise to go into carmaking rather than shipbuilding, for it is difficult to find the testimony of anyone who served aboard an Eagle who didn't detest it. The ships didn't sink, but they did almost everything else possible to make their occupants unhappy at sea. Still, a few Eagles stayed in service right through World War II.

Despite the lack of fondness the ship commanded, its very existence represented a great achievement for Knudsen. Ford came to him first on November 11 when the sirens and church bells were still heralding the armistice.

"Well, William, the war is over."

Knudsen said he knew that.

"How quickly can you get this Army stuff out of here?"

"Right away, if you say so, Mr. Ford."

"I wish you would."

"All of it?"

"All of it, whether finished or not. Pack it up in boxes and put it out in the yard."

That was that for Ford and the Great War. The skeptical Vulcan had done his part, and now he wanted all the crap he'd had to make put out in packing crates in his factory yard under the winter rain until the army came to take it off, or it rusted away.

And just as he didn't want the detritus of the war cluttering up his factories, neither did he want its profits cluttering up his soul. He had pledged to return to the government every penny he made above his plant costs.

This of course impressed the public—"the only rich man of note who . . . refused to coin money out of the blood of nations"—and as late as 1941, with an even bigger war coming on the boil, the Ford company's Cincinnati branch manager was urging his salesmen to remind people of "Ford's refusal to accept personal profit from war work."

Twenty years before that an exuberant biographer had written that Henry Ford refunded to the government the entirety of his war profits, which amounted to $29 million. This made enough of a splash to cause Andrew Mellon, secretary of the Treasury, to turn his grave ascetic's face to a letter. Mellon said that as far as the Treasury knew, Ford, rather than not keeping a single cent of his war profits, had not returned one. (Mellon's letter was not quite that harsh, but its meaning was clear.)

Ford's ever-evolving sense of publicity knew this would not be a good battle to join. He said he was eager to work with the Treasury to determine the exact amount he owed, and pay it. Ford's all-but-omniscient student David L. Lewis puts the company's war profits at a satisfyingly precise $8,151,119.31. With taxes deducted this would have shrunk to about half, and by the time it got close to Ford's own pocket he had profits of $926,780.46. No contemptible sum in 1922, but one Henry Ford was then in the position to pay as casually as he might have tipped his barber.

He never did. About this time, Samuel Marquis wrote, "The isolation of Henry Ford's mind is about as perfect as it is possible to make it." Ford was working toward that isolation now: He was beginning to move away from virtually everyone who had helped him succeed.

CHAPTER 15

The Expert

The Rouge rises; the Dodge brothers sue; "we don't seem to be able to keep the profits down"; sandbagging the shareholders; probing Ford's ignorance in court: "Did you ever hear of Benedict Arnold?"

While Ford was jettisoning his war leavings, one thing he definitely didn't want the military to make off with was the factory in which Knudsen was building the Eagle boats, "Now the famous 'B' building of the Rouge River Ford Plant," remarks Knudsen's biographer in 1947.

A few miles south of the city, where the Detroit River and the Rouge meet, Ford had as early as 1915 envisioned a factory that would do it all. That is to say, make a car from dirt and sand and wood and other basic elements dug and cut from Ford holdings. It was to be an industrial fortress, a city-state really. Knudsen's biographer notwithstanding, nobody would refer to it as the Rouge Plant any more than they would call the great natural wonder the Falls of Niagara. It would simply be the Rouge.

The plant was a titanic early exercise in what came to be known as

253

vertical integration. Largely invented by Andrew Carnegie as he came
to own not only the mills that forged his steel but the mines that supplied them, it allowed the industrialist to control every step in the creation of his product. Ore would come from Ford mines, timber from
Ford forests, rubber from Ford's Brazil plantation to feed his own tire
factory (one of the sorriest results of his disdain for experts: He hoped
people with scant horticultural knowledge might somehow master this
very demanding tree on the job). Ford steamers would bring the ore
across the Great Lakes (he never quite managed to acquire the Lakes
themselves) to a steel plant. Ford was feeling uneasy about the quality
of his steel. How much, he asked Sorensen, would a proper steel plant
cost? Thirty-five million dollars or so, Sorensen guessed. "What are
you waiting for?" said Ford.

He had given his government things it needed during the war, and
it had given him what he needed when it was over. To accommodate
the Eagle boats, the ship channel that fronted the Rouge had been
dredged by military engineers, a turning basin dug, everything necessary to feed the Rouge. Glassworks, paper mill, ore docks where the
ten-story-tall, thousand-ton Hulett unloaders reached with delicate
reptilian grace right down into the holds of ships to take out fifteen-
ton mouthfuls of iron ore. Coke ovens. Rolling mills. Cold-drawn
steel shops. Ten thousand acres cross-hatched with 100 miles of railroad track, and 120 miles of conveyors bringing supplies that always
arrived waist-high in front of 100,000 workers.

Not yet, though; not with the drying up of the Eagle contracts.
Despite his enormous resources, despite his "what are you waiting
for?"s, Henry Ford still needed money to build the Rouge. One of the
ways he came up with it was to stop paying dividends to his shareholders.

At least, that's how it seemed to John and Horace Dodge, and with
reason. Ford announced in 1916 that henceforth he would be paying

dividends of 5 percent monthly on the company's comically low book capitalization of $2 million. He told the brothers in August that this would allow him to put $58 million into expanding his plant. At the same time he cut the price of the Model T by sixty-six dollars. Even with Highland Park running at full capacity, the supply of cars could not meet the demand for them, and this meant, the brothers calculated, that Ford had just torn up $40 million of company profits for no reason at all.

The Dodges were no longer supplying any parts to the Ford Motor Company. Three years earlier, in 1913, they had been shopping in a downtown department store when they ran into Howard Bloomer, their friend and lawyer ever since they'd retained him to look after the seven hundred dollars they had raised to found their machine shop.

Bloomer surprised them by asking, "Why don't you brothers build your own car?"

John said they had headaches enough—let Ford and Couzens cope with the myriad difficulties of putting an automobile in the hands of a buyer.

Bloomer reminded them that their contract with Ford allowed either party to cancel it on a year's notice. What if Ford did that? "Your plant equipment is too heavy to have it all depending on one customer. You've got too big an investment not to safeguard it better than you are doing."

John, still merely amused by Bloomer's suggestion, asked the lawyer if he didn't believe in the business acumen of Andrew Carnegie, and quoted the steelmaker's apothegm: "Put all your eggs in one basket, and then *watch that basket.*"

"Yes, I believe that," Bloomer said, "if you own the basket. The basket belongs to Ford; the eggs belong to you. What is to prevent Ford from kicking over his basket and breaking your eggs?"

Bloomer went to the brothers' office the next day to press his argument, and that July the Dodges told Ford that their agreement would come to an end on July 1, 1914. Despite their initial misgivings they quickly created a popular automobile. Their car was more expensive than the Model T, and thus no competition to Ford, but they were relying on his dividends to get it firmly established. Ford had stopped paying all but the most derisory dividends to his shareholders in order to invest in his own plants. As the Dodge brothers' friend had told them, it's fine to put all your eggs in one basket as long as you have control of the basket. Ford, in this case, suddenly decided the basket was his and was going to keep all the eggs.

The Dodges told Ford: All right, if that's how you want to do things, just buy us out and you'll have a free hand. Ford said he'd already given them a fortune on their initial investment, and he wasn't interested in adding to it by buying them out.

The brothers took him to court. They got a restraining order against Ford's using company funds for the Rouge—or any plant expansion— and brought suit demanding the company pay out to the shareholders three-quarters of its cash surplus, which would come to nearly $40 million.

Ford went to the press. It had stung him on the Peace Ship, but he thought he would look good in the coming fight. He told the *Detroit News*, "And let me say right here that I do not believe that we should make such an awful profit on our cars. A reasonable profit is right, but not too much. So it has been my policy to force the price of a car down as fast as production would permit, and give the benefits to users and laborers."

In the state circuit court, he faced the Dodges' attorney, Elliott G. Stevenson. Pugnacious and capable, Stevenson knew what he had to do: make the case that the first responsibility of any company was to its stockholders. But there seemed to be no way to get there without asking Ford questions that the carmaker welcomed. The more Stevenson pressed Ford on the witness stand, the more petty and querulous the prosecutor seemed. Aside from one outburst when Ford told Stevenson, "If you sit there until you are petrified, I wouldn't buy Dodge brothers' stock," the carmaker was calm, restrained, and sounded like a benefactor of all humankind.

"Now," Stevenson challenged him, quoting the *Detroit News* interview, "I will ask you again, do you still think that those profits were 'awful profits'?"

"Well, I guess I do, yes."

"And for that reason you were not satisfied to continue to make such awful profits?"

Ford looked apologetic. "We don't seem to be able to keep the profits down."

". . . Are you *trying* to keep them down? What is the Ford Motor Company organized for except profits, will you tell me, Mr. Ford?"

"Organized to do as much good as we can, everywhere, for everybody concerned."

That shut Stevenson up for the day, but he had to return to the theme the next morning. He again asked Ford what was the "purpose" of his company.

"Give employment, and send out the car where the people can use it . . . and incidentally to make money. . . . Business is a service, not a bonanza."

"*Incidentally* make money?"

"Yes, sir."

Stevenson moved from incredulity to sarcasm: "But your controlling feature . . . is to employ a great army of men at high wages, to reduce the selling price of your car, so that a lot of people can buy it at a cheap price, and give everyone a car that wants one?"

Ford punctured the mocking summary by agreeing with it. "If you give all that," he said, "the money will fall into your hands; you can't get out of it."

Ford won the sympathy of the public, but Stevenson won his case. The court told Ford he had to drop his Rouge plans, and within ninety days pay a dividend of $19,275,385.36. Ford appealed the decision and in February 1919, a state superior court ruled that he could proceed with the Rouge, "but it is not within the powers of a corporation to shape and conduct a company's affairs for the merely incidental benefit of shareholders and for the primary purpose of benefiting others." The dividend stood.

Because Henry Ford was the main shareholder, most of the payment went right back to him. The trial had evidently made him restless, though, for on December 30, 1918, he resigned as president of the Ford Motor Company. Edsel took his place, and Henry went west with Clara on a vacation in Southern California.

On March 5, 1919, the *Los Angeles Examiner* ran this headline: "Henry Ford Organizing Huge New Company to Build a Better, Cheaper Car."

He was leaving his company because of the Dodge suit, Ford told the California reporters. The court's ruling had made it clear to him that he was not free to operate as he saw fit, and his only possible course was "to get out, design a new car." After all, "the present Ford car was designed twelve years ago." The new one would be a better automobile at about half the price.

What would become of the old company? Ford acted as if this particular question had never occurred to him. "Why, I don't know exactly what will become of that."

With the same tone of bemusement, one of Ford's lieutenants wrote, "Mr. Ford's recent announcement has caused quite a stir in this community. In fact, I do not believe any of the shareholders are at all pleased over it."

Certainly the Dodge brothers weren't. They had their lawyer, Stevenson, say, "There would be no attempt to keep either Mr. Ford or his son in the firm if they simply wished to retire, but Henry Ford is under contract to the Ford Motor Co. and he will not be allowed to leave the firm and start a competing business."

Ford might have replied that this was exactly what the Dodge brothers had done to him; or he might have said that he wasn't in competition at all since the new car would be far less expensive than the Motel T. Instead he told the press, "The present Ford Motor Company employees number about 50,000 in the actual manufacture of its cars. Our new company will have four or five times that number." All those workers would be making something entirely fresh: "None of the old car will be used in the new manufacture. . . . It will have a new motor and new fixtures." And it was "well advanced, for I have been working on it while resting in California." It might cost $250.

Edsel tried to reassure the dealers, who were at least as worried as the stockholders, that they were in no imminent danger: "We know a new car could not possibly be designed, tested out, manufactured, and marketed in quantity [in] under two or three years." Then he added the hazy but disturbing statement that "we expect to make it a competitor to the streetcar rather than the Ford."

At the same time, agents began to approach the Ford stockholders, expressing cautious interest in acquiring their Ford Motor Company shares, civilly suggesting that it might be a good time to sell.

It is a powerful testament to what Henry Ford had accomplished that the shareholders didn't at once see that the new company was a ploy, and its soon-to-be-produced car a fantasy. But look what Henry Ford *had* done. They began to agree to sell.

Couzens did not. He had been right there when his partner figured out the Model T. He knew Henry Ford would no sooner abandon that car than he would his wife or his son. He had also watched while Ford used an identical stratagem to buy out Malcomson. Couzens stayed out of the negotiations as the bidding started at $7,500 per share and the price rose and finally settled at $12,500. Then he said he was willing to sell, but only at $13,000.

John Anderson, who had grown from the eager, timid young lawyer who wrote his father the long letter begging for five thousand dollars into a gentleman of leisure, found out what was going on through a man named Stuart Webb, who was representing undisclosed parties that wished to buy his shares. Anderson had already told Webb he would sell only if all the other shareholders wanted to. On July 3, 1919, "Mr. Webb called on the telephone and said he had a document which he thought might interest me." Anderson told him to come over. The document "proved to be an option running to Edsel Ford, giving him the privilege of buying Mr. Couzens' stock in the Ford Motor Company for $13,000 a share.

> Well, I read that option over and it was certainly a distinct surprise to me, because this was the first time I had any inkling who the purchaser of the stocks was to be. Mr. Ford had denied in the press that he was interested in buying the stock. . . .
> "Well," I said to Mr. Webb, "I see Mr. Couzens is getting more for his stocks than is being offered me."

Webb unhappily agreed that this was true, and that there was nothing he could to about it.

Anderson said, "I don't care, Mr. Webb. If there is anybody in that organization who is entitled to a little bit more than anybody else in case of a general sale, it seems to me it is Mayor Couzens [he was then mayor of Detroit]. It was due to his efforts that the Company became a success."

Webb, surprised and relieved, handed Anderson a sheaf of papers and asked if he might go over them and give his answer on Monday, which was July 7.

Anderson's account of where he went to think it over reflects in a most appealing way his grateful wonder at the path his life had taken since his fond, doubting father had reluctantly written the check.

"Well, the next day was the 4th of July. I . . . was all alone. The family had gone away to the seashore, and there was nobody there but the servants. I had a room up on the third floor in the corner of my house, that I call a den. It is a room surrounded by shelves, with books on them, and a table in the center."

In this unique chamber, Anderson studied the figures and came to realize that if he sold he'd be getting a good deal less than his shares' true value. Because he was the only stockholder who had not committed himself to selling, he was in a position to exact more money, but did he want to "present to Mr. Ford the picture, as it inevitably would have been presented to him, that I was holding him up?" All his old colleagues had signed the agreement; if he held back, he'd be upsetting their plans. On the other hand, had he been too generous in his initial response to Couzens's getting more for his own shares?

All of these thoughts ran through my mind. I figured out, supposing I do refuse unless I get two or two and one-half million dollars more money, then the tax thing came,—where will that land me? It meant a difference of about $600,000 or $700,000. And I said to myself, "By Jove," as I thought over what Mr. Ford had done for me; as I thought of the house I was in, and the room, and contrasted it with my humble home in 1903 when the Company started; the advantages I had had in the meantime, and the ability to give up the daily practice of law; the opportunities afforded to travel; all of these things I could trace directly to my association with Mr. Ford in the Ford Motor Company, and I said to myself:

"John Anderson, are you going to be an ingrate, or are you going to be a man?"

And I decided that I would try not to be an ingrate.

On Monday Anderson told Webb yes, and then the deal moved so quickly that the newspapers reported it completed four days later, on July 11. Anderson got $12.5 million, having already received dividends of nearly $5 million. Couzens received $30 million. The estate of John Gray, who had gone to his grave still full of doubts about the wisdom of investing in motorcars, took in $26 million.

Henry Ford, who so distrusted Wall Street and all the haughty financial bastions of the East, had to swallow his pride to ask for a $75 million credit to cover his buyout. He did so grimly, but when everything was settled, he found he had climbed to a summit nobody had achieved before. John D. Rockefeller never owned much more than a third of Standard Oil, and Rockefeller himself had been surprised to learn how little America's foremost financier had been worth when J. P. Morgan died in 1913. But by the end of 1919 Henry Ford held the largest company ever in the hands of one person. His operation was worth half a billion dollars, and he owned it as completely as he did his piano and his birdhouses.

The $250 wonder car started its phantom engine and silently backed away to park itself forever alongside the one-man submarines and their pill-bombs.

———————∿∿∿∿∿∿∿∿∿———————

Nineteen nineteen, that year of triumph and consolidation, also turned out to be one of the most painful of Henry Ford's life, and one that would change it.

Samuel Marquis wrote that Ford "seems to shirk encounters in which it will be necessary for him to say unpleasant things. In other words, he hates a quarrel but he loves a good fight. He is of Irish descent. He keeps his eye on his opponent—many eyes on him in fact—and is master in the art of waiting. This is one of the reasons I think he enjoys lawsuits, of which he has had his share: they are usually so long drawn out. There are so many courts of appeal, and the more the merrier."

He found little merriment in his tangle with the *Chicago Tribune*. In a rare moment of partisan heat, Nevins writes that "it grew out of an editorial that even in the history of the *Tribune* stands forth as peculiarly silly and obnoxious."

The trouble went back to 1916 when, with Pancho Villa and his men active along the Mexican border, President Wilson summoned the National Guard. The *Tribune*, at this time in its career full of martial ardor, had its correspondents get in touch with big corporations to see whether they planned to support their employees who went after Villa. The *Tribune*'s man in Detroit somehow got the Ford company's treasurer, Frank Klingensmith, on the phone. Without consulting his boss or anyone at all, Klingensmith said that any Ford worker who went would lose his job. He later denied this in court, and indeed it wasn't true: Eighty-nine Ford employees served along the border, and they all got back their old jobs or better ones. The answer was good enough for the *Tribune*, which ran an editorial under the heading "Ford Is an Anarchist." It said, "If Ford allows this rule of his shop to stand, he will reveal himself not merely as an ignorant idealist, but as an anarchistic enemy of the nation which protects him in his wealth."

Ford might have let this pass unchallenged, but his lawyer, Alfred Lucking, urged him to take the *Tribune* to court. Ford didn't need much urging; as Marquis observed, he enjoyed speaking from the pulpit of the witness chair. He cavalierly told Lucking, "Well, you'd better start suit against them for libel."

Lucking did, demanding $1 million in damages. He began with a bad misstep. Had he simply sued over the terms "anarchist" and "anarchistic," words that had long been recognized as libelous by courts, he would likely have won a swift and early victory. But he chose to cite the entire editorial, and thus the word "ignorant." Marquis wrote that "there are hundreds of men figuring prominently in the business world of no greater erudition than [Ford], but on matters with which they are not familiar they have the gift of silence and a correspondingly low visibility."

Ford by now was eager to speak on any topic. He said he had brought the suit largely because he wanted "to educate people." He didn't know how little he knew, but he was about to find out.

As the suit gathered momentum, it attracted more and more attention. Ford's attorneys didn't want it tried in Chicago on *Tribune* ground, and the *Tribune* didn't want it in Detroit. Both sides finally agreed on Mount Clemens, a quiet little resort town—it had sulfur springs—twenty miles northeast of Detroit. There Ford set up his own news bureau to make sure his side of the story reached the smaller towns where he felt his strongest support lay.

The trial began on May 12 before a jury of eleven farmers and a road builder. One of the jurors told the court that although he owned a Model T, "that would not prejudice me against Mr. Ford."

Ford was up against his old adversary Elliott Stevenson, only this time Stevenson would not be questioning him on the one subject Ford knew more about than anyone on earth. Three years earlier Ford had told a *Chicago Tribune* reporter, "I don't know much about history, and I wouldn't give a nickel for all the history in the world. It means nothing to me. History is more or less bunk. It's tradition. We want to live in the present and the only history that is worth a tinker's damn is the history we make today. That's the trouble with the world. We're living in books and history and tradition. We want to get away from that and take care of today. We've done too much looking back. What we want to do, and do it quick, is to make just history right now. The men who are responsible for the present war in Europe knew all about history. Yet they brought on the worst war in the world's history."

Ford's lawyers discovered that Stevenson would try to ratify their client's ignorance by questioning him about American history and they hastily put together a history lesson for him. It didn't go well. E. G. Pipp, a newspaperman helping Ford, remembered that Lucking might begin with,

> "Now don't forget this; remember the evacuation of Florida. . . ."
> But Ford would be out of his seat, looking out of the window.
> "Say, that airplane is flying pretty low, isn't it?" he would ask.
> Again Lucking would steer him to the chair, but Ford would hop
> to the window with: "Look at that bird there; pretty little fellow isn't
> he? Somebody's feeding it, or it wouldn't come back so often."

While these tutorials ran their barren course, the trial commenced with a great deal of testimony about the meaning of "anarchy" and evocations of the violence along the Mexican border to demonstrate the peril the nation had been in when Ford was urging pacifism. Some honest-to-God Texas Rangers had been imported to tell about gunfights with Villa's men.

Despite the presence of such exotic beings walking out in the streets of Mount Clemens, Ford was the main event. He took the stand on July 14. This was the beginning of the trial's third month, and the newspaper correspondents had developed a heartfelt slogan: "Out of Mount Clemens by Christmas." But they were all engaged and alert when Ford took the stand.

Stevenson approached him. There were to be no questions about the morality of doing shareholders out of their profits.

"You call yourself an educator? Now I shall inquire whether you were a well-informed man, competent to educate people."

Stevenson brought up Ford's already well-known comment about history.

"Did you say that?"

"I did not say that it was bunk. It was bunk to me but I did not say—"

Stevenson quickly put in, "It was bunk to you?"

"It was not much to me."

"What do you mean by that?"

"Well, I haven't much use for it. I didn't need it very bad."

Stevenson wanted to attach the bunk remark more firmly to Ford. He'd been trying to buffalo his witness with elaborate words, and now he asked a high-flown question. "What do you mean? Do you think we can provide for the future and care wisely with reference to the future in matters like preparation for defense, or anything of that sort, without knowing the history of what has happened in the past?"

The answer didn't go the way the lawyer hoped.

Ford spoke of the conflict he had tried to stop: "When we got into the war, the past didn't amount to much for us."

"Will you answer the question, Mr. Ford, please?"

"I thought I was answering it as well as I could. History usually didn't last a week."

"What do you mean, 'History didn't last a week'?"

"In the present war . . . airships and things we used were out of date in a week."

"What has that to do with history?" Stevenson asked in disgust. Although his was probably the best legal mind in the trial, Stevenson had missed Ford's point. Naturally the man who had been changing history with machines answered the lawyer in mechanical terms, but the obsolete airships stood as an emblem of a century of certainties and customs that had withered even as the war pursued its annihilating course. History, Ford was saying, is both malleable and perishable, and its lessons vital to one era can become platitudes and archaisms, mere chatter, in, as he put it, a week.

Stevenson pressed on with the *Tribune*'s labeling Ford an "ignorant idealist."

Ford said, "Well, I admit I'm ignorant about some things. I don't know anything about art."

Stevenson wanted to know if Ford was "ignorant of the fundamental principles of this government."

"I suppose it's the Constitution."

"What does 'fundamental principles of government' mean?"

"I don't understand."

"What is the fundamental principle of government?"

"Just you," said Ford. (Actually, given its brevity, a pretty good answer in the face of a question that was seeking a civics lecture.)

"Is that the only idea you have on it?"

Ford replied, again not absurdly, "This is a long subject."

Stevenson went on to ask if there had been any revolutions in America. Ford said, "There was, I understand."

"When?"

"In 1812."

"In 1812, the Revolution?"

"Yes."

"Any other times?"

"I don't know."

This went on for days, and it got worse. Savoring a kind of litigatory bloodlust, one of the *Tribune* lawyers told a reporter, "This lawsuit is like the tenth baby in a family. We didn't want it but now that we have it we wouldn't take a million dollars for it. It is worth that to show Ford up."

Sometimes Ford scored against his opponents. Stevenson asked him, "What was the United States originally?" Ford paused, but not because he was stumped, and then tartly replied, "Land, I guess." He was able briefly to reprise his Dodge trial testimony when Stevenson asked him to define the word "idealist." Ford said that it was "a person that can help to make other people prosperous."

Ford enjoyed few such moments. What was the Monroe Doctrine? "A big-brother act." Did he know the United States Capitol was burned in 1812? "I heard so." What is ballyhoo? "A blackguard or something of that nature." Treason? "Anything against the government." Anarchy? An answer inspired by editorial cartoons he must have seen: "Overthrowing the government and throwing bombs."

Finally, this excruciating exchange:

"Did you ever hear of Benedict Arnold?"

"I have heard the name."

"Who was he?"

"I have forgotten just who he is. He's a writer, I think."

The case went on until August 14, when the patient jury received it and rendered a verdict in ten hours. The decision held the *Tribune* guilty of libel. Ford was awarded damages of six cents (one reporter wanted to know how he planned to spend it).

A correspondent for the *Literary Digest* during the trial saw Ford in a characteristic pose. "He is sitting in a chair that is tilted back against the wall. His thin knee is clasped in his long hands; good-natured patience dwells upon his face. . . . When a question is asked him he rubs his hand across his long jaw, a rural gesture; he speculatively moistens his lips, lowering his eyes when he wants to think, leaning forward when something interests him. Henry Ford sitting in court with crossed legs, suggests the country store philosopher."

This sagacious disinterest was a pose, and one it must have been very difficult for Ford to maintain. The man who loved practical jokes but never wanted to be the object of them was now, he knew, the butt of a national joke. The *New York Times* said, "Mr. Ford has been submitted to a severe examination of his intellectual qualities. He has not received a passing degree." The *New York Tribune* found him "deliciously naive and omniscient and preposterous." The *Post* said simply, "This man is a joke."

John Reed, who had become disillusioned with Ford because of what he saw as the pernicious meddling of the Sociological Department, came back to his side during the trial, taking pity on the "slight boyish figure with thin long sure hands incessantly moving . . . the fine skin of his thin face browned by the sun; the mouth and nose of a simpleminded saint."

The *Ohio State Journal*, acknowledging the carmaker's humiliating performance, allowed that "we sort of like old Henry Ford, anyway." Editorials in small-town newspapers said that their readers didn't give a damn about the War of 1812.

Ford took no comfort in patronizing kindness. The generous instincts that had led to the five-dollar day and the Peace Ship began to warp and tarnish under the acid-drip of his memories of those days on the stand. They had cured him forever of seeking the witness chair as a speaker's podium. The ordeal fortified his growing insularity and irrigated many unexamined prejudices, while seeming to have taught him no lessons at all.

That isn't quite just. The trial did spur him to earn his private degree in history, just as he'd earned his engineering degree, all by himself, putting what he'd learned on display in a great museum. But whatever good might emerge from the suit was distant. Its ills were immediate.

It made him angry, and convinced him that he had no true allies.

We don't have much to thank Lucking for. Had he not persuaded Ford to sue the *Tribune*, and then bungled the case from the outset, the impulse that launched the ill-planned Peace Ship might have evolved throughout the 1920s into something more sophisticated and effective that benefited the entire country. Ford had the means and the energy to affect things at that level.

Nevins says "the scars which the *Tribune* suit left upon Henry Ford were thus a public misfortune." By "public misfortune" Nevins means a national one. The trial had stifled Ford's altruistic instincts, and left him open to frittering away much of his time and fortune on vagrant enthusiasms that were as random and powerful as they were short-lived.

CHAPTER 16

The International Jew

The problems of civilization traced to their source; the Dearborn Independent; *Liebold; "LET'S HAVE SOME SENSATIONALISM"; "Jewish Degradation of American Baseball"; two U.S. presidents ask Ford to stop his campaign; he carries it on for ninety-one issues of the* Independent; *Ford apologizes, saying he had no idea what was in his newspaper.*

In 1917 the *New York Herald* asked a reporter to go out to Detroit and put ten questions to Henry Ford. This sounds like a compact and relatively easy assignment, but it wasn't. The reporter, William C. Richards, knew that Ford combined the trying qualities of being a publicity-seeking extrovert and making himself impossible to get near. Richards managed it, though, and asked his ten questions.

"It was the first time I had talked to him and what I remember most was his candor in saying he did not know the answers to four of the questions and would not try to guess." He answered four others at once, and "the ninth he dismissed as a trick one—which it was—and over the last he paused, as if rolling around in his mouth a medicine of tart bite, and could not make up his mind whether to swallow or spit it out. . . .

"Lastly, Mr. Ford," Richards began confidently, but then immediately lost his nerve—laying, he said, the "onus" of the question "squarely" on his editor. "The *Herald* wishes to know how you feel to be the world's first billionaire."

Ford wasn't quite that yet, but as Richards put it, "The green was an easy chip shot away." As the carmaker took in the question, "he squirmed in his chair and twisted a leg over one arm of it, and then his eyes lost their equanimity and he exploded with an earthy vulgarism. I remember writing to the editor, 'In answer to Question Ten Mr. Ford said, "Oh, shit!" Your problem is what to do with it.'"

The problem of what to do with the billion, however, was all Ford's, and he wasn't finding it easy to solve.

The war he'd failed to shut down would be over in a year. The Model Ts would keep coming, a long, unvarying black stream that Sorensen was beginning to get sick of looking at. Black, because after 1915 that was the only hue offered. This was not, as folklore durably holds, because black paint dried more quickly, but simply another step in the endless effort to speed and simplify production. Ford quoted the famous phrase about the customer being able to have any color as long as it was black in his autobiography, but he didn't originate it. Like the Ford jokes, it came from everywhere.

The "Oh, shit!" was a cry of frustration. He was getting bored. He saw the decade ahead, saw it being populated with millions and millions of new Model Ts, and couldn't see beyond that. He had perfected the Model T, and you can't further perfect perfection. The fierce, brief blaze of the five-dollar day had guttered in the wartime prosperity. Ford was paying a six-dollar day now, and its inauguration had made no impact whatever. He could see, too, that the steady pressure of war had brought his production methods to many plants sooner than ever would have happened in time of peace. He'd always shared his industrial techniques, never tried to stymie rivals with patent suits, but now there were a good many freshly equipped establishments that might be competitors.

That wasn't what made him restless, though. He missed the high calling of the Selden suit, the Peace Ship, and jousting with the Dodge brothers. Surely he missed the days when Americans were adopting into their families a car, *his* car, more quickly and wholeheartedly than they had embraced any other invention ever. Even having bought out his stockholders couldn't assuage his desire to act on the largest possible stage. He'd thought the libel suit might give him a taste of that. Instead it was a searing disappointment, but not a chastening one.

After that first interview, Richards, who came to know Ford quite well, wrote "what stuck in my memory in the intervening years was not so much the expletive as his frank admission of ignorance, the fact he had no answers for four questions and would not talk—at least at the moment—of things he knew nothing about. . . . The hour would come when he would tackle the toughest without awe or misgiving and often without knowledge. He would pass judgment quickly on world controversies, needing no more than a single sentence for the panacea."

And so he came to find an answer to the most pressing problem in the world, the canker that fomented wars and kept them going, with all their blighting of constructive labor, the hidden catalyst that drew men from their lathes and plows and put them at one another's throats. Ford's answer was as simple and complex and efficient as his Model T. It was the Jews.

Why? In his scrupulous study *Henry Ford and the Jews,* the historian Neil Baldwin takes it back to what he calls "McGuffeyland." The readers included the maneuverings of Shakespeare's Shylock, but millions of other American children read them and didn't come away thinking themselves in the grip of a worldwide Jewish conspiracy.

Although there were few Jewish workers in Highland Park, the younger Ford never spoke of his animus against them as a people. Still, there was a general feeling in the Midwest of his youth that the distant forces controlling the all-powerful abstraction known as Wall Street included Jewish bankers and stock manipulators whose "orientalism"—a word of the time that often referred to Jews rather than Asians—was hostile to the stalwart values of farm and church.

Then there was Ford's growing anger about the "parasites" who did no work themselves but lived off the labors of others through returns on investments. Though none of the parasites he'd had to buy out to gain full control of his company was Jewish, at some point he began to see the Jews as a race of moneylenders who shunned honest labor. He once offered a thousand dollars to anyone who could show him a Jewish farmer.

If they could profit from the sweat of others, so could they from the blood of others. Rosika Schwimmer said that even before the Peace Ship sailed Henry Ford, after speaking to her "briskly and logically" about his pacifism, abruptly came out with, "I know who caused the war—the German-Jewish bankers! I have the evidence here"—he patted his breast pocket—"Facts! The German-Jewish bankers caused the war. I can't give out the facts now, because I haven't got them all yet, but I'll have them soon." Schwimmer said that Ford's tone had abruptly lost its intelligent vigor of seconds earlier: Now he was speaking with "that lack of conviction with which a schoolboy would recite something about the supreme happiness of being good and virtuous."

In 1918 Ford got a platform on which to display his goodness and virtue. He bought a feeble local weekly called the *Dearborn Independent*, and hired E. G. Pipp—the highly competent, liberal-minded veteran newspaperman who would witness the futile tutorial efforts at Mount Clemens—as editor, and Fred L. Black, a salesman who understood printing costs, as business manager. They were promised complete editorial independence save for a feature to be called "Mr. Ford's Own Page." That would be under the control of the general manager, Ernest Liebold.

Liebold did any number of things for Ford.

When Julian Street went seeking the carmaker, he came first to the Highland Park plant, "so full of people, all of them working for Ford, that a thousand or two would make no difference in the look of things. And among all these people there was just one man I really wanted to see, and just one man I really wanted not to see. I wanted to see Henry Ford, and I wanted not to see a man named Liebold, because, they say, if you see Liebold first you never do see Ford. That is what Liebold is there for. He is the man whose business in life is to know where Ford *isn't*."

Liebold had been keeping track of where Ford wasn't since 1911. Henry Ford, who knew exactly how much every part in his Model T cost to manufacture, who would happily buy a hundred-thousand-dollar machine to save a few pennies a day, who had used his command of prices to battle all his rivals until he had none, was surprisingly casual about his own money. One day Clara, going through a suit of his before sending it out to be cleaned, felt something in a trouser pocket. She reached in and withdrew a creased and battered but perfectly live check for seventy-five thousand dollars.

Clara, who was still thrifty enough regularly to darn her husband's socks, was appalled. She asked Couzens to find her husband someone to handle his business mail, and he said he thought Liebold would do a good job of it.

Born in Detroit in 1884, Liebold trained in business there and was working at a savings bank when his obvious capability caught Couzens's eye. Ford's lieutenant brought him aboard a newly founded bank, and when Ford himself wanted to save an ailing private bank in Dearborn, he gave the job to Liebold. He did so well that Ford put his money in what had become the Dearborn State Bank, and soon had such confidence in Liebold that he let him handle his personal finances. Holding power of attorney for Henry and Clara, Liebold managed every Ford family business that didn't directly involve car-making. He was never officially employed by the Ford Motor Company, but he had greater access to Ford, and more influence over him, than almost anyone who was.

Liebold was so trusted that he apparently wrote his own salary checks. Nearly as competent as Couzens, he served Ford as business manager, executive secretary, and when a hospital needed building in Dearborn, he saw that it got built. When Ford bought a dilapidated railroad Liebold helped get the line in shape and sold it for a $9 million profit. Naturally Ford gave him a role in the *Dearborn Independent.*

It was impossible to find anyone who could question Liebold's integrity. It was equally impossible to find anyone who liked him. That suited Liebold. "I make it a rule not to have any friends in the company," he told Fred Black. "You must be in a position where you don't give a God-damn what happens to anybody."

That suited Henry Ford: "Well, when you hire a watchdog, you don't hire him to like everybody who comes to the gate."

Liebold was proud of his German heritage, which to him encompassed an implacable anti-Semitism.

The first issue of the *Dearborn Independent* under Ford's ownership and Pipp's direction came out on May 11, 1919. The best that can be said is that it was harmless. Between gray halftones, columns of text warned against monopoly, recounted agricultural developments, picked up various stories from other papers, and voiced the faded Populist enthusiasms of twenty years earlier. The *Detroit Times* remarked that it was "the best periodical ever turned out by a tractor plant." Another Detroit paper—almost certainly the only midwestern daily ever to swipe at a rival by invoking Samuel Taylor Coleridge—said the *Independent* was "tranquil as a Peace Ship upon a painted ocean."

"Mr. Ford's Own Page," smoothed and expanded from whatever he might have said by William Cameron, was an anthology of pithless epigrams: "Opportunity will not overlook you because you wear overalls."

Despite the interest aroused by Ford's participation, the circulation reached only 56,000 during the first year he owned it, and cost him $284,000 in losses. The next spring the readership dropped to 26,000.

Pipp thought the remedy might be a fiction contest. Joseph J. O'Neill, who had come from the *New York World* to help with the press office at Mount Clemens, did not. In a fourteen-page memo that reads as if it were designed to be heard through a gale, he wrote, "PUSSY FOOTING and being afraid to hurt people will keep us where we are. . . . ONE SINGLE SERIES may make us known to millions. A succession of series of FEARLESS, TRUTHFUL, INTERESTING, PLAIN-SPOKEN articles, if properly handled . . . will make a lasting reputation . . . LET'S HAVE SOME SENSATIONALISM."

He was right about establishing a lasting reputation. From that day to this it has cost the Ford Motor Company untold millions of dollars, and cast a shadow over its founder that has yet to entirely lift. O'Neill hadn't suggested any particular subject for the *Independent*'s sensational series. Pipp said the topic was Liebold's doing. Shortly after it had been chosen he wrote, "The door to the Ford mind was always open to anything Liebold wanted to shove in it, and during that time Mr. Ford developed a dislike for Jews . . . I am sure that if Mr. Ford were put on the witness stand he could not tell to save his life just when he started against the Jews. I am sure that Liebold could tell." Fred Black agreed: Ford's secretary "did have a fertile field to work on, but if I were to put the number one blame on anyone, I would put it on Liebold."

Pipp saw what was coming, and he quit the *Independent* in April, a month before the journal began presenting what he called Ford's "gospel of bitterness and poison-gas race-hatred."

That began on May 22, 1920, when "the Ford International Weekly (5¢ an issue $1.00 per year) *The Dearborn Independent*" ran its front-page headline: "The International Jew: The World's Problem."

The story began, "The Jew is again being singled out for critical attention throughout the world. His emergence in the financial, political and social spheres has been so complete and spectacular since the war, that his place, power and purpose in the world are being given a real scrutiny, much of it unfriendly. . . .

"The single description which will include a larger percentage of Jews than members of any other race is this: he is in business. It may be only gathering rags and selling them, but he is in business. From the sale of old clothes to the control of international trade and finance, the Jew is supremely gifted for business." And so on. And on, and on, and on for ninety-one issues. "Does a Jewish Power Control the World Press?" (Yes); "Does a Definite Jewish World Program Exist?" (Yes); "Are the Jews a Nation?" (Who knows? So many have come into America uncounted that they may already be close to taking over the country.)

Liebold found a useful ally in his campaign when he got his hands on a copy of *The Protocols of the Learned Elders of Zion,* recently translated into English. This invention of the czarist secret police had emerged in the first years of the century. It is usually called a forgery but, as the late Christopher Hitchens furiously strove to establish, a "forgery" means that there exists an authentic original that has surreptitiously been copied. The *Protocols* are a hoax or, if that word might suggest mere prankishness, a fraud. They purport to record the seven highest leaders of the Jewish faith plotting world domination through usury and the corruption of gentile traditions and morals.

Liebold seized on the *Protocols* to help fight back every assault of the hydra-headed Jewish campaign to destroy America: "Jewish Supremacy in the Motion Picture"; "Jewish Degradation of American Baseball"; "How Jews in the U.S. Conceal their Strength." The *Independent* continued also to run innocuous stories in every issue. That of August 6, 1921, includes in its cover lines, "Teaching the Deaf to Hear With Their Eyes," and, "Many By-Products from Sweet-Potatoes," but the dominant one is "Jewish Jazz—Moron Music—Becomes our National Music."

Cameron was writing much of this. Gifted, loyal to his boss, alcoholic all his adult life, he got the *Independent's* editorship after Pipp left in disgust. Ordered by Liebold and Ford to go dig up all the facts about the Jewish conspiracy, he turned in a report that said he'd instead discovered "what a wonderful race they were, and how little he had known of their history, and what a magnificent history it was." That, at least, is what he said to interviewers years later. He did not stress to them his long-held belief that the British had descended from the only true lost tribe of Israel.

In any event he was Ford's man, and he did Ford's work.

Of course American Jews were surprised to be told by somebody almost all of them admired that they were responsible for pornography, short skirts, urbanization at the expense of the farm, increased public drunkenness, exorbitant rents, salacious Broadway shows, lewd nightclubs, and, for that matter, nightclubs. (In her 1981 biography of Ford, Carol Gelderman makes the shrewd suggestion that he may have been lashing out at the Jews as a scapegoat; that some sunken part of him feared the Model T had done more to bring the moral disintegration he deplored than had any conclave of "International Jews.") The financier Bernard Baruch was above the provocations of the *Dearborn Independent.* When reporters asked him about the accusations that he was the "proconsul of Judah in America," and a "Jew of Super-Power," he replied, grinning, "Now, boys, you wouldn't expect me to deny them, would you?"

Not many of the campaign's victims could laugh it off so easily. When the Jewish press complained, Liebold answered, telling the editors that they should shut up and keep on reading the articles so that they could "get a new light on the Jewish situation," because "all fair-minded Jews must help rid the world of the peril that threatens."

Rabbi Leo Franklin, head of Beth El, Detroit's leading reform temple, who had spoken so warmly in favor of the five-dollar day and begged its recipients to make themselves worthy of their benefactor, wrote in his diary, "Such venom could only come from a Jew-hater of the lowest type, and here it is appearing in a newspaper owned and controlled by one whom the Jews had counted as among their friends."

Franklin took this as more than an assault on his people. He had been Ford's neighbor on Edison Avenue, and his close friend. So close, that Ford sent him a new Model T every year. When one arrived a little later that spring, Franklin told the chauffeur to take it back: He couldn't accept it. Ford was surprised and shaken, and called right away. "What's wrong, Dr. Franklin? Has something come between us?"

Apparently Ford believed with Liebold that any responsible Jew would be grateful to have the venality and ruthlessness of most of his people pointed out to him, so he could help correct them. Franklin said what was wrong a few days later in a local paper: "Few thinking men have ever given any credence to the charges offered against the Jews. But his publications have besmirched the name of the Jews in the eyes of the great majority, and especially in the small towns of the country, where Ford's word was taken as gospel. He has also fed the flames of anti-Semitism throughout the world."

American Jews never launched a formal boycott against Ford products. About as close as they came was when Connecticut congregations mounted a parade in Hartford to honor Chaim Weizmann and Albert Einstein. Four hundred cars were to take part, but "positively no Ford machines permitted in line." Albert Kahn took a calm, almost philosophical view, at least twenty years later when he said Ford "is a strange man. He seems to feel always that he is being guided by someone outside himself." Kahn was pragmatic enough not to sever his architectural ties with his most important client once the attacks were under way. But he never again met with Ford personally.

Nor did the *Independent*'s campaign sit well with many gentiles. William Howard Taft, William Cardinal O'Connor, and Woodrow Wilson urged Ford to drop this "vicious propaganda."

As he usually did with his new business ventures, Ford made Clara and Edsel part of the *Dearborn Independent*: she was vice president; he, secretary treasurer. When "The International Jew" began its long run, they resigned.

Ford's dealers couldn't resign, but they did protest. It wasn't just the reputation of the newspaper that was suffocating their business; it was their having to sell a subscription to it along with every Model T. This played particularly poorly in the big towns, where many dealers simply tore a few pages out of the phone book, copied the addresses, bought subscriptions themselves, and every so often sent a check off to Detroit to cover the payments of their unwitting subscribers.

But the *Independent*, though its circulation grew to over six hundred thousand, was not a great success in the small towns, either. When an agent in Virginia, Minnesota, asked for the articles to stop because his landlord was threatening to evict him, Liebold helpfully suggested he buy his own building where he would be immune from such pressures. Other agents were more blunt: A New York dealer wrote that everything would be better if Ford put his money into improving his car instead of hawking his newspaper. Ford's curt answer to all such protests was, "If they want our product, they'll buy it."

Then, in January 1922, while Liebold was gathering evidence that Abraham Lincoln had been assassinated by "Jewish internationalists" angered at the president's wartime adoption of greenback dollars, Ford came into Cameron's office and said, "I want you to cut out the Jewish articles."

Pipp, who had started his own newspaper, and often vented his disillusionment with Ford in its pages, wrote, "There was amazement. Some who were supposed to be on the inside of things hopped around like hens with their heads cut off."

The reasons for the abrupt cessation are still unclear. Ford at the time was toying with the idea of running for the presidency, and that may have something to do with it, although Pipp believed that Gaston Plaintiff, Ford's main New York dealer and a man he trusted, had persuaded him that the series was destroying sales. Ford himself, at his most maddeningly capricious, told Cameron that he was planning to develop a new "money standard"—which is to say a new economic system—and naturally he needed Jewish help. Cameron thought of the ninety-one straight issues of the *Independent* Ford had devoted to Jewish scurrility. "They won't do it," he said. Ford was blithe: "Oh, yes, they will. We can work with them."

He didn't try to for very long. In April 1924 the *Independent* began warning the nation about "Jewish Exploitation of Farmer Organizations."

Aaron Sapiro, a well-known Chicago attorney, had spent years drafting contracts that would coordinate and strengthen the scattered efforts of southern cotton planters and West Coast fruit growers. Now he was working to recruit dissatisfied midwestern wheat farmers into a marketing cooperative. "A Band of Jews is on the Back of the American Farmer," said the *Independent*. They were "bankers, lawyers, money-lenders, advertising agencies, fruit-packers, produce-buyers, experts," and at the head of them all was Aaron Sapiro.

Ford had picked on the wrong Jew. Sapiro could be obstinate and impulsive, and not always wise in his choice of lieutenants, but he was smart and tough, and he was a fighter. He sued Henry Ford for $1 million.

By now Ford had long outgrown his relish for disseminating his views from the witness stand and he went to great lengths to avoid being subpoenaed. Meanwhile, Cameron stood in the breach.

For the better part of a week Sapiro's incredulous lawyer listened to the editor blandly but unshakably asserting that Henry Ford had no idea what ran in his own newspaper. Never mind the copious assurances by Liebold and Cameron in promotional campaigns that "the *Dearborn Independent* is Henry Ford's own paper and he authorizes every statement occurring therein," and that "we never step out on any unusual programs without first getting his guidance"—Ford had never read a line.

Not even on "Mr. Ford's Own Page"?

No.

Had he ever mentioned Mr. Sapiro to Mr. Cameron?

No. The staff had an absolutely free hand. Henry Ford had never heard of Aaron Sapiro before he brought his lawsuit. Cameron had never spoken with Ford about "any article" on "any Jew."

The Sunday evening before Ford was to appear in court he was heading back to Fair Lane along Michigan Avenue when a Studebaker sideswiped his coupe and sent it down a fifteen-foot embankment and into a tree. The facts of the accident remain clouded to this day—it's not even clear whether Ford was alone in his car—and the papers made much of it: "Ford Injured by Assassins: Hurled Over River Bank in Car." He wasn't badly hurt, but he was banged up enough to keep off the stand for the next few days, while the case dissolved amid accusations of jury tampering and the judge declared a mistrial.

This gave Ford the room to settle with Sapiro out of court, which he eagerly did.

He went further. To Cameron's astonishment, and Edsel's, he issued a sweeping apology not only to Sapiro, which was part of the settlement, but to the Jewish people in general. He worked on it with two associates of his, and two distinguished Jewish public figures, the former congressman Nathan D. Perlman and Louis P. Marshall, head of the American Jewish Committee. Marshall turned over the initial draft certain that much wrangling was to follow. "If I had his money," he wrote a colleague, "I would not make such a humiliating statement."

Ford didn't change a word.

He began by saying that he had "given consideration to the series of articles concerning Jews . . ." but ". . . in the multitude of my activities it has been impossible for me to devote personal attention to their management or to keep informed as to their contents." So he entrusted the reports to "men whom I placed in charge of them and upon whom I relied implicitly.

"To my great regret I have learned that Jews generally, and particularly those of this country not only resent these publications as promoting anti-Semitism, but regard me as their enemy. Trusted friends . . . have assured me in all sincerity that [the articles justify] the righteous indignation entertained by Jews everywhere toward me because of the mental anguish occasioned by the unprovoked reflections made upon them.

"This has led me to direct my personal attention to the subject, in order to ascertain the exact nature of these articles. As a result of this survey I confess I am deeply mortified." Ford says he was horrified to learn that his newspaper was suggesting Jews were trying to control "the capital and industries of the world," and dismayed to discover the presence of the "exploded fictions" of the *Protocols*.

"Had I appreciated even the general nature, to say nothing of the details, of these utterances I would have forbidden their circulation without a moment's hesitation . . . I deem it my duty as an honorable man to make amends for the wrong done to the Jews as fellow-men and brothers, by asking their forgiveness for the harm that I have unintentionally committed . . . and by giving them the unqualified assurance that henceforth they may look to me for friendship and good will."

There was a sparkle of mockery in the celebratory ballad issued by the Broadway hitsmith and producer Billy Rose:

> *I was sad and I was blue*
> *But now I'm just as good as you*
> *Since Hen-ry Ford a-pol-o-gized to me*
> *I've thrown a-way my lit-tle Chev-ro-let*
> *And bought my-self a Ford Cou-pe . . .*

And the *New York Herald Tribune* wasn't buying a word of it: "Nobody but Mr. Ford could be ignorant of a major policy of his own newspaper. Nobody but Mr. Ford could be unaware of the national and international repercussions of this policy of anti-Semitism." But in general the Jewish public seems to have been remarkably tolerant of the about-face. The *Jewish Daily Forward* said that Ford's "frank and courageous repudiation of the attacks on Jewry will have a tremendous effect in undoing the harm that has been done." Louis B. Mayer wrote from Hollywood that he was "thrilled" by the "stand which you have courageously taken in reference to the Jewish people."

Ford paid the $160,000 court costs, and shut down the *Dearborn Independent*, ending Liebold's career as de facto editor, but keeping him on his staff.

He could not, however, shut down *The International Jew*, a book drawn from the interminable series. It has kept bobbing to the surface in the publishing cloacae of the world's capitals ever since. By 1933 it had run through twenty-nine editions in Germany alone. Henry Ford is the only American mentioned in *Mein Kampf*: Although the Jews were "increasingly the controlling master" of American labor, wrote Adolf Hitler, "one great man, Ford, to their exasperation still holds out independently."

In the decades to come the Ford Motor Company would work with steady patience and intelligence to undo this part of the reputation their founder had bequeathed it.

Possibly Ford would have been more interested in the content of his apology had the Sapiro trial and his recantation taken place in any year other than 1927, when he was worrying about matters he found more urgent than angry customers deserting him for Chevrolet, or even further humiliations on the witness stand.

CHAPTER 17

The End of the Line

Edsel; his powerless power in the company; Evangeline Dahlinger and her houses and horses; the "executive scrap heap"; how to join it: suggest changing the Model T; sales dwindle; Edsel fights; the last Model T; what the car had done.

"**H**enry, I don't envy you a damn thing except that boy of yours." This was John Dodge talking with Henry Ford on November 1, 1916, at Edsel Ford's wedding. The remark rings with bluff bonhomie, but it may also have been truly felt. Everybody who ever met him seems to have liked Edsel Ford.

He was shorter than his father, and darker, but the greater differences between them were not physical ones. Edsel shrank from personal publicity. During all his years as president of the Ford Motor Company he seems never once to have spoken at a business-related press conference. When Ford publicists wanted to take his picture at an event, he would usually wave them off with, "See if you can't get father to do that. He likes that sort of thing. I don't." The *Philadelphia Inquirer* once groused that the single longest statement Edsel ever made to the press was "See father."

He shared his father's fascination with the automobile, which he had loved from his earliest memory (and of course he had earlier memories of automobiles than almost any American of his generation), but he took a wider view of what one should be. When Henry Ford sought beauty in a car, he looked to the machinery beneath the skin. Edsel thought the skin mattered, too.

He'd driven his scarlet Model A runabout when he was ten. When the Model T was a year old and he sixteen, he had the company build him a sports version. Despite his implacable feelings on the matter, Couzens allowed it to be sold for two hundred dollars beneath cost. The result was by far the handsomest Model T of its year: a two-seater lower to the ground than any other Ford, with the steering shaft canted closer to the horizontal. It was dashing enough to earn Edsel's father's approval.

The boy had already made himself so popular around the factory that the workers never resented carrying out his projects. Edsel was modest, alert, and cheerful. Decades later none of that had changed. His secretary, A. J. Lepine, wrote that he "had a keen mentality . . . and bright, observing, intelligent eyes. . . . He had a sense of humor, quick laugh, and a bright smile. He also had a very good memory . . . and he was even-tempered and well-controlled. . . . He never said anything sarcastic or resentful about people. He expressed his disapproval with silence. . . . He never used profanity. Well, hardly ever. He might come out occasionally with some apt expression . . . but he didn't use cheap language."

Edsel married Eleanor Lowthian Clay, whom he had met at dancing school. She was the niece of H. L. Hudson, founder of Detroit's leading department store and, according to one newspaper account, "the wealthiest merchant in the city."

Both Fords were fortunate in their marriages. Eleanor was every bit as loyal to Edsel as Clara was to his father (though Edsel never felt it necessary to invent an honorific to bestow upon her), and just as important, they enjoyed the same things, and each other.

But in that closeness lay seeds of the troubles that would grow between father and son. When Clara and Henry built Fair Lane, they put in a bowling alley, a swimming pool, a golf course, and other amenities they believed would keep their only son on hand. They expected him and his bride to move in once the Hawaiian honeymoon was over, but instead the newlyweds built a house in Grosse Pointe, the nest of gentry that alarmed and disgusted Henry.

Edsel was following the almost inevitable course of second-generation wealth. He wanted to be near the friends he'd made in the school his father sent him to, and thus became part of a society that tended to smoke, and, worse (but just slightly) from Henry's point of view, drink. Edsel drank and apparently smoked with them, although Sorensen says he never saw Henry's son with a cigarette in his hand. Clara seems to have been more alarmed by the smoking, but then she had held firm against Henry on her favorite beer, Rolling Rock, which the man who managed the Ford farms made sure was always close to hand however far Clara traveled from the Pennsylvania brewery that made it.

"For all their ambition for Edsel to make a name for himself," wrote Sorensen, "Father and Mother Ford never wanted their son to grow up. They wanted to keep him close to themselves and to guide his every thought." His move to Grosse Pointe among what the Fords saw as his louche friends opened a rift between the generations that would never quite close.

The Fords lived well, but were nothing like the racketing, feckless moneyed young whose doings fascinated novelists and moviemakers as the 1920s began. Sorensen, who was quick to celebrate his own tireless dedication to his Ford duties, nonetheless said, "Edsel worked hard and was always on the job early."

That job was at first secretary-treasurer of the Ford Motor Company, which Couzens vacated when he quit in 1915. Edsel took it over, and walked a steep road for the rest of his life. Once the Dodge brothers began their suit, his father wouldn't attend board meetings, and Edsel was introduced to those always barbed gatherings at their most tumultuous.

Greater tumult was on the way. When the nation entered the war, Sorensen immediately drew up draft deferment papers for Edsel, with Henry Ford's grateful support. Edsel would have nothing to do with them. He told Marquis, "There is one job in this war I do not want and will not take, and that is the job of a rich man's son." Both Marquis and Sorensen argued hard against his stand. Edsel was no figurehead: He was running the business side of the company, and he had shown himself to be thorough, organized, sensible, and productive. If he wasn't privileged to receive his father's occasional thunderclap of intuitive genius, neither would he sneak out of a meeting at the first pinch of boredom and spend the rest of the day watching a sparrow take a bath.

Edsel gave in. He took the deferment and stayed with the company throughout the war. "And it was a martyrdom," wrote Marquis, "as we knew who saw him day after day going steadily about his work, facing the great problems, and shouldering the enormous responsibilities in changing over from a peace basis to a one hundred per cent war basis one of the largest industries in the country." E. G. Pipp said, "It took more courage for Edsel Ford not to put on a uniform than it would have to put one on."

Not surprisingly, Theodore Roosevelt disagreed. The one man in America who, with the possible exception of Flo Ziegfeld, was as thirsty for public attention as Henry Ford had begun fussing years before about the carmaker getting more of it than he deserved. Roosevelt kept up a mutter of general complaint—"Henry, like Barnum, has been a great advertiser"—until the war and Edsel's deferment gave him something to sink his formidable teeth into: "The expenditures on behalf of pacifism by Mr. Ford in connection with the Peace Ship . . . [were] as thoroughly demoralizing to the conscience of the American people as anything that has ever taken place. The failure of Mr. Ford's son to go into the army at this time, and the approval by the father of the son's refusal, represent exactly what might be expected from the moral disintegration inevitably produced by such pacifist propaganda. Mr. Ford's son is the son of a man of enormous wealth.

If he went to war he would leave his wife and child"—Eleanor had in September given birth to her and Edsel's first son, Henry Ford II— "immeasurably distant from all chance of even the slightest financial strain or trouble, and his absence would not in the slightest degree affect the efficiency of the business with which he is connected."

Part of the animus in this statement must come from the fact that Roosevelt's youngest son, Quentin, had recently been killed flying a pursuit plane on the Western Front, but part probably comes from TR's desire to keep Henry Ford out of the Senate. Despite their disagreements over the Peace Ship, President Wilson asked him to run in 1918, and in response Ford was conducting one of the most lackadaisical political campaigns in American history. During its entire course, he did not give a single speech.

The Democratic candidate's near-invisibility failed to keep the campaign from becoming vicious, and much of its spleen was directed at Edsel. "Why not send the indispensable Edsel to the Senate?" asked the papers. One editor wrote that on the day Quentin Roosevelt was shot from the French skies, Edsel and his wife were giving a party for some of their rich friends beneath the more hospitable ones above a Detroit country club. Ford's opponents said, "He kept *his* boy out of the trenches by Christmas."

This would have been hard on anybody, and it was very hard on Edsel Ford, who was far from thick-skinned. Despite the draft-dodger taunts and his father's inert campaign, Henry Ford came close to winning. Twenty-two hundred more votes and he would have beaten his Republican opponent and, very possibly, have put America in the League of Nations (one more Democratic vote in the nearly split Senate and the matter would have been up to Wilson's vice president to decide).

While this defeat gave Henry Ford yet another resentment to chew on, the Dodge trial arrived—Edsel spent as much time on the stand as his father, and impressed both sides with his unshowy grasp of company management—and then came the buyout, and the libel trial.

During the chimera of the $250 car, Edsel became president of the company, and held the position for the rest of his life. It proved different from the presidency of any other company, as the founder was not only the new president's father, but he never handed over the wheel.

Sorensen wrote that "Henry Ford's idea of harmony was constant turmoil." He early began pitting his lieutenants against one another, giving them overlapping authority to see which turned out to be tougher in defending what he thought was his own territory. Throughout, Ford would innocently warn one against the other as if he were a well-meaning neighbor who had overheard something at a party.

Edsel hated turmoil. He knew that an operation the size of the one his father owned guaranteed as much of it as any human enterprise required. Don't throw your most spirited managers against one another like fighting cocks, he believed: Get the best you can out of them by fostering cooperation.

This approach held no appeal to Henry Ford, and he was worried that it showed a streak of softness in his son. For years he said, "Edsel needs to be tougher." The way to toughen him was to harry and contradict and poke at him until he screamed. But Edsel wouldn't scream. The only complaint anyone ever seems to have had against him was that he should have been stronger in defying Henry Ford.

That wasn't in his nature. He always deferred to his father, not because of any kind of filial cowardice, but through a deep respect for what his father had accomplished. Cut off again and again, often in the most humiliating way, in the midst of initially approved projects that would have advanced the company, Edsel would only say, albeit sometimes on the verge of tears, Father invented this. He's the boss.

Even before Henry Ford began to harass his son, he turned against his managers. This was at the dawn of the 1920s. The Model T had done everything it was going to do, save continue to pour wealth on its creator. Ford became increasingly jealous of the men who had helped him invent the car. One of the half dozen most famous people in the world seems to have felt he was receiving insufficient recognition.

In the early years, back when he had the gift that Edsel would inherit for making friends, Ford had been happy to share credit with his colleagues. Wills did as much as Ford did to create the *999*, the

Ford Times said in 1908, and three years later the magazine ran a photograph with the caption: "Mr. Henry Ford and Mr. C. H. Wills, the two men who developed the Ford car."

With the advent of the five-dollar day there would be only one man. The change took place quickly. Sorensen wrote, "After the name Henry Ford became a household word, men in the Ford Motor Company who might temporarily get more publicity than he did aroused his jealousy, and one by one they were purged."

Marquis saw what was happening, and how the wise Ford employee responded to it. Praise—any praise at all—belonged to the boss alone. "Every time anyone handed John R. Lee a bouquet for his bigness of heart he tossed it over to Henry, and when there was no one around explained what it was all about. And Henry kept the flowers."

About the same time Edsel started his tenure as president, his father began to discard even the flower-bearers.

Around 1920 "a judge of national repute" told Marquis, "I have a great admiration for Henry Ford, but there is one thing that I can't understand, and that is the inability to keep his executives and old-time friends about him." Marquis said it was not a matter of inability but disability. "He can't help it. He is built that way."

Couzens was one of the first to go—over a legitimate disagreement, it is true, but Ford could have kept him if he'd tried.

If Ford and Couzens had never enjoyed much more than an allegiance of shared goals, Ford and Wills were at first close friends. Just as Wills's boyhood type case had supplied the Ford emblem, so had his mechanical vision helped supply the Model T itself. Wills grew tired of having one responsibility after another taken away from him, but his departure may have reflected something more than Henry Ford's increasing impatience with anyone who wasn't Henry Ford.

———————

During his time at the company, Childe Harold Wills had gained the reputation of being what the era called a ladies' man. When word began to go around that he was leaving, a young engineer named

Harold Hicks, who had gotten a job working directly for Henry Ford, impudently asked the boss if women had anything to do with Wills's departure. "Women!" Ford was amused. "Why Hicks, women won't do you any harm. You can screw any woman on earth excepting only one thing—never let your wife find out."

Henry Ford didn't say many things like this, and the statement may have been an ebullient half declaration of something that was going on in his life then. Perhaps it was another symptom of the same restlessness that had started him hounding his executives out of their jobs, although such impulses have shown up in men far more tranquil than Ford.

Womanizer or not, Wills had no trouble gathering attractive females about him in his work, and he didn't take long to notice Evangeline Côté.

She was a French Canadian who joined the company at sixteen to support her family after her father fell ill. Smart, energetic, spirited, and ambitious, she entered the stenographic department in 1909 and by 1912 was running it.

As soon as Wills became aware of her, he made Côté his private secretary. During the incandescent years of inventing the assembly line that followed, Ford and Wills were often together and Ford got to know her. Before long she became his special assistant.

Save for her admiration for Henry Ford, which was genuine and which would last for three decades, Evangeline Côté was the opposite of Clara Ford. No fussing around a flower garden for her: She was as athletic as her boss, and as confident, too. She became the tristate women's harness racing champion, and then the first woman in Michigan to get a pilot's license, whereupon she acquired a Curtiss flying boat.

She did not accomplish all this on a stenographer's salary.

Henry Ford seems to have taken to her immediately. Most men did; she was short—just over five feet tall—with a jaunty athlete's body and an insolent, merry, confiding smile.

She was eight years younger than a man named Ray Dahlinger, whom Ford had come to like and trust. Dahlinger had been a thirteen-dollar-a-week floorwalker in a Detroit department store when he met John Anderson's partner Horace Rackham shopping there with his wife. Dahlinger saw his chance, and was persuasive enough to talk the shareholder into finding him a job at the young company. He moved from the assembly line to just off it, taking the finished cars through brief, sputtering tests to determine they were ready for shipment. Ford often liked to pick a brand-new car at random and see how it did, and he noticed Dahlinger, took a shine to him, and sometimes chose him as his personal driver. When the Peace Ship sailed, Dahlinger served as both bodyguard and monitor over the considerable amount of cash his boss had brought to cover expenses. Back in America, Dahlinger did not return to the factory, but took up an amorphous role at Fair Lane: chauffeur, landscape consultant, handyman, and, later, overseer of all Ford's farms, and a test driver. (He was the cause of much frustration to Ford engineers in this last role, as after each run he would provide—and not enlarge upon—only one of two diagnoses: "Damn good"; or "No damn good.")

Henry Ford evidently saw a way to remove Evangeline Côté from any licentious ploy Wills might be planning by getting her to marry Ray Dahlinger. He pressed the suggestion on them both, and they took him up on it in February 1918.

The couple immediately went on Ford's personal payroll and moved into his wedding gift, a big, modern farmhouse in Dearborn, where he would spend hours talking things over with them. The farmhouse was followed by a summer home on Lake Huron with a seaplane-docking ramp and, of course, the Curtiss. Then, a three-hundred-acre tract with three hundred head of cattle to occupy it and, a year after that, a Tudor manor house a mile up the Rouge from Fair Lane: nine fireplaces, eight bathrooms, a refrigerated fur-storage vault, a half-mile racetrack for Mrs. Dahlinger's horses, a six-car garage, and a show barn that Ford told his architect Edward Cutler, who contributed much to Greenfield Village, should be fitted out as an apartment for Mr. Dahlinger to live in.

Dahlinger couldn't have been happy about this last: A letter to his wife survives in which he wrote, "You said about twin beds. I think they're made only for sick people, not people that love each other . . . I wish our room would have *one* bed just for *you* and *me*. Is that alright to say that?"

On April 9, 1923, Evangeline Dahlinger gave birth to a son in the Henry Ford Hospital. Henry Ford arrived there immediately, looked the baby over, and quickly hired Nurse Lynch, the head of the maternity ward, to go to the Dahlingers' home and take care of the baby, which was to be named John. She stayed with the family for twenty-four years.

A month later Ford sent John a present somewhat beyond his comprehension, a Shetland pony, and the infant's parents the turned-wood cradle his mother had rocked him in sixty years earlier.

Ford never made the least effort to hide his liking for Mrs. Dahlinger, and she would be near him for the rest of his life. The impertinent Hicks and many others believed the child was his. Ford spent a good deal of time with the boy—it was John whom he told he had invented the modern age—but the evidence is circumstantial nonetheless, especially in Henry Ford's case. Here was a man perfectly capable of developing a benign interest in a couple of his workers and rewarding them in the most openhanded ways.

Still, there is no other passage in his life quite like this one. John Côté Dahlinger believed he was Ford's son and in 1978 published an aggrieved memoir making the claim.

Certainly John Dahlinger received treatment the equal of what the bastard son of any royal Henry ever enjoyed. The just-postnatal Shetland pony was followed by a miniature but fully motorized roadster, and a scale model working tractor that couldn't have cost much less than a real one. When John was seven he got a Ford Model T race car that had been dashingly modified to run the Indianapolis 500 and, still warm from the contest, further modified to let the pedals reach its young owner's feet so the boy could drive the car around his mother's horse track.

John was imported to Fair Lane as a playmate for Clara and Henry's grandchildren, who at first accepted his presence as children will, but later began to wonder about it, and, as they grew, to draw away from him. Dahlinger, who called his putative father by his last name, wrote, "Ford didn't have a hell of a lot of tenderness, but I got the feeling he liked having me around, and that was sometimes enough to give me a nice feeling of security."

Some of the stories Dahlinger tells in his memoir are clearly quarried directly from Nevins, but now and again there is one that rings absolutely true to his own experience. "Ford had a thing about jew's-harps. He thought they were wonderful." This is the lyre-shaped musical instrument, slightly more exalted than a kazoo, that you play by putting its two metal arms between your teeth, thus making your mouth the resonator, and plucking its single metal tongue. "He always had a couple in his pocket and more in the car. If I didn't have mine with me, he would give me another. And he was always handing them out to little kids around the Village."

When Dahlinger was eight, he came upon Ford "sitting on a stump, his back to me, looking out over the Rouge River and playing a jew's-harp as if he had an audience of thousands.

"He didn't know I was behind him, and I guess he thought he was alone. When he had finished, all you could hear were the sounds of birds, and he took a little bow. Not exactly a bow; he nodded his head to the birds."

John Dahlinger writes that Ford was always pressing him to take over some large sector of the business. But he makes much of his own independent streak. He demanded to go east to attend the Deerfield Academy in Massachusetts, where he received letters from his mother like this one, about the upholstery of a car he wanted shipped to him from Detroit.

> *Here is the paint sample, also the leather—you see I haven't seen the blue leather 'til late last night, and then waited 'til this a.m. for sunlight—this is the Zephyr Blue—We would have to go outside for the other blue and it would take too long now.*

But in the meantime I can get busy and get other samples. . . .
It seems that US Royal Cords [tires] *can not be bought from Ford*
Motor Company—Mr. Edsel's orders, but Harold is going to find
out today if we can't take a set of Firestones and trade with some
US dealer and pay whatever is necessary if you much prefer Roy-
als—better let me know about that. Mom.

John Dahlinger eventually ended up running not, say, the Ford
marketing department, but a Detroit nightclub.

His mother and father became ever closer to Henry Ford, Ray
handling the landscaping of Greenfield Village as well as the farms,
Evangeline doing any number of jobs, from furnishing the rooms in
Greenfield to lecturing in them dressed in period costume.

She was a real force in the creation of the Village. When Henry Ford
was vacationing down South, she wrote Frank Campsall—the secretary who had far too late replaced Ernest Liebold in Ford's regard—
knowing that the final recipient of the letter would be Henry Ford,
"The trees are moving into the village fast and furious and it's starting
to look real nice. There are five maples at the Edison house now and
you know it looks like they had been there always. You know there's
something real homey looking about that old place, sort of a mellow
and lived-in look. The McGuffey house is being set up O.K. and it
is starting to take on a look of having always been in just that setting—with that very severe and substantial old Lincoln Court-house,
it seems as though you just naturally expect to see a log cabin in the
offing. You know what we mean, Lincoln, log cabins, books, education, McGuffey—don't they seem kind of all to belong together? Took
some pictures, thought the boss might enjoy looking at them."

Once, during the two decades that reporters were asking Ford
about anything from pancake recipes to the British parliamentary system, one of them wanted to know what he felt about why men often
embarked on extramarital affairs in middle life. Ford said it was in
effect a twenty-four-hour virus: They are "simply trying to hold onto
their youth. I say to the woman whose husband is in this situation:

Treat it like the measles! It's a disease that strikes a lot of people. That's all it is, at the most. Help your husband through it. Stand by. Don't let it hurt you. Don't let it break up your home."

Clara didn't. She came to rely on both Ray and Evangeline, and toward the end of her life formed a friendship with the latter.

She insisted on having Ray on the estate as long as she lived. When she died in 1950, it was the third generation of Fords who had him abruptly locked out of his office. Evangeline ended her days in a nursing home. When her son visited her and asked for confirmation that Henry Ford had been her father, she would say, "I don't want to talk about it."

Clara Ford didn't miss much. It is absurd to suppose she didn't have feelings about her husband's thirty-year friendship with Evangeline Dahlinger. Whatever those feelings might have been, some of them were impressively spacious. On the last night of her husband's life, Clara Ford summoned Evangeline Dahlinger through a storm so that she, too, could be at Henry Ford's side when he died.

While Mrs. Dahlinger tended her trotting horses and her seaplane, Frank Klingensmith, to whom Ford had entrusted much of Edsel's education around the plant, joined Wills on what Samuel Marquis was beginning to call "the executive scrap heap." Norval Hawkins, a sales manager who had come to the company in 1907, went, and so did the Sociological Department head whom Marquis so admired, John Lee. "The Ford executive," Marquis wrote, "has added to those two certainties in life—death and taxes—a third, that is discharge."

LeRoy Pelletier, Ford's first great advertising man, had lit on the company briefly in 1907 and left behind him a slogan that was famous for decades. The next year it went up in lights on the Temple Theatre in downtown Detroit, blazing out the message: "Watch the Fords Go By." In 1922, people who worked for the company were trading the mordant catchphrase, "Watch the Ford executives go by."

In one case it is possible that Ford acquired a company for the main purpose of firing its owners. Henry Leland and his son Wilfred had founded the Lincoln Motor Company in 1917. Both father and son stayed true to the exacting standards that had made the elder Leland the most respected machinist of his day, and they were building a car of the highest mechanical quality. They and it got caught in the brief but sharp depression of 1921, and Henry Ford paid $8 million for the company. Helping an old friend out of a tight spot, people said approvingly. But Ford didn't see Henry Leland as an old friend; he saw him as the somber martinet who had driven him away from his second company. He assured the Lelands that they would be left alone to run their business as they saw fit, and then turned Sorensen loose on them. In months, the Lelands had left their company.

Whatever his father's reason for the purchase, it greatly pleased Edsel. "Father made the most popular car in the world," he told his friends. "I would like to make the best car in the world." He maintained the engineering standards while putting designers to work on the car's somewhat dowdy body—Henry Leland, like Henry Ford, cared little for outward appearances—and by the end of the decade was selling a luxury car that many believed edged out the Cadillac and even the mighty Duesenberg. A decade later Edsel created, in the Lincoln Continental, what Frank Lloyd Wright declared the single most beautiful automobile ever built.

One day in March 1921 William Knudsen wrote to Edsel. The next morning Henry Ford was in Knudsen's office: "What's the matter, William? Edsel tells me he has a letter from you, saying you are resigning."

"Yes, Mr. Ford."

"What's the matter, William?" Ford asked again in his most guileless manner.

Knudsen wouldn't quite tell him. "Well, Mr. Ford, I've thought it over very carefully, and I've made up my mind to quit."

Knudsen did, however, tell his friend and colleague William Smith, who had been with him when he first showed Ford the stampings from the Keim Mills. Smith, like Knudsen, had come to the Ford

Motor Company when it bought Keim, and Henry had sent him over to ask Knudsen to stay.

Knudsen said to him, "My job with Mr. Ford, since 1918, was being production manager. Is that right?"

Smith nodded.

"All right. Well . . . starting a few months ago, there have been quite a few times when I have found that my shop instructions on production matters were countermanded or ignored. I did not like it when I found it out and I still don't like it. I found out who was countermanding them and who was nullifying them. It was Mr. Ford. I asked him about it. He just smiled, and didn't say much."

Knudsen said he couldn't work for someone who didn't have confidence in him, and that the lack of confidence had been shown in a particularly unpleasant way: "If I'm doing something wrong, he ought to tell me about it and not go out in the shop and tell other people."

It was Ford's company, Knudsen went on, and he realized that "he has every right to run it as he sees fit. Mr. Ford and I have never had any serious arguments, any serious differences in opinion about how things should be run in the shop. We are not going to have any now. To keep from this, I am going to quit."

Smith said he understood, and would tell the boss only that he couldn't change Knudsen's mind.

At least one Ford manager seems to have been as fortunate in his marriage as the Fords were in theirs. When Knudsen told his wife he'd just thrown away a sixty-five-thousand-dollar-a-year job she laughed, hugged him, gave him a kiss, and said, "That's good. Now we can have some sort of peace around our place."

Knudsen was capable and Knudsen was popular, traits for which Henry Ford had dwindling patience. The man who had built his career by running a friendly shop, by being so congenial that people would give up their weekends to cut gears and turn crankshafts for him, now complained that "some organizations use up so much energy and time maintaining a feeling of harmony that they have no force left to work for the object for which the organization was created. . . . I pity the poor fellow who is so soft and flabby that he must always have 'an atmosphere of good feeling' around him before he can do his work. . . . Not only are they business failures; they are character failures also. . . . People have too great a fondness for working with the people they like."

Knudsen, however, had been dealing with something more volatile than an agreeable working atmosphere. At about the time he was clearing out the leavings of war production at the Rouge, he approached his boss.

"Mr. Ford, this war has changed our whole industrial setup."

"How do you mean?"

"I mean, we've learned to do a lot of different things with different materials. I think we are going to have to make a whole lot of everything because the people are going to want a whole lot of everything. . . . With the war ended we've got a lot of equipment, a lot of buildings, a lot of blast furnaces. We've got to use them."

"What have you in mind, William?" Ford never called Knudsen Bill, and Knudsen certainly never called him Henry.

"Well, Mr. Ford, the day is coming, and you know it, when maybe 80 or 90 per cent of all the motor cars sold in this country will be in the low-price field."

"What is it you have in mind, particularly?"

"The Model T."

Knudsen showed a surprised Ford some drawings he'd had made at the Rouge plant, and explained them. "I think we ought to start in and refine our product. We can do it in three ways. We can make the same car we have been making for less money; we can make a better car for more money; or we can make a better car for the same money."

Knudsen would have been justified in a satisfied little pause before he concluded, "*This* one we can make for the same money."

Ford kept studying the drawings. "This car has a gear shift," he said finally.

"Yes."

"What color?"

"The customer would be given the choice."

"Is it heavier than the Model T?"

"A little, not much, and the lines are different, too."

"So I see." Of course he did. "How long will it take you to get into production with this new model?"

"A few months, maybe six."

"How long will it take you to get into production on the Model T?"

"Sixty days."

"There's your answer."

Did Knudsen know this conversation had ended his career at Ford? Likely he did; he understood cars, and he understood Henry Ford, as far as that was possible. He knew both that the Model T had to evolve, and that its creator would be remorseless toward any apostate who suggested significant changes.

———~~~~~~~———

Knudsen would have heard what happened two years before he joined the company, when the founder returned with his family from visiting his overseas plants in 1912. On his first day back at work, Henry Ford discovered that Wills and some of his other lieutenants had prepared a homecoming surprise for him.

The Model T was already five years old, and they'd been working on an improved design. They were pleased with the results, and were so sure their boss would be that they parked the prototype in front of his office for him to discover. The car was less boxy than its parent, lower and more than a foot longer, altogether a better-looking machine.

It caught Ford's eye, and he went over and walked around it, hands in pockets. The new model had four doors. On his third or fourth circuit Ford paused before one of them and, according to a company accountant named George Brown who was watching from a safe distance, "He takes his hands out, gets hold of the door, and bang! He ripped the door right off! God! How the man done it, I didn't know! He jumped in there, and bang goes another door. Bang goes the windshield. He jumps over the back seat and starts pounding on the top. He rips the top with the heel of his shoe." At no point did Ford say anything, and of course by the time he was through working on the top he didn't have to.

Wills was eventually shunted into purchasing, and Joseph Galamb took his place in engineering and design. He, too, ventured into the fraught territory of changing the car. In 1914 Ford was driving fast along a country road when the rear wheels left the ground and the car threw its inventor into a ditch.

Galamb laid the blame on a radius rod, and set about designing a stronger one. Ford wouldn't consider it. "He was practically killed with the old rod," Galamb said years later, "but he still didn't want it changed."

Ford had told Galamb, "Your job is going to be to watch it so that nobody will make a change on that car." He said he was worried about production costs, and he did pay close attention to them. But, as his response to Wills's improvements suggests, there was more to it than that. The Model T represented the culmination of his life's work, and he had come to see it not only as a mechanical force but as a moral one. It was exactly as much automobile as people needed, and no more. One fundamentalist Dunkard sect forbade its members to drive Buicks, but approved of the Model T because it was not "haughty and sinful."

Garet Garrett wrote that Ford "was always sensitive to the slur that Model T was not a finely made car. In early Ford practice there was no fetish of precision. That is why the Model T was noisy and rattled; that was why it also possessed the animal qualities of the mountain ass, such as hardihood, extraordinary powers of endurance, phlegmatic courage and a kind of cheerfulness when not too much abused."

Here again, as so many who owned one have suggested, the car has the spirit of a living thing. Ford himself said that for all their endless uniformity every Model T drove a little differently.

David L. Cohn, who ran a New Orleans department store before becoming a popular historian, enlarged on this in 1944: "It was discovered, when earnest men compared notes, that no two Model Ts were temperamentally alike; they reacted to different stimuli and drew their strength from different sources. Consequently no man could pass on to his brother the secret of his own success because success was a combination in constantly varying proportions, of prayer, prestidigitation, and intuition. Only the vulgar would expect such mystical elements could be reduced to a mathematical formula, and the owners of the Model T, scorning such attempts, were content to move about the world each with his secret locked in his breast."

If this sounds as though the author finds in the Model T a little ribbon of mysticism passing through the case-hardened heart of the Machine Age, Henry Ford might have agreed with him. He always saw his car as an idea as well as a machine, and attempting to tamper with its design may have come to represent to him a sort of spiritual insolence.

He could hector and goad those in his company who did, and eventually fire them. But he couldn't fire the president—only hector and goad him more and more. Edsel took it, year after year, and did not make life easier for himself by steadily pushing to improve the Model T. He believed that all the constantly renewed production equipment, all those house-high machines his father would replace the minute something better came along to keep the plant the most modern in the world, were beginning to be in the service of producing an antique.

He was always respectful to his father, never publicly contradicted him on anything. When a delegation of Ford dealers visited Detroit to urge that a modern ignition system replace the once-revolutionary magneto, a Ford executive named William Klann brought the request to Henry.

"You can do that over my dead body," Ford said. "That magneto stays on as long as I'm alive."

Afterward, Klann spoke to Edsel. "Didn't you think your dad made a mistake?"

"Yes," said Edsel, "he did; but he's the boss, Bill."

Still, Edsel stood his ground, glum and fatalistic and always deferring to his father, but unbending in the certainty that sometimes flashed tiny defiance from his wrists: His cufflinks bore in Latin the legend, "All Things Change."

He had few allies. Sorensen boasts in his autobiography about his valiant support of Edsel in the face of his father, but nobody in the shop at the time noticed this fealty. Before one of the daily luncheons where Ford talked things over with his managers, Edsel got Sorensen and Martin to say that they'd back him in his proposal that the company consider hydraulic brakes for its cars.

Edsel made his pitch. When he was finished, his father stood up and said, "Edsel, you shut up!" He looked around the table. Martin and Sorensen returned the glance in bland silence.

Later, when Edsel was promoting a six-cylinder engine, Ford said, "We have no intention of introducing a six. We made sixes twenty years ago [for the costly Model K]. The Ford car is a tried and proved product that . . . has met all the conditions of transportation the world over. . . . We do not intend to make a six, an eight, or anything else outside our regular production. It is true that we have experiments with such cars, as we have experiments with many things. They keep our engineers busy—prevent them from tinkering too much with the Ford car."

He showed his distaste for the six in a more vivid way. Lawrence Sheldrick, who followed Galamb in his engineering post, had worked with Edsel to develop a six-cylinder engine. Edsel thought he'd gotten his father's permission to build a prototype. It was finished and about to be tested when Ford called the engineer. "Sheldrick, I've got a new scrap conveyor that I'm very proud of. It goes right to the cupola at the top of the plant. I'd like you to come and take a look at it. I am very proud of it."

When Sheldrick arrived on the high platform he was surprised to find Edsel there with his father. Henry signaled, and the conveyor started crawling upward. The very first thing it was bearing toward the scrap heap below was Edsel's six. As the engine dropped into oblivion, Henry said, "Now don't you try anything like that again. Don't you ever, do you hear?"

Ford had been adding to the executive scrap heap, too. As the Rouge grew, the plant's gravitational pull became greater than that of Highland Park. Not only was the Rouge bigger—bigger than any industrial plant on earth—but things were going to be done differently there. Sorensen was in charge.

"Let's get rid of the Model T sons of bitches," he said.

One of them, Samuel Marquis, had been trying to establish the services of his Sociological Department in the new factory. Sorensen had consistently blocked him. Ford assured Marquis that nothing had changed: Don't worry about Charlie. Charlie was in control, though, and he told Ford that Marquis was getting in the way of production.

The mutual discontent, Sorensen wrote, "all came to a head one day in [1921] when Mr. Ford asked me to come up to his office. . . . When I arrived I found Dean Marquis there. I had no more than entered when he sailed into me for 'interfering' with him and his staff. It was a surprising accusation, but that did not take me back half so much as the vigor of his language. I had always treated clergymen with deference. Many times in my life I have been called an s.o.b., but never before or after was I called one by a supposed man of God—in fact, that day I heard from Dean Marquis some words I'd never heard before."

Unlikely, but Sorensen's horror at being exposed to such language was allayed when Ford backed him instead of the minister.

Marquis was amazed and infuriated, and then, for a long time, bitter. He felt a friend had betrayed both him and a great mission. A few days later he quit—the only high Ford employee to do so, Clara remarked: All the rest were forced out or fired.

Marquis thought he'd been forced out, and he went off to write a book about it. His wife tried to dissuade him—think of the thirty-five thousand dollars a year Mr. Ford used to pay you, she said. She did get her husband to cut out some of his harshest passages, but *Henry Ford: An Interpretation* is stingingly frank, yet judicious. It is also fair-minded, very well written, and touching. More than just a record of grievances, the book is an elegy to a cause and a friendship with a man that Marquis believed was visibly being consumed by his worst impulses.

Ford's "puzzling mixture of opposing natures," Marquis wrote, "are generally accompanied by outward changes in physical appearance. To-day he stands erect, lithe, agile, full of life. . . . Out of his eyes there looks the soul of a genius, a dreamer, an idealist,—a soul that is affable, kindly, and generous to a fault. But tomorrow he may be the opposite. He will have the appearance of a man shrunken by long illness. The shoulders droop, and there is a forward slant to the body when he walks as when a man is moving forward on his toes. His face is deeply lined, and . . . the affable, gentle manner has disappeared. There is a light in the eye that reveals a fire burning within altogether unlike that which burned there yesterday."

Marquis says Ford's executives would recognize this storm warning and do what they could to prepare for the gale that followed. "Old policies are swept away. New policies are set up. Departments are turned inside out and upside down, or altogether done away with. . . . Desks are removed on one or two occasions with an ax. The men who worked at them return to find them gone, and possibly their jobs gone also. Men are discharged without warning, and no reason is given them in response to their inquiry."

Marquis was realist enough to know that business sometimes had to be hard. "A major operation may be necessary to save the life of an industry, but just because there must be a major operation is no reason why you should engage the services of a butcher and not a surgeon."

With his leaving, though, there would be more butchers than surgeons in the Ford Motor Company. The Sociological Department withered, and then disappeared.

Marquis ends his short book with two hopeful chapters devoted to what he believes will be the coming beneficent reign of Edsel. "I credit him with an intellectual breadth and balance, with a sympathy and tolerance of mind, an understanding heart, a less ruthless manner of putting down his foot, than I credit to the father. The son is a composite in whom is to be found much of the father's ability, broad humanitarian impulses, together with certain elements of strength inherited from his mother . . . I can see no reason to fear that the House of Ford will suffer at the hands of the son."

What the House of Ford got instead was Harry Bennett.

—————∿∿∿∿∿∿∿∿∿—————

Here is how Harry Bennett described the departure of Samuel Marquis.

> Under Dean Marquis the Sociology Department had a staff of investigators who visited every employee. . . . They asked the wives how much money their husbands saved, how much they brought home, whether they drank, whether they had any domestic difficulties. If a workman had kept out of his pay a few dollars for a crap game or a glass of beer, he was in trouble. . . .
>
> I felt the whole setup was a stupid waste of time and money for the company and petty tyranny over the employees . . . I criticized the whole thing to Mr. Ford, and he said, "Well go ahead and stop it." So in 1921 I ended the Sociology setup as it existed, and Dean Marquis left the company.

Who was this man who could saunter into Henry Ford's office and get him to shut down a department? One of the strangest figures in American industrial history, given the eminence he achieved at the Ford Motor Company.

Bennett wrote that "during the thirty years I worked for Henry Ford I became his most intimate companion, closer to him even than his only son." Sorensen made the same claim—"We had a business relationship closer than even his family had with him, and in many ways I knew him better than his family"—but in terms of intimacy, Bennett had Sorensen beat.

His career is in ways a preposterous, grimy fairy tale. Harry Bennett was born in Ann Arbor in 1892. His father, a sign painter, was killed in a brawl when Harry was two. He joined the navy as soon as he was old enough, and liked the life, even though moving coal on a cruiser in 1915 was about the hardest job one could find in the post-medieval world. He took up boxing and excelled at it. Although he stood five seven and weighed 145 pounds, he was physically fearless. All his life he would take on anybody of any size at the least provocation and with a ferocity that usually prevailed.

When his tour of duty ended in 1916, he planned to reenlist, but wanted to have a little fun ashore first. He got as far ashore as the Customs House in Battery Park in lower Manhattan, and there managed to ignite a spontaneous fistfight with a customs official. "I gave a good account of myself—" Bennett said, "until a big cop got me by the back of the collar." Whereupon Arthur Brisbane, the most famous journalist of his day, walked over and asked the policeman, "What's going on?"

"Oh, I've got a tough one here," he said. And on the basis of this, and apparently nothing else other than that Bennett turned out to have been born in Michigan, Brisbane decided to take him to Henry Ford, who was visiting New York.

Bennett wrote, "When Brisbane and I arrived at 1710 Broadway, Ford sales headquarters in New York, he at once introduced me to Mr. Ford. Mr. Ford was already in his fifties, he had sharp, gray eyes and heavy eyebrows, and was of medium height and a spare build. He was alert and almost nervously quick. As I was to learn later, he was a grasshopper in his capacity for locomotion, and got in and out of a car with a jackknife motion that made men years younger seem awkward."

Bennett added, "I wasn't very impressed."

Not impressed by being rescued from a potentially bad situation by one famous American and hurried uptown into the presence of a more famous one? Nope, said Bennett—it's just the way I am.

Still, he got interested when Ford asked, "Can you shoot?"

"Sure I can."

Ford said, "The men who are building the Rouge are a pretty tough lot." Bennett wasn't alarmed to learn this. Ford said, later, that he wanted the sailor to be his "eyes and ears." Bennett said that all he wanted was to go back to sea. Ford persisted, and Bennett made a concession. "Well, I won't work for the company, but I'll work for you."

And so he did, to the dismay of almost everyone else in the company.

The Rouge was, as its owner said, a pretty rough place, but not too rough for Harry Bennett. In his first few minutes there he "turned to a giant Polish foreman I saw" and said, "Where can I find Mr. Knudsen?"

"Why do you want to see him?"

"That's my business," Bennett replied, and "without another word the big Pole clipped me on the jaw and knocked me down."

The foreman stooped and helped Bennett to his feet. "The next time you're asked a question," he said, "don't get so cocky."

"'Thanks,' I said. Then I pushed his chin up with my left and swung with my right. Only his jaw didn't come down, as I had expected, and I hit him on the neck. The blow not only laid him out, but left him speechless as well. He went around the Rouge whispering for weeks."

The incident, which could have been taken whole from a Popeye cartoon, concisely prefigures Bennett's tenure at the Ford Motor Company. Bennett became the head of the Ford "Service Department," a grotesque successor to the old Sociological Department. It, too, was interested in the workers, but only to make sure they didn't loaf, or steal, or communicate with one another. Most important, they must not whisper a word about organizing, although Ford's battles against the United Automobile Workers union, which would be ferociously and disastrously led by Bennett, lay over the rim of the next decade.

After hiring Bennett, Ford lived in a thickening atmosphere of apprehension. He was worried that he or members of his family would be kidnapped, and he trusted Bennett to shield him. Bennett fertilized Ford's imagination with illusory plots, but he also made friends with gang leaders, whom he offered food concessions at the Rouge in return for protection. Henry Ford came to believe him an indispensable protector.

Bennett must have possessed considerable charm along with his belligerence. It shows in *We Never Called Him Henry*, an autobiography he published in 1951. It is "as told to Paul Marcus," but it carries a persuasive sense of its subject speaking. Bennett tells engaging stories, casually throwing in the occasional detail that rings absolutely true. Who could doubt this description of Liebold? "A short bull neck and close-cropped hair; for some reason, his coat collar always stood out about three inches from the back of his neck." The book's tone is affable, even avuncular, and yet every now and then there comes through a note of what most of his colleagues saw in Bennett: "Edsel, who had a mild voice and quiet manners, was built like his father—slender and long-legged. He was a nervous man; when he got angry, he threw up. He was just a scared boy as long as I knew him." Which was up to his death. Sometimes, although not in his autobiography, Bennett would refer to Edsel as "the weakling."

It is Edsel's tragedy—and Henry's, too—that the father believed this. The United Auto Workers organizer Walter Reuther, long after he had been victorious in the labor wars, but still a man not likely cavalierly to praise a car magnate, said, "I believe fully and completely that Edsel Ford was a decent human being and a man who hated with every drop of blood what was going on there at the plant. I know he knew it because he talked about it. I told him what was going on, but I didn't have to because he already knew. He hated it, but he was completely without power to do anything about it. He was helpless. His soul bled. . . . He was a decent man and he cared. I felt sorry for him. I still do."

What Edsel and Reuther saw happening was an increasing corrosion of working conditions. Reuther, who began his career at Ford on the shop floor in Highland Park sitting at a bench handling small parts, was shifted to the Rouge and ordered to do the same job on his feet. "You can't work with those fine tolerances standing up," he said. "You need to be firmly planted. But that wasn't the big difference. Those two places were different as day and night. Highland Park was civilized, but the Rouge was a jungle. The humanitarianism that

Henry Ford had shown so dramatically in his early days just didn't exist anymore. Sorensen and Peter Martin were in charge of production and that's all they cared about. I didn't think they were sociologically aware that the harshness and speedups for which they were responsible, combined with the terror and brutality for which they weren't, actually interfered with production. The Rouge was a jungle because of one man, Harry Bennett. His gangsters ran that company. He was a mean man, a neurotic man, a man with a gangster mentality. It was absolutely fantastic that a man like that could reach the position he did with a great company like Ford."

The Ford Motor Company never paid Bennett for his work. Liebold occasionally doled out his salary, which Bennett later complained was "peanuts," and Henry Ford would augment it with things like houses and yachts. For it was Ford who was setting the tenor at the Rouge. Bennett never directly defied him any more than Sorensen did.

After a while the head of the Service Department had three thousand men under him, all of them hard, many of them criminals. Henry Ford liked that. He thought it picturesque when Bennett would brandish a handgun, and enjoyed firing .32 pistols with him in the target range in Bennett's Rouge office. He suggested that Bennett build not a house but a "castle"—ramparts, towers—in his Detroit suburb. There should be secret passageways, too, Ford said, and both men enjoyed this adolescent's paradise. Bennett raised lions there, and would take them for walks in the Rouge. Once, as a practical joke his boss must surely have enjoyed, he smuggled one into the back of a departing friend's car. (The animal ended up dead in a Detroit police station. Bennett explained that "it had hanged itself.")

Ford also liked Bennett's willingness to take a swing at anyone. Bennett said Ford's attitude could be summed up as, "Harry, let's you and him have a fight."

Bennett claimed he once pulled off his coat to fight Ford's son. Edsel declined. Not John R. Davis, a sales manager and supporter of Edsel's. Henry Ford managed to provoke a row between Davis and Bennett, but as soon as his security chief threw the first punch, Ford hurried out of the room. This put a damper on the scrap: Antagonists though they were, Davis and Bennett both believed that while Ford loved stirring up a fight, he never wanted to see the blood.

Ford encouraged Bennett's high-strung savagery, and was complicit in how his paladin got rid of Frank Kulick.

We last saw Kulick in Ford No. 1 falling behind in the 1909 New York–Seattle race after a local had given him bad directions. Kulick couldn't get lost on an oval track, though, and for years he proved nearly unbeatable. Ford hired him as a racing driver about 1904, the year his twenty-horsepower car shut down a ninety-horsepower Fiat and a sixty-horsepower Renault. In 1907 a rear wheel disintegrated and put his car through a fence. "The old man wouldn't let me have a differential," Kulick said of Ford, "and the strain was such it broke the wheels." The driver's kneecap was shattered, his leg broken in two places, and he seemed to have internal injuries.

Ford may have been stingy with his equipment, but it's a good thing he was there to see the race, for his swift, intuitive sense of action found a solution. While spectators were muttering around the bleeding Kulick in worried futility, Ford borrowed a saw from somebody, sheared off the top of a touring car parked nearby, laid a plank across it, and in this improvised ambulance got Kulick to a hospital. The driver was in a brace for two years and limped for the rest of his life. But he was racing again by 1910, winning more often than not. Until 1927, when Henry Ford fired him.

Kulick went to his boss as soon as he got the word. Of course Mr. Ford knew nothing about it. Clearly distressed, he told Kulick to go to Mr. Sorensen, who would put him back to work at once. Sorensen handed the driver off to Harry Bennett, who needed him to fix a car that was misbehaving. Kulick found that the camshaft had been badly ground. He turned a new one and got it installed in the car despite a puzzling swarm of small obstructions from Bennett's men. Then he asked Bennett to come check it.

The engine was running beautifully. Too noisy, Bennett said. Kulick didn't understand. Bennett told him to lie on the dashboard and put his ear next to the hood to listen to the engine from the outside, and "we'll take it for a ride."

Kulick took his place. Bennett put his foot down hard, bounced out of the plant, and swung the wheel sharply enough to send Kulick rolling in the dust and grit of Miller Road. Bennett sped back inside the factory.

When Kulick picked himself up and limped back to the plant gates, Bennett's men wouldn't let him through.

Bennett wrote, "I believe Mr. Ford thought of me as a son." Bennett and Edsel had been born just a year apart, and the former showed all the combative spirit that Ford tried to implant in the latter. "Harry gets things done in a hurry," he told people. Bennett never made it into the executive dining room, but Ford liked bringing him to board meetings. After a few minutes of cowed remarks from the directors, Ford would jump up and say, "Come on, Harry, let's get the hell out of here. We'll probably only change what they do anyway."

The historian Julie Fenster, who believes that the influence of Couzens on Ford's career is decisive, remarked that "I think the white-collar strongman was replaced by the blue-collar strongman." Bennett might also have proved satisfactory to Ford in other ways. Couzens was tough enough, but he never spared Ford from his promiscuous acerbity. Bennett was just as tough on everyone *but* Ford. So was Sorensen, although he had technical abilities that may have made Ford jealous. Bennett could offer all that enticing brutality free of enviable talents.

Ford spent as much time as he could with Bennett, had lengthy conversations with him every evening, gave him more and more troops to police the Rouge until, by the early 1930s, people around the plant were asking one another: Who invented the Gestapo first? Henry or Adolf?

A worker named Al Bardelli, who came to the Rouge as a teenager in the 1920s, said of Bennett's men, "They were all rotten, no-good sons of bitches. You couldn't go to take a crap without one of the bastards following you into the rest room. Take too long and you were out of a job."

Drive a Buick, and you were out of a job, too. Knudsen's old story about the worker who got the Sociological Department's permission to buy a car and then announced he was getting a Buick lost its point as a joke. If a worker showed up in a Rouge parking lot in an Essex or a Hudson or anything but a Model T, he'd be told he was late. When he protested that he was on time, he was fired.

Those other cars were beginning to look pretty good, as Edsel well understood. He kept pressing his father in perhaps the sole area in which Henry didn't want his son to display some spirit: Change the car; the car must change.

And it did, some. Henry Ford had ordered that no Model T could be built that made an earlier one obsolete, but as the Ts flowed out of Highland Park and the Rouge in the millions they went through a slow evolution both in their scant decorations and their mechanisms. Leather upholstery gave way to leatherette after 1912, the same year a smart little Torpedo Roadster died after its twenty-four-month life. A water pump on the first twenty-five hundred models was deemed too expensive, and abandoned for the "thermo-syphon" cooling system, which took advantage of the fact that heated water rises, and thus left the matter in the hands of Newton and God. Sheet steel replaced wooden bodies, and the car lost its sole gleam of panache in 1916 when a painted steel radiator replaced the brass one. A year later, the fenders grew a gentle crown to smooth their original squared-off geometry, and in 1919 the car finally could have an electric starter.

Ford, a believer in suffrage and women's rights in general, had long campaigned for them to drive the Model T. Very early in his company's life he ran ads showing female drivers rolling joyfully through the countryside in the billowing road costumes of the day. But although many women did master it, that often vicious starting crank spared neither sex.

As the 1920s went on, Edsel pressed for the Model T to get lower, handsomer, more convenient. He won small victories, and the car of the mid-1920s was different from its predecessors: It was softer, rounder, how the 1908 prototype might have looked had it been reshaped by a gentle fall of snow. This car had wire wheels and lighter connecting rods, but in every significant way it was the same machine.

———————vvvvvvvvvvvvvv———————

Alfred Sloan had come a long way from Newark and his Hyatt roller bearings. He had done well with them—so well that he got worried. The bulk of his business rested on massive orders from a few car companies, Ford among them. If they decided to start making their own bearings, Hyatt would be done for.

So Sloan sold it, and in 1923 Pierre du Pont made him president of General Motors. The new president's largest decision was also his first: "to determine whether we would operate under a centralized or decentralized form of administration. Decentralization was analogous to free enterprise. Centralization, to regimentation. [Here he would have been thinking of the most centralized of all great companies.] We decided on free enterprise. . . .

"We would set up each of our various operations as an integral unit, complete as to itself. We would place in charge of each unit an executive responsible, and solely responsible, for his complete activity."

While Sloan was building this managerial structure a friend came to him and said he had met a big fellow who seemed to have a lot on the ball. Would Sloan speak with him?

"As soon as I saw him I remembered him. 'You are Knudsen, of course! I had some business with you at Ford's some time ago.'"

They talked. Sloan explained he had developed "a General Staff similar in name and purpose to what exists in the army" to coordinate the efforts of his managers. He had no particular job to offer Knudsen at the moment, but he'd like him to join the staff and see whether he might help.

Knudsen said that was fine with him.

"How much shall we pay you, Mr. Knudsen?"

"Anything you like. I am not here to set a figure. I seek an opportunity."

"It was not long after that," wrote Sloan, "that he was made general manager and chief executive of the Chevrolet Motor Division, in complete charge of that entire business." Soon enough Knudsen was again earning what Ford had been paying him.

———————～～～～～～～———————

Sloan once remarked that the Ford organization was "run like a northern lumber camp." If so, for a while in the 1920s that seemed a fine arrangement. Between 1921 and 1926 Ford built more than half the trucks and automobiles sold in America. Production peaked in 1923, with 1,866,307 Model Ts, and on Halloween two years later the plant turned out 9,109 in a single day.

In 1924 the ten millionth Model T came off the line and was driven from New York to San Francisco along the Lincoln Highway, a road that was both unimagined and unimaginable the year the car was born. After the trip it posed for a photograph beside the original Quadricycle of 1896. In the picture, Henry Ford stands—dressed in the neat gray suit—to the left of his first car, his head slightly inclined toward it. In between the two automobiles is Edsel, solemn and composed, his hands clasped before him with a gravity that somehow gives the celebratory photograph a funereal air. Both cars look like relics to us now, but even in 1924 many people thought that the Model T was following the Quadricycle into antiquity. Edsel was one of them.

Two years later the industry journal *Motor* wrote that Ford's tremendous sales figures were at once real and illusory. "Ford ate up his primary market with amazing rapidity, but it was not until last year that he reached 'the point of diminishing returns.' In the biggest year the industry as a whole ever had, his domestic sales actually fell off slightly."

In 1921 Americans had a choice of just three touring cars selling for under a thousand dollars, two of them Fords. Five years later they could choose among twenty-seven models made by ten different companies—and "if the roadsters and coupes are counted there are under $1,000 today 41 models."

In 1925 the Ford Motor Company sold 200,000 fewer cars than it had the year before. That was still 1,675,000 automobiles, but during the past two years Knudsen's sales of Chevrolets had risen from 280,000 to 470,000.

Henry Ford fought back, as he always had, by cutting prices—finally to $290. The Chevrolet cost $525 with its roomy body, longer wheelbase, and stick shift, and Knudsen built 520,000 of them. As the Dodge brothers had put it when they started to build their own car, "Think how many Ford buyers would like to own a real automobile by paying only a little more." Chevrolet stood second to Ford in car sales during 1925.

That same year, Ford revived colors—phoenix brown, gunmetal blue, highland green, and fawn gray—and nickeled the T's radiator. "Yes," said a New York dealer, "you can paint up a barn but it will still be a barn and not a parlor."

Henry Ford's heart was not in any of the changes. His car jolted through the mid-1920s with an oil lamp still casting its sallow glow on the license plate. He was experimenting with a new engine, an X-eight, with four cylinders pointing up, four down. It ran, but not well, as road dirt constantly fouled the four lower plugs. Perhaps Ford was pursuing this bizarre configuration because he felt that only something truly radical was worthy to replace his car; or perhaps he was doing the same thing he told the reporter he did with his engineers: keep them busy experimenting so they wouldn't have time to be "tinkering" with the Model T.

Months passed and sales fell, while Chevrolet's grew by a third and Knudsen's plant expanded to produce a million cars. The Ford Motor Company was fighting not only the competition but itself. As secondhand Model Ts came on the market, they cut into the sales of the not-so-different new ones. And anybody who found a good secondhand Buick for the price of a new Ford was likely to choose it instead. For a while the Ford company was making only two dollars in profit on every car it sold.

The public mood of sardonic fondness for the car began to curdle.

The Keith-Albee Vaudeville circuit was said to have imposed a ban on Ford jokes—they were stale—and the ones going around had lost their undertone of affection:

Q: Why is a Ford like a bathtub?
A: Because you don't want to be seen in one.

Before expiring completely, the Ford joke devolved into a final form that the humor magazine *Judge* called "Lizzie Labels," or, when the editors were in a loftier mood, "Ford epigrams." These were slogans painted on the sides of Model Ts by teenagers and college students who had bought their cars fourth- or fifth-hand for about the price of a steak dinner.

"Henry makes 'em faster 'n you can wreck 'em"; "Ford runabout—runabout a mile and stop"; "Lincoln's poor relation."

Most of the labels had shifted from referring to the qualities of the car to advertising what might go on inside it: "Shy girls walk home"; "Capacity 5 gals"; "Peaches, here's your can"; "I'm a wanderer of the waistlands"; "I take 'em young and treat 'em rough"; "Mayflower—many a Puritan has come across in it"; and "Chicken, here's your coupe." ("Chicken" being the forgotten World War I–era slang term for an attractive young woman that lasted into fairly recent times in its truncated form of "chick.")

Henry Ford refused to notice the change of tone in the raillery. He held fast to the idea that an automobile was basic transportation. Alfred Sloan understood that it had grown up to become an object of desire as well. An engineer speaking of the difference between the cars in the T's natal year of 1908 and those of 1926 wrote, "It is like comparing a sleek greyhound with a mid-Victorian pug dog. . . . Our cars should be made fashionable and given style appeal, because it is our most important asset. No one cares about engines; their satisfactory functioning is taken for granted. In fact, we turn in a car with a perfectly good engine and buy a new car because the new one appeals to our style sense, our desires and our developing needs. The automobile is not merely a machine. . . . Cars produce a form of emotional thrill."

The Ford company tried to put some emotional thrill into its aging star by resuming advertising in a campaign that featured paintings of russet-haired young women gathering boughs in an autumn bower while a Model T waits nearby ready to "take you there and back in comfort, trouble-free. Off and away in this obedient, ever-ready car, women may 'recharge the batteries' of tired bodies, newly inspired for the day's work."

Henry Ford had second thoughts about the campaign. "I think we'll have good times if we don't do too much advertising. A good thing will sell itself. . . . You've just got to let people know where to get it, that's all."

This graveyard whistling did no good. The Ford executives did no good. Sorensen and Martin were for killing the Model T, but wouldn't say so, because they'd seen what happened to the people who did.

The man who finally spoke up to Henry Ford was named Ernest Kanzler. Business heroism is of course on a different scale from military heroism. Nevertheless, Kanzler must be accounted an uncommonly brave man. He knew just what he was doing and what it would cost him.

He was a close friend of Edsel's, and his brother-in-law. Trained as a lawyer, he impressed Henry Ford, who put him in charge of production at Highland Park, where he quickly cut inventory costs by $40 million. When Knudsen left, Kanzler became second vice president of Ford, and it was under his and Edsel's guidance that production reached the plateau of 2 million cars a year, which the company would not again approach until 1955.

Everything Henry Ford should have seen as a success grated on him. He was jealous of Kanzler's friendship with his son, and possibly jealous of his son, too. Once he grumbled that "both Edsel and Kanzler should have been bankers," a profession less honorable in Ford's view than the pickpocket's. Kanzler, he said, "was getting too big for his britches."

In January of 1926 Kanzler put in Ford's hand a letter of unusual frankness. "I write certain things I find it difficult to say to you. It is one of the handicaps of the power of your personality which you perhaps least of all realize, but most people when with you hesitate to say what they think."

What Kanzler thought, what they all thought, was, "We have not gone ahead in the last few years, have barely held our own, whereas competition has made great strides. You have always said you either go forward or go backwards, you can't stand still. . . .

"The best evidence that conditions are not right is the fact that with most of the bigger men in the organization there is a growing uneasiness because . . . they feel our position weakening and our grip slipping. We are no longer sure when we plan increased facilities that they will be used. The buoyant spirit of confident expansion is lacking. And we know we have been defeated and licked in England. And we are being caught up [with] in the United States. With every additional car our competitors sell they get stronger and we get weaker."

Ford never replied to Kanzler, and he was gone in six months. Edsel wanted him back, and his wife pleaded with her father-in-law with tears on her cheeks. Henry Ford was adamant. But the letter had done its work.

Ford blamed his slipping sales on dealer laziness. In June he cut 41 percent of his San Francisco branch and fired twenty-five employees in Seattle. But despite such flailings, he seems to have made up his mind by the end of 1926. Galamb thought Edsel was too reticent ever to confront his father about the car, but Sorensen wrote that "Edsel had quite an argument with Henry Ford lasting a long time, but he finally forced his father to give up the Model T. That was Edsel's victory."

Right before Christmas Henry Ford pledged that "the Ford car will be made in the same way." Then, with 1927 less than a week old, he said that the company would experience a "little let-down"—that is, make fewer cars—"which will give us an opportunity for closer inspection that will be in every way desirable." This might have sounded vague, but the press and the public fastened on his next sentence: "We are not contemplating any extraordinary changes in models, although, of course, the whole industry is in a state of development."

On May 25 every paper in the country carried the news that the Ford Motor Company would be replacing the Model T.

The next morning, engine block number 15,000,000, wearing a bright coat of paint to distinguish it from its fellows, started its way along the line at the Rouge. As with the move to Highland Park years before, there were no noisy ceremonies, no band, no mayoral remarks. The engine was complete by ten o'clock, when the company's eight longest-lasting employees—Wandersee and Kulick, Martin and Sorensen among them—each helped stamp the serial number onto the block. All of them were the Model T sons of bitches Sorensen had wanted to get rid of, and all of them save him would soon be gone.

Then the engine went to Highland Park, where Henry and Edsel were waiting. The car's progress is well filmed. We see the engine lowered onto the chassis, and Edsel and Henry walk along beside it while the body, "The Fifteen Millionth Ford" painted in silver on its sides, drops down over the car's vitals.

Henry and Edsel walk through the factory not quite side by side. Henry is a few paces ahead, bent forward stiffly as if moving against a wind. Edsel is behind, walking like a modern person, someone who has grown up in the century that his father invented for him and all the rest of us. Both look as if they are strangers called together on some distressing errand—to identify a corpse, or explain themselves to the Internal Revenue Service.

Edsel gets behind the wheel of the Fifteen Millionth and Henry climbs in beside him. They drive a few hundred yards and then stop to pick up Sorensen and Martin. Sorensen lounges in the right rear seat, his grim, handsome face expressionless, or perhaps slightly vexed by this intrusion into his working day. Martin seems to have much more trouble than an engineer should buttoning his overcoat, and briefly jumps out of the car to adjust it. Then Edsel leads a parade of other cars beneath a sky that even ninety-year-old black-and-white newsreel film shows is leaking desultory rain. At one point, while Martin and Sorensen are settling themselves, Henry Ford, in the background, puts his right hand to his forehead and draws it slowly down over his face in a gesture that might be a kind of tic, but that any 1927 movie audience would identify as grief.

———◦◦◦———

Some newspapers reported the car's passing with a brief flurry of warmed-over Model T jokes. But most sensed the end of an extraordinary epoch, and saw the Model T off with warmth and respect. Arthur Brisbane, who had blessed the Ford Motor Company with Harry Bennett, was appalled. He at once bought a new Model T sedan and Model T truck, and wired Ford that he should keep production going in one of his plants, manufacturing five hundred thousand Model Ts a year. Other admirers of the car found this unlikely, and took steps to compensate. An elderly woman in Montclair, New Jersey, bought seven Model Ts in order to make sure that the car would outlive her. A Toledo resident bought six, but found the supply insufficient: The sixth quit on him in 1967.

Despite the Ohio man's having had to say good-bye to his friend forty years after it was built, the Model T will be with us forever.

It had drawn, from its spindly rear axle, as a spider casts its web, thousands and then tens of thousands of miles of new roads that gentler, prettier cars could navigate. It had given birth to a national culture that Americans were already taking for granted at the time of its death.

When, in *The Great Gatsby*, the twenty-nine-year-old Nick Carraway, driving home from dinner at Daisy and Tom Buchanan's Long Island mansion in 1922, notices that "already it was deep summer on roadhouse roofs and in front of wayside garages, where new red gas pumps sat out in pools of light," he is looking at perfectly familiar things that had not existed when he was a boy.

The departing Model T left us the landscape we know today—gas stations, suburbs, parkways, hot-dog stands shaped like hot dogs, motels, and much that goes with all that: vacations and spending money, for instance. The Model T lived a long time for an automobile, but a short one in which to transform a nation.

The novelist and critic James Agee took a lengthy and rapturous inventory of the still-fresh automotive world a few years later, certain his readers would understand what he was saying, and so do we eighty years later:

> The automobile you know as well as you know the slouch of the accustomed body at the wheel. . . . You know the sweat and the steady throes of the motor and the copious and thoughtless silence and the almost lack of hunger and the spreaded swell and swim of the hard highway toward and beneath and gone and the parted roadside swimming past. . . . Oh yes, you know this road; and you know this roadside. You know the roadside as well as you know the formulas of talk at the gas station, the welcome taste of a Bar B-Q sandwich in mid-afternoon, the early start in the cold bright lonesome air. . . . God and the conjunction of confused bloods, history and the bullying of this tough continent to heel did something to the American people—worked up in their blood a species of restiveness unlike that any race before has ever known. . . . The American in turn and in due time got into the automobile and found it good.

Henry Ford understood that people liked to move around, and he had showed them how to do it in a new way, with a machine whose dowdy looks belied its revolutionary soul. There had never been anything like the Model T before, and there will never be again, because what it did could happen only once in a civilization.

"The Model T was a pioneer," its creator said. "It had stamina and power. It was the car that ran before there were good roads to run on. It broke down the barriers of distance in rural sections, brought people in those sections closer together, and placed education in the reach of everyone." If this last might seem a non sequitur, it reflected Ford's most closely held convictions, and given the machine's socializing power, and its capacity to generate wealth, the statement is hard to gainsay.

Everyone who owned a Model T, or even just rode in one, had a supply of stories about the car. One of these might serve as a good epitaph for the vexing, indefatigable machine. On a black May night in 1917 a man named Howard A. Doyle, a driver with the American Field Service bringing in wounded French soldiers on the Western Front, was flogging his Model T ambulance across the glutinous moonscape of Verdun. "We got within a mile of the fort," Doyle wrote, "when we struck a big abrupt hole filled with mud and water, and dropped. I thought we would come out in China. My Frenchman thought that the car had broken the axle, but I gave it a little more gas and put her into low and she walked right out. Up half a mile, we smashed into another huge hole, and went right down to the chassis that time. Personally I thought it was hopeless even to try to get out. But still I thought I would give her a try. So I again started the motor and shoved her into first, and to my extreme surprise I went up out of this hole and climbed up the side of it like a cat, and kept agoing."

Epilogue

The Model A; "The Rouge is no fun anymore"; buying every steam engine; "Maybe I pushed the boy too hard"; the reluctant armorer of Democracy; to bed by candlelight.

Number 15,000,000 wasn't the last Model T. Henry Ford made 458,781 more before he finally turned off the tap.

Nineteen twenty-seven was not, of course, the final year of the Ford Motor Company. "I'm sixty-three and facing the hardest task of my life," its owner said, as he set to work on the T's successor.

The whole country watched. Automobile sales fell everywhere during a boom time while Americans waited to see what Ford would do next. Henry Ford symbolically swept away all he had done before when he decided that the new car would be called the Model A. When in August Edsel announced that it would be available late in the year the public was, to say the least, interested. Only Lindbergh's transatlantic flight drew more attention in 1927. Crowds gathered everywhere for the car's unveiling. In Manhattan, said the reporter for the *New York World*, "the excitement could hardly have been greater had Pah-Wah, the sacred white elephant of Burma, elected to sit for seven days on the flagpole of the Woolworth Building." The *New York Sun* wrote that "it was just exactly as if Mr. Mellon had thrown open the doors of the Sub-Treasury and invited folks to help him count the gold reserve."

The Model A didn't come quickly, because it couldn't, even with the full pressure of the Rouge behind it. Forty thousand machine tools, perfect for building a Model T, useless for any other task, had to be scrapped. Given how thriftily close together they stood, every difficulty magnified itself.

The metallic cries of the big machines' uprooting echoed all across the country. Thirty assembly plants in America and a dozen around the world suffered the same brutal rebirth.

In a way, the new car was worth the wait. The Model A was a fine automobile. Just as the Model T still looks ugly today, so does the A still look handsome. People immediately started calling it "the baby Lincoln." It had the stick shift and gauges of its competitors, and its hurried gestation had brought out flashes of the young Henry Ford. At one point that summer he jumped behind the wheel of a prototype and banged away across a stony field. "Rides too hard," he said at the end of his spin. "Put on hydraulic shock absorbers." Hydraulic shocks were unknown on modestly priced cars, and this flash of Ford intuition gave his engineers many long nights and lost him millions in potential profits.

Within two weeks of its debut the Ford company had received four hundred thousand orders.

A *Detroit Times* cartoon showed Henry Ford driving off smiling in a sleek new car while "Lizzie," her radiator sadly steaming, stands abandoned around a bend in the road behind him.

There were songs, of course, and one of them became quite a hit:

> . . . *They used to park her in a lot,*
> *For that they charged two bits,*
> *But now they charge you nothing,*
> *And you park her at the Ritz.*

She once had rattles in her wheel,

But now she's full of "sex appeal . . ."

She's like all the other vamps,

Pretty shape and lovely lamps,

HENRY'S MADE A LADY OUT OF LIZZIE!

The Model A bore out Edsel's abilities. It offered good looks and impressive mechanical sophistication for almost the same price as its predecessor. But it couldn't change the world. Another car had already done that.

By the end of the year the Ford Motor Company had turned out eight hundred thousand Model As. But Knudsen sold more than a million Chevrolets.

———\~\~\~\~\~\~\~\~\~———

In 1933 Henry Ford said, "The Rouge is no fun anymore." It hadn't been for years. Sorensen wrote that "after Ford started Greenfield Village and the Museum at Dearborn, he seldom came to the Rouge plant. . . . In his later years he actually put more hard work into the museum than he did into the Ford Motor Company."

His communications with an English Ford agent named Herbert Morton reflect the way he went about it. Britain was the cradle of the Industrial Revolution and Ford asked Morton whether it would be possible to put together a complete collection of steam engines from the very first ones, the huge, slow seventeenth-century Newcomens that had gasped water out of mines. Morton said he thought he could do this: Steam engines lived long lives and Britain wasn't so voracious as America in devouring the artifacts of its recent past. But, Morton said, "the cost . . . would be enormous." Ford thought that over. "Well, I'll tell you—I'll spend ten million dollars." He got his steam engines.

From the start people condescended to his museum and village. His early biographer Keith Sward, diligent and hostile, set a tone that lasted: "The favorite of those who have made the grand tour at Dearborn is Ford's vest-pocket village. The miniature community is running over with nearly every outward souvenir of the years of Henry Ford's youth. Plain gravel roads wind through the village. Gas street lamps stand at every corner. The only mode of transportation is provided by several horse-drawn hacks. An imitation New England chapel graces the far end of an immaculately tended village common. An original Cape Cod windmill stands on the premises—said to be the oldest relic of its kind in existence. Ford doted on its mechanism. He had the shaft remounted on ball bearings. Moored at the dock in an artificial lagoon lies an old stern-wheeler, long since retired from service on the Suwanee. The proudest specimens of the village are an ancient apothecary shop and an original old-time country store. Both are internally complete, with all the fixings. In quaint little shops, scattered here and there, hoary handicraft workers ply their trades full time. These artisans include a glass blower, a village blacksmith, a cobbler making shoes by hand and a wizened photographer at work in a tintype studio."

In fact Henry Ford was doing more than building a mountain of butter churns. "History is being rewritten every year from a new point of view," he said, "so how can anybody claim to know the truth about history?" He chose, as he always did when he was at his best, history's tangible leavings. Ford could see any mechanism with an intimate understanding that verged on the uncanny. He could look at a dozen identical carburetors spread out on a workbench and point to the one that wasn't working properly. He could handle a valve or a rifle breech and know "what the man who made them was thinking, what he was going at." In this sort of understanding, he found that "there's a beauty in machinery, too. A machine that has been run fifteen years tells its own story."

He meant it. "I have not spent twenty-five years making these collections simply to bring a homesick tear to sentimental eyes. It's serious, not sentimental."

But of course sentimentality will put its not entirely spurious gloss on every useful object. Often in the Ford Museum I have heard a six-tyish man like me, transfixed by a Chevy Bel Air or a Mercury Comet, cry from his heart, "God, I loved that car."

This happened on a more exalted level when Ford first showed Edison his reconstruction of his Menlo Park laboratory in 1929. Edison said, "You got it ninety-nine per cent right."

What's the one percent? Ford wanted to know.

"The floor's too clean." Edison grinned, then wept, and said he could sit right down and start working with his old tools.

Later that day, at a banquet celebrating the fiftieth anniversary of the electric light bulb, Will Rogers pointed to Ford and said without a trace of his occasional folksiness, "It will take a hundred years to tell whether you have helped us or hurt us. But you certainly didn't leave us where you found us."

The museum shows us that journey as the man who made it saw the way he had come. No bankers, no law offices in Greenfield Village, but amid the pretty plantings and tall old trees we see the history of industrial America asleep in machines that still look every bit as potent as they did when they were wide awake, flinging electricity and messages and motor carriages out across the land.

It is the most interesting museum I know. In support of this possibly silly-sounding statement, I offer my wife, a publishing executive who has never given ten seconds' thought to the planetary transmission.

Some years ago, when I was at *American Heritage*, a magazine devoted to our history, I told Carol that we were going to Dearborn in December. She wasn't pleased. "Why the hell can't you work for a travel magazine? We could be in St. Bart's! But, no, we're going to Detroit for Christmas."

We took a room in a hotel at Henry Ford's museum and explored it. At the end of three gray, icy, fascinating days, Carol said, "Let's stay for just one more day."

The institution that is now called the Henry Ford didn't leave us where it found us, either.

Henry Ford's absorption in his museum did not prevent him from sending Sorensen and Bennett against his son. "Who is this man, Bennett," Clara once burst out, "who has so much control over my husband and is ruining my son's health?"

Edsel had endured, with a dogged, somber courage, all his father's taunts and torments. Well might they have made him sick. If so, they manifested themselves in stomach cancer. Surgeons removed half of the stomach, and then the Ford cow proved its malevolence. Even though Henry had said, "The cow must go," as long as it was hanging around, its milk was not to be tinkered with: No pasteurization was permitted on any Ford farm. Those farms supplied the Ford offices, and the raw milk seems to have added to Edsel's afflictions an all-but-untreatable undulant fever.

His father thought Edsel's friends and late hours were to blame, and wanted his chiropractor to heal his son.

Edsel died on May 26, 1943. He was forty-nine years old.

"Maybe I pushed the boy too hard," was about all Ford said, but Edsel's death dealt him a blow from which he never recovered. He had little to say about reincarnation. Instead, he built in Greenfield Village a replica of the brick garage on Edison Avenue where father and son had once worked amicably together forty years earlier.

With Edsel's death, Henry Ford announced he was resuming his duties of running the Ford Motor Company. For months, he had thought World War II was a hoax gotten up by munitions makers to sell field guns and newspapermen to sell stories.

Sorensen knew better, and took on the tremendous project of building, at Willow Run, a small creek outside of Ypsilanti, a plant that would make heavy bombers. When magazines began hailing Sorensen as Master of the Rouge and the wizard of Willow Run, Ford

saw the stories, and that was the end of Sorensen. "My last days with
him were rather formal. The day before I left for Florida I went over to
Dearborn to say goodbye to the staff there. On my way out I ran into
Mr. Ford. I told him I was leaving in the morning and not coming
back. He made no response except to say, 'I guess there's something in
life besides work.' He followed me to my car. We shook hands, and I
was off. I never saw him again."

———∿∿∿∿∿∿∿———

Charles Sorensen left the Ford Motor Company in the midst of an
achievement he saw as larger than having been one of the Model T's
creators. He called the Willow Run plant "the biggest challenge of
my life." He had proposed to build B-24 Liberator bombers on an
assembly line exactly as the Model T had been made, even though a
single one of the Liberator's four engines was far more complex than
a Model T.

In early January of 1941 Sorensen flew to San Diego to visit Consolidated Aircraft, which had designed the Liberator, and discovered
that the company was having trouble turning out one bomber a day.
This was hardly surprising; the plane was new, and it contained 1.2
million parts. Nevertheless, the government wanted thousands of
them. As Sorensen looked over the half-finished planes, his mind went
back to "when we were making Model N Fords at the Piquette Avenue
plant. That was before Walter Flanders rearranged our machines and
eight years before we achieved the orderly sequence of the assembly
line and mass production. The nearer a B-24 came to its final assembly
the fewer principles of mass production there were as we at Ford had
developed and applied over the years. Here was a custom-made plane,
put together as a tailor would cut and fit a suit of clothes."

As always, Sorensen expressed himself bluntly, and of course the air
force response was "How would you do it?" Sorensen realized, "I had
to put up or shut up."

He put up, the next morning. He'd gone back to his room in the

Coronado Hotel thinking, "To compare a Ford . . . with a four-engine
Liberator was like matching a garage with a skyscraper, but despite
the great differences I knew the fundamentals applied to high-volume
production of both, the same as they would to an electric egg beater
or a wristwatch."

He was back in the slapped-together room with the blackboard
and Wills and Henry Ford in his mother's rocking chair. No Wills or
Ford this time, but Sorensen remembered his boss saying, "Unless you
can see a thing, you cannot simplify it. And unless you can simplify it,
it's a good sign you can't make it."

Sorensen spent the night with the Consolidated production figures,
breaking operations down into ever-smaller segments. "And instead of
one bomber a day by the prevailing method I saw the possibility of
one B-24 an hour by mass production assembly lines."

He sketched out on a piece of Coronado stationery a bomber
plant "a mile long and a quarter mile wide, the largest single industrial
building ever." In 1956 he wrote, "I still have that sketch, signed by
Edsel Ford . . . and I still get a kick out of it."

Edsel had agreed to a $200 million project without knowing
whether the government would back him. The air force did balk a
bit, but soon signed on. Willow Run put its first bomber in the air
nineteen months later. The unprecedented operation had a troubled
beginning, and during the first months some journalists and plant
workers—there were fifty thousand of the latter—started referring to
the factory as Will-It Run? But in a couple of years Willow Run was
turning out 650 heavy bombers a month, and by war's end had built
8,600 of what remains America's most copiously produced warplane.

—————∿∿∿∿∿∿∿—————

The immense factory early became seen as a symbol of America's
industrial muscle, and in September of 1942 Sorensen got word that
President and Mrs. Roosevelt planned on paying it a visit.

This would be FDR's first view of an airplane plant, and Sorensen put on a great show for him. He had made sure Willow Run was wide enough to drive a car its entire length, past a panorama that began with sheets of aluminum being offloaded from freight cars and ended with the finished planes shuddering on runways while aircrew who had been awaiting each one (thirteen hundred beds were provided for them) tested the virgin engines.

Sorensen said the afternoon would have been perfect, save for the presence of the owner. When the president arrived, he suggested Henry Ford sit in the backseat of the waiting Lincoln between him and Mrs. Roosevelt. Ford did, Edsel perched on a jump seat facing the First Lady, and Sorensen on one in front of FDR.

Roosevelt, fascinated and in full coruscation, at once impressed the staunchly Republican Sorensen with both his charm—he immediately started calling his guide "Charlie"—and his shrewd, swift understanding of what he was being shown. So did his wife, who often asked the driver to stop so she could find out what a particular group of workers was up to. The visit had been scheduled to last for about thirty minutes; it took an hour and a quarter.

Sorensen was not a man easily discomfited, but as his guests rolled past welders and stamping machines, he became increasingly aware that his boss (whom he had already infuriated by referring to FDR as "the boss") was touring his $200 million holding in fuming silence. "Sitting between the Roosevelts, who were good-sized people, he was almost hidden. He could not enter into the spirit of the event. When Edsel and I tried to look at him he would glare at us furiously."

Henry Ford detested FDR. At this time in his life he even sometimes suspected the president was plotting, in concert with General Motors, to take his company away from him. He had fought the New Deal—if there was to be paternalism for workers, *he* was going to dispense it—and here was the New Deal's author shining and chuckling and calling one of Ford's own hirelings "Charlie," while Edsel (who had always liked FDR and had sent him a Model A, requesting in return a "signed photograph") chatted with the First Lady. "No one," said Sorensen, "could resent others receiving attention as Henry Ford could. When he was around, the spotlight was for him." As the workers cheered their president, Ford scowled and pouted and said not a word during the entire journey.

Roosevelt acted throughout as if he hadn't noticed his seatmate's mood (fat chance), and once they were back in the sunlight with the big airplanes starting their engines around them, the president put all his irresistible cordiality into making his farewells.

Sorensen said, "It was one of the worst days, up to that time, that I ever spent with Henry Ford."

There wouldn't be too many others. He resigned in March 1944, with, as he had every right to point out, "Willow Run ahead of schedule."

———————————

Henry Ford hated not only Franklin Roosevelt, but the entire war. Having gone from believing it a hoax, he moved to thinking all the combatants equally at fault. He softened some on this when the Luftwaffe bombed his British factories, but he still forbade the Ford company from making Rolls Royce engines for British warplanes, even though Edsel had already promised to.

At the last press conference he ever gave, on his seventy-ninth birthday in the summer of 1942, he said the war had been "precipitated by greed, lust for power, and financial gain; it won't end until some sense of sanity has returned to those who believe in armed might for selfish gain."

This was the old Peace Ship impresario talking. The Ford plants were entirely given over to war production then, but he would have stopped them if he could—indeed, would have taken all the tools of war from their users' hands. He had lost any chance of that, however, thirty years earlier when he first set his production lines moving.

Henry Ford's life is spiky with ironies. In a small way by developing the Cadillac and in a far larger one by driving William Knudsen to another shop, he can claim responsibility along with Alfred Sloan for the success of General Motors. His unceasing demands for a more capable son while he relied on Harry Bennett make for a much sadder irony. His yearning for a one-room-schoolhouse America tenanted by small farmers while using all his unique powers to annihilate such a possibility is an irony that echoes throughout our history.

But it is the irony that flickered about his final years that had the greatest consequences. He disliked every war, but particularly the one on offer after he moved into his eighties.

By the time that war was over, America had sent it 300,000 airplanes, 12 million rifles, 90,000 tanks, nearly that number of landing craft, 147 aircraft carriers (Germany was never able to launch even one), and close to 1,000 other warships. In his fine recent history *The Storm of War*, Andrew Roberts writes, "Grossly to oversimplify the contributions made by the three leading members of the Grand Alliance in the Second World War, if Britain had provided the time and Russia the blood necessary to defeat the Axis, it was America that produced the weapons."

It was Henry Ford who produced the weapons. That was never his goal, of course, but without the industrial techniques he developed in 1913, America couldn't have done it. Over the years those techniques would surely have come about—time brings all her children to life sooner or later—but would they have been here when Hitler started battering down the dikes of civilization?

———∿∿∿∿∿∿∿∿∿∿———

Under Harry Bennett the company got into such a ramshackle state that the United States government may have come close to ratifying Henry Ford's fears by taking over the plant. Instead, they sent for his grandson Henry Ford II, who was training for Pacific duty in the navy, and wanted to stay there.

The service said—with more urgency than it had about his father—that he was needed in Detroit. He came, this twenty-four-year-old man who was generally considered to be a good-humored playboy, and found that Bennett had made the Rouge a dangerous place.

Once, years later, after he had rebuilt the tottering company, he got drunk with John Bugas, a sometime FBI man who had been hired into the Ford fold by Bennett and, once there, hated it. He had sided with the young Henry.

Bugas started talking about what it had been like then, in the days when both of them felt they had to carry revolvers into their offices. Harry Bennett was that scary.

"Henry," Bugas said. "Why did you bother? You didn't have to do it. Why didn't you just go out and play?"

Henry II answered the question for the only time anyone knows about. "My grandfather killed my father in my mind. I know he died of cancer, but it was because of what my grandfather did to him."

In the end, Bennett went without any gunplay, and Henry II became head of the company. That wasn't an easy transition. Henry Ford wanted to keep full control. Clara the Believer sided with Eleanor the daughter-in-law: Give it over to your grandson. Henry Ford gave his grandson the control he had never yielded to Edsel. Possibly they made the unprecedented threat of selling their Ford Motor Company stock. Whatever pressure they applied, it finally proved sufficient.

———wwwwwww———

John McIntyre, a Scottish immigrant, for twenty-five years had charge of Henry Ford's particular pride, the powerhouse at Fair Lane. McIntyre was with his boss often, and saw him change. "After Edsel died, I met Mr. Ford on the path going up to the kitchen, and I wasn't six inches from him; he walked right past me and looked down at the cement. He didn't even see me. It just seemed to me that his mind was on the boy, and he was gone. When the boy left, it just seemed to take something out of him."

Afterward, strokes made Henry Ford more remote. Around Thanksgiving in 1946, while McIntyre was at work on the grounds, Clara Ford came by taking her husband for a walk. "I was fixing the two radiators for the swimming pool. . . . He didn't even know me. He just looked at me and never even smiled. Mrs. Ford asked me what was the matter, and I told her two of the radiators wouldn't shut off and I said, 'I have to change the valves, Mrs. Ford.'

"She said, 'I suppose these things have to be done.'

"Mr. Ford never spoke, never said a word."

Half a year later, on April 7, 1947, McIntyre, coping with a spring storm, checked to make sure the powerhouse could handle it. "On that Tuesday night we had a couple of motors from the Rouge plant, and I saw when I went down that they wouldn't take the load. They were smoking pretty bad, and I thought . . . I would go up and warn the butler, Mr. Thompson, that if anything should go wrong . . . they would be in darkness that night. He went in and saw Mr. Ford and Mr. Ford rose from the living room and he came into the hallway and shook hands with me."

"Hello there, Scottie," he said. "Are you having trouble?"

McIntyre thought him "more like himself that night than I had seen him in eighteen months."

"Well, I just came up to warn Mr. Thompson here that I was afraid we weren't going to hold the lights for you tonight. I thought maybe if you or Mrs. Ford woke up in the middle of the night and found the lights were out, it would be nice for me to come and tell you ahead of time."

"That's all right, Scottie." Ford smiled and tapped him on the shoulder. "I know you will all stick by me; you've always done it for years. I never worry about these things. You fellows are pretty good." He nodded to Thompson and then said, about the motors, "Don't pay attention to them. Just leave them alone, and they will be all right."

"That was ten minutes to nine," McIntyre remembered. "My motors blew up at 9:25, but they were already in bed by that time."

The rain was falling hard, the Rouge high, the power plant useless. Henry Ford wanted a glass of milk, drank it, and went to sleep. He woke in a couple of hours complaining that his throat was dry. Clara spoke with him and then went and woke up the maid, Rosa Buhler, and told her, "I think Mr. Ford is very sick." With the telephones out and the roads awash, Buhler and the chauffeur did very well summoning a doctor, but he didn't get there in time, and even had he been able to could likely have done nothing but record "cerebral hemorrhage."

The next day there would be telegrams from Harry Truman and Winston Churchill and Josef Stalin, and the day after that a hundred thousand people filing past a bier in Greenfield Village. But right then there were only Clara and Henry Ford in the tall, shadowy room. She held him and asked him to speak to her, while around their bed the candles and oil lamps that had survived the remaking of a world stood calmly doing their old duty, just as were the two hundred thousand registered Model Ts still traveling the roads of the Republic.

A NOTE ON SOURCES, AND
ACKNOWLEDGMENTS

In his introduction to a badly needed 2007 reissue of Samuel Marquis's *Henry Ford: An Interpretation* (Ford had seen to it that most copies of the original 1923 edition disappeared), the historian David L. Lewis wrote that by 1976 he'd already published more than a million words about the man. Many of these had appeared in his excellent *The Public Image of Henry Ford*, which came out that year. He went on: "I probably know more about Ford's life and work than any other writer. But I cannot say that I have completely sorted him out, nor am I sure that I shall ever fully understand him." Making Marquis again available in 2007, Lewis added, "Thirty-one years and millions of words later, I feel the same."

In his own ninety-year-old book, Marquis says pretty much the same thing, and so, too, do a surprising number of people—it might even be safe to say all of them—who worked with Henry Ford.

Such statements about the man's inscrutability were not meant to be cautionary, but they struck me that way when I began the research that led to this book. So did the remark of a friend who, when I told him my subject, said, "Isn't that story about as well known as the Nativity?"

Sure: the Man Who Put the Nation on Wheels, the Man Who Said History Is Bunk, the Anti-Semite, the Greatest of All Twentieth-Century Industrialists. The man who has already been the subject of scores of books.

But he got his hooks into me almost the same way he did his earliest colleagues, when I first went through his museum in Dearborn years ago. The place is personal in a way that I find hard to describe, but I left it feeling drawn to its creator as if I'd met him, even as if I bore him some vague obligation.

When I got to know him better, I liked him more, and less: The slim gray spirit suddenly blazing with the possibilities of the whole twentieth century and drawing disciples to his heat, the friend of all humankind, the friend of nobody, the most famous living American going from being a great man to a rather awful one within what seems the span of a single year.

The story fascinated me, and this book is a story: not an attempt to turn new ground (the ground has long been turned by more capable historians than I), nor a technological history where, again, students (like David Hounshell) have advanced far more than I ever will. But early I began to sense the emotional ties between Henry Ford and the Model T. Each incarnated the flaws and virtues of the other so closely that I can't think of a parallel in all our industrial history. As far as I know, nobody has written exactly that story, and I hope this effort may find a space open on the large shelf.

From the start, I came across things I hadn't known—for instance, that Ford gambled his late-blooming career on building and campaigning race cars in which none of his backers had the least interest. I remembered only the sketchiest details of the Selden suit; I don't believe I could have said a thing about James Couzens.

Henry Ford was, in his way, as busy a man as his friend Thomas Edison, and had as widespread interests. Although my story ends early, with the demise of the Model T, it is incomplete even in its own truncated terms. There is nothing here about the aviation career that produced the durable Ford Tri-Motor, or about its inventor's efforts to decentralize his industry so that smaller factories, set down in farm country, would produce Model T parts for some of the year, and still allow their workers to plant and harvest their own food. Nor is there anything about Ford's lifelong dietary and agricultural obsessions that sometimes had his guests sitting down in dread to a dinner that would begin with soybean canapés and pass on through soybean bread, soybean soup, soybean croquettes garnished with soybeans, soybean ice cream, soybean pie, and soybean coffee.

I see that I have not once mentioned the other name the Tin Lizzie universally bore, which was "flivver." (Nobody knows where it came from, although *The Oxford English Dictionary* unhelpfully explains that it can also mean "a destroyer of 750 tons or less." For some reason, the word has always grated on me.)

All these omissions and a thousand more are covered in the myriad books, very many of them of exceptional quality, that have followed in the path the Model T and its maker cut.

The three stout piers that support so much Ford research are the volumes that make up the history by Allan Nevins and Frank Ernest Hill. Published between 1954 and 1963, they trace the company's fortunes from Henry Ford's beginnings until the early 1960s (they missed the Mustang only by months).

These books run to nineteen hundred pages, and although their production was strongly backed by the Ford Motor Company, they are admirably frank and thorough, and they draw on the talents of many fine people. William Greenleaf, for instance, who was largely responsible for the chapter on the Selden suit, later wrote the classic 1961 history of it, *Monopoly on Wheels,* which has just been reissued by Wayne State University Press—and a good thing, too, as far as I'm concerned: Over the years the first edition has been so avidly sought that it is hard to find even in libraries, and the cheapest copy I could locate for sale before Wayne State came to my rescue was going for $895.

The Ford company also conducted extensive interviews—over three hundred of them—with people who had been there at the dawn, everyone from floor-sweepers to Liebold. A good many of the quotations in this book represent memories at least four decades old; still, those who are remembering what was said had really been there to hear.

The company's hundredth anniversary in 2003 inspired several histories, among them Douglas Brinkley's *Wheels for the World,* which is lively and comprehensive and engaging. Nearly two decades earlier, in 1986, the historian Robert Lacey surprisingly deviated from recording British royalty to write about what might be seen as its American counterpart, and produced *Ford: The Men and the Machine*: It's racy, highly readable, and solid.

Many good books focus only on Henry Ford, and not his company's later life. Steven Watts's *The People's Tycoon* is the most recent and diligent, divided into chapters that address various facets of this endlessly faceted man: "Entrepreneur," "Folk Hero," "Victorian," "Positive Thinker," and so forth. Anne Jardim, in *The First Henry Ford,* wrote a study that is shrewd, canny, and well worth finding. But it was published in 1970, still the high noon of Freudian psychology in America, and the narrative occasionally stops for a bolus of Freudian speculation presented as solid medical diagnosis, which makes those passages—but only those—feel as much a relic as the planetary transmission.

There are innumerable accounts by Model T drivers, all carrying the wistful sense of fond annoyance with which one recalls a loyal but difficult friend. Roscoe Sheller's memoir *Me and the Model T* vividly follows its author from enthusiast to dealer; a fine little book called *The Ford Dealer Story,* published by the company on its fiftieth anniversary, contains several particularly good tributes and diatribes.

The memory—actually, the immediate experience—of driving the car lives on in several websites that crackle with intimidating exactitude. Take this exchange, which cropped up on a site called "The Ford Barn." The questioner has bought a Model T ("with a bill of sale but no title") and although the "engine #3373006 places this component as 1919," how can he determine the year of the frame and body?

A Florida enthusiast helps him out: "Motor # is Sept 1919, does it have a starter and generator? Electric start began in 1919. If original to a Sept 1919 chassis, look for wishbone bolted below the axle. And the running board brackets should be forged with tapered like ends. Those brackets were changed to pressed steel U shape in 1920." Make sure the gas tank is round (an oval one wasn't coming until the next year) and see that "the drive shaft end that mounts to the rear axle should have exposed bolt shafts." Then the car will be a pureblood 1919 through and through.

The Model T keeps a-going.

————————∿∿∿∿∿∿∿————————

As is the case with anyone who has written a book outside of solitary confinement, I have received more friendly support on this one than I can possibly acknowledge.

Among those to whom I owe particular gratitude are: my friend Ellen Feldman, who interrupted her own writing to read mine and offer valuable advice and equally valuable enthusiasm; Colin Harrison, my editor, who amiably saved me from a constellation of solecisms in the initial manuscript, and wholly salvaged the ending; the copy editor (every writer's invisible but indispensable ally), Sean Devlin; André Bernard, who assured me from the start that people really would tolerate yet one more book about Henry Ford; my history-teacher son, William, another early and helpful reader; my daughter, Rebecca, who never once interfered with the work (and who made clear there would be hell to pay if I mentioned her older brother and not her); my agent, Emma Sweeney, who was initially a bit dubious about the topic, but who encouraged me throughout; my former boss (and nobody ever had a better one) Tim Forbes, whom I believe was the first person to speak with me seriously and knowledgeably about what Ford accomplished; and finally to the John Simon Guggenheim Memorial Foundation, which immensely heartened me by discerning enough virtue in this project generously to offer me the means to complete it.

And my wife, Carol, who has seen me through this, and worse.

BIBLIOGRAPHY

Agee, James. "The American Roadside." *Fortune,* September 1934.

Alvarado, Rudolph, and Sonya Alvarado. *Drawing Conclusions on Henry Ford.* University of Michigan Press, 2001.

Automobile Manufacturers Association, Inc. *Automobiles of America.* Wayne State University Press, 1962.

Bak, Richard. *Henry and Edsel: The Creation of the Ford Empire.* Wiley, 2003.

Baldwin, Neil. *Henry Ford and the Jews: The Mass Production of Hate.* Public Affairs, 2001.

Barnard, Harry. *Independent Man: The Life of Senator James Couzens.* Wayne State University Press, 2002.

Beasley, Norman. *Knudsen, A Biography.* McGraw-Hill, 1947.

Bennett, Harry. *We Never Called Him Henry.* Fawcett, 1951.

Botkin, B. A. "Automobile Humor: From the Horseless Carriage to the Compact Car." *Journal of Popular Culture,* Spring 1968.

Bridenstine, James A. *Edsel and Eleanor Ford House.* No date, no publisher (but it's worth your while: a lovely house and a handsome book).

Brinkley, Douglas. *Wheels For the World: Henry Ford, His Company, and a Century of Progress, 1903–2003.* Viking, 2003.

Bryan, Ford R. *Clara: Mrs. Henry Ford.* Ford Books, 2001.

———. *Friends Families and Forays: Scenes from the Life and Times of Henry Ford.* Ford Books, 2002.

———. *Henry's Attic: Some Fascinating Gifts to His Museum.* Wayne State University Press, 2006.

———. *Henry's Lieutenants.* Wayne State University Press, 1993.

Burlingame, Roger. *Henry Ford: A Great Life in Brief.* Knopf, 1955.

Cabadas, Joseph P. *River Rouge: Ford's Industrial Colossus.* MBI Publishing, 2004.

Casey, Robert. *The Model T: A Centennial History.* Johns Hopkins University Press, 2008.

Chandler, Alfred D., Jr., ed. *Giant Enterprise: Ford, General Motors and the Automobile Industry, Sources and Readings.* Harcourt, Brace & World, 1964.

Clymer, Floyd. *Henry's Wonderful Model T, 1908–1927.* McGraw-Hill, 1955.

———. *Treasury of Early American Automobiles, 1877–1925.* Bonanza, 1950.

Cohn, David L. *Combustion on Wheels: An Informal History of the Automobile Age.* Houghton Mifflin, 1944.

Collier, Peter, and David Horowitz. *The Fords: An American Epic.* Summit Books, 1987.

Collins, Tom. *The Legendary Model T: The Ultimate History of America's First Great Automobile.* Krause Publications, 2007.

Dahlinger, John Côté. *The Secret Life of Henry Ford.* Bobbs-Merrill, 1978.

Dos Passos, John. *U.S.A.* Library of America, 1996.

Edmonds, J. P. *Development of the Automobile and Gasoline Engine in Michigan.* Franklin DeKleine Company, no date.

"1895 Chicago to Evanston Race: The Greatest Race in American History." *Horseless Age Magazine,* 1895.

Fahnestock, Murray. *The Model T Ford Owner.* Lincoln Publishing Company, 1999.

Ferguson, Eugene S. *Engineering and the Mind's Eye.* MIT Press, 1992.

Flink, James J. *America Adopts the Automobile, 1895–1910.* MIT Press, 1970.

———. *The Automobile Age.* MIT Press, 1988.

Ford, Henry. *Edison as I Know Him.* American Thought and Action, 1966.

———. *My Life and Work.* Doubleday, 1922.

———. *The International Jew: The World's Foremost Problem.* CPA Book Publisher, 1995.

"Ford at 100." *Autoweek.* June 16, 2003.

"Ford a Winner in the Munsey Reliability Run." *Ford Times,* October 15, 1909.

Ford Division, Ford Motor Company. *The Ford Dealer Story.* 1953.

Friends of France: The Field Service of the American Ambulance Described by Its Members. Houghton Mifflin, 1916.

Garrett, Garet. *The Wild Wheel: The World that Henry Ford Built.* Pantheon, 1952.

Gelderman, Carol. *Henry Ford, the Wayward Capitalist.* St. Martin's Press, 1981.

Genat, Robert. *The American Car Dealership.* MBI Publishing, 1999.

Gerber, John. *O Marvelous Model T! A Diary of a Great Model T Expedition in 1928 From Pittsburgh to the West Coast and Back.* Maecenas Press, 1991.

Grandin, Greg. *Fordlandia: The Rise and Fall of Henry Ford's Forgotten Jungle City.* Metropolitan Books, 2009.

Greenleaf, William. *Monopoly on Wheels: Henry Ford and the Selden Automobile Patent.* Wayne State University Press, 2011.

Gunther, John. *Inside U.S.A.* Harper, 1947.

Halberstam, David. *The Reckoning.* Morrow, 1986.

Havighurst, Walter. "Primer From a Green World." *American Heritage,* August 1957.

Henry Ford Museum Staff. *Greenfield Village and the Henry Ford Museum.* Crown Publishers, 1978.

Herndon, Booton. *Ford: An Unconventional Biography of the Men and Their Times.* Weybright and Talley, 1969.

Hershey, Burnet. *The Odyssey of Henry Ford and the Great Peace Ship.* Taplinger, 1967.

Hooker, Clarence. *Life in the Shadows of the Crystal Palace, 1910–1927.* Bowling Green State University Popular Press, 1997.

Hounshell, David A. *From the American System to Mass Production, 1800–1932.* Johns Hopkins University Press, 1984.

Hughes, Jonathan. *The Vital Few: The Entrepreneur and American Economic Progress.* Oxford University Press, 1986.

Hyde, Charles K. *The Dodge Brothers: The Men, the Motor Cars, and Their Legacy.* Wayne State University Press, 2005.

Jardim, Anne. *The First Henry Ford: A Study in Personality and Business Leadership.* MIT Press, 1970.

Jensen, Oliver, and Joseph J. Thorndike, Jr. *Ford at Fifty, 1903–1953.* Simon & Schuster, 1953.

Karp, Walter. "Greenfield Village." *American Heritage,* December 1980.

Keats, John. *The Insolent Chariots.* Lippincott, 1958.

Kimes, Beverley Rae. *The Cars That Henry Ford Built: A 75th Anniversary Tribute to America's Most Remembered Automobiles.* Princeton Publishing, Inc., 1978.

———. "Henry's Model T." *Automobile Quarterly,* vol. X, no. 4, 1972.

———. "Young Henry Ford." *Automobile Quarterly,* vol. X, no. 2, 1972.

Kraft, Barbara S. *The Peace Ship: Henry Ford's Pacifist Adventure in the First World War.* Macmillan, 1978.

Lacey, Robert. *Ford: The Men and the Machine.* Little, Brown, 1986.

Latham, Caroline, and David Agresta. *Dodge Dynasty: The Car and the Family that Rocked Detroit.* Harcourt Brace Jovanovich, 1989.

Leonard, Jonathan Norton. *The Tragedy of Henry Ford.* Putnam, 1932.

Levine, Leo. *Ford: The Dust and the Glory—A Racing History.* Macmillan, 1968.

Lewis, David L. *100 Years of Ford: A Centennial Celebration of the Ford Motor Company.* Publications International, Ltd., 2003.

————. *The Public Image of Henry Ford: An American Folk Hero and His Company.* Wayne State University Press, 1976.

Lewis, Eugene W. *Motor Memories: A Saga of Whirling Gears.* Alved Publishers, 1947.

MacManus, Theodore F., and Norman Beasley. *Men, Money and Motors: The Drama of the Automobile.* Harper, 1929.

Marquis, Samuel S. *Henry Ford: An Interpretation.* Wayne State University Press, 2007.

Maxim, Hiram Percy. *Horseless Carriage Days.* Harper, 1937.

May, George S. *A Most Unique Machine: The Michigan Origins of the American Automobile Industry.* William B. Erdmans, 1975.

McGuffey, William Holmes. *McGuffey's Fifth Eclectic Reader.* Van Nostrand Reinhold, no date.

McShane, Clay. *Down the Asphalt Path: The Automobile and the American City.* Columbia University Press, 1994.

Merz, Charles. . . . *And Then Came Ford.* Doubleday, Doran & Company, 1929.

Meyer, Stephen III. *The Five Dollar Day: Labor Management and Social Control in the Ford Motor Company, 1908–1921.* State University of New York Press, 1981.

Miller, Ray, and Bruce McCalley. *The Model T Ford: From Here to Obscurity: An Illustrated History of the Model T Ford, 1909–1927.* Sierra Printers, 1971.

Morison, Elting E. *Men, Machines and Modern Times.* MIT Press, 1966.

Musselman, M. M. *Get a Horse! The Story of the Automobile in America.* Lippincott, 1950.

Nevins, Allan, and Frank Ernest Hill. *Ford: The Times, the Man, the Company.* Charles Scribner's Sons, 1954.

————. *Ford: Expansion and Challenge, 1915–1933.* Charles Scribner's Sons, 1957.

————. *Ford: Decline and Rebirth, 1933–1962.* Charles Scribner's Sons, 1963.

Newton, James. *Uncommon Friends: Life With Thomas Edison, Henry Ford, Harvey Firestone, Alexis Carrel & Charles Lindbergh.* Harcourt Brace Jovanovich, 1987.

Olson, Sidney. *Young Henry Ford: A Picture History of the First Forty Years.* Wayne State University Press, 1963.

Partridge, Bellamy. *Excuse My Dust.* McGraw-Hill, 1943.

————. *Fill 'er Up! The Story of Fifty Years of Motoring.* McGraw-Hill, 1952.

Pipp, Edwin Gustave. *The Real Henry Ford.* Pipp's Weekly, 1922.

Post, Dan R. *Model T Ford in Speed and Sport.* Post-Era Books, 1974.

Presto Publishing Company. *Funny Stories About the Ford: Uncanny Stories About a Canny Car, Vol. II.* 1915.

Quaife, Milo M. *The Life of John Wendell Anderson.* Privately printed, Detroit, 1950.

Rae, John B. *The American Automobile: A Brief History.* University of Chicago Press, 1965.

Rae, John B., ed. *Henry Ford.* Prentice-Hall, 1969.

Richards, William C. *The Last Billionaire: Henry Ford.* Charles Scribner's Sons, 1948.

Roberts, Andrew. *The Storm of War: A New History of the Second World War.* Harper, 2011.

Ruddiman, Margaret Ford. "Memories of My Brother Henry Ford." *Michigan History,* September 1953.

Saal, Thomas F., and Bernard J. Golias. *Famous But Forgotten: The Story of the Automotive Pioneer and Industrialist Alexander Winton.* Golias Publishing, 1997.

Scharff, Virginia. *Taking the Wheel: Women and the Coming of the Motor Age.* Free Press, 1991.

Sheller, Roscoe. *Me and the Model T.* Binford & Mort Publishing, 1965.

Simonds, William Adams. *Henry Ford and Greenfield Village.* Frederick A. Stokes Company, 1938.

Sinsabaugh, Charles. *Who, Me? Forty Years of Automobile History.* Arnold Powers, Inc., 1940.

Sloan, Alfred P., Jr. *Adventures of a White-Collar Man.* Doubleday, 1941.

Smith, Orlando J. *A Short View of Great Questions.* Brandur Company, 1899.

Sophir, Jack, Jr. *Get a Horse!* Wayne County Press, 1989.

Sorensen, Charles E. *My Forty Years with Ford.* Norton, 1956.

Steinbeck, John. *Cannery Row*. Viking, 1945.

Stephenson, Albert B. "Secrets of the Model T." *American Heritage,* July 1989.

Stern, Philip Van Doren. *Tin Lizzie: The Story of the Fabulous Model T Ford*. Simon & Schuster, 1955.

Street, Julian. *Abroad at Home*. Century Company, 1914.

Sward, Keith. *The Legend of Henry Ford*. Rinehart, 1948.

Villard, Oswald Garrison. *Fighting Years: Memoirs of a Liberal Editor*. Harcourt, Brace, 1939.

Volti, Rudi. "Why Internal Combustion?" *American Heritage of Invention and Technology,* Fall 1990.

Wamsley, James S. *American Ingenuity: Henry Ford Museum and Greenfield Village*. Abrams, 1985.

Watts, Steven. *The People's Tycoon: Henry Ford and the American Century*. Knopf, 2005.

Wik, Reynolds M. *Henry Ford and Grass-roots America*. University of Michigan Press, 1973.

Wood, John Cunningham, and Michael C. Wood, eds. *Henry Ford: Critical Evaluations in Business and Management*. Routledge, 2003.

INDEX

A CONVERSATION WITH RICHARD SNOW

What made you decide to write this book?

A couple of things. One is the quote that gives the book its title. I came across Ford making that megalomaniac boast—"I invented the modern age"—and it sounded crazy. But the more I learned about him, the more it seemed that if any individual could justify that claim, it was Henry Ford. But he'd gotten his hooks into me before that, when I went to his enormous museum in Dearborn. I know Detroit isn't generally high on the list of vacation destinations, but I would guiltlessly urge anyone to go there and visit what is now called The Henry Ford. It's like a Disneyland that's good for you. I've been there half a dozen times since, and there's always something fresh and beguiling about it. Where else can you stroll from the Wright brothers' bicycle shop—with a stop in the house they grew up in—and ten minutes later be in the laboratory where Edison worked out the electric light? It conveys the strangely powerful spirit of Henry Ford at his best.

But how can he really have invented the modern age?

Well, you'll notice he didn't say, "I made a hell of a lot of automobiles." He claimed authorship of the world we live in, and I think he was talking about more than his phenomenally successful Model T—he was talking about the way he made them. The system of mass production that he inaugurated changed everything so completely that as his inheritors we don't even see his influence—it's as transparent as the air we breathe. But it basically built the middle class that is the object of so much anxious discussion today, and it gave us the industrial heft necessary to prevail in the great, cataclysmic conflict of the last century, the Second World War.

A lot of people still think he invented the automobile.

No—he didn't really invent much of anything, except that one enormous thing, which was a process rather than a single machine. But that's not to take anything away from the Model T. It was a very good car for its time, but if he hadn't been able to deploy it in staggering numbers—fifteen million of them before he turned off the tap—the Model T would be as forgotten today as the Apperson Jackrabbit or the Thomas Flyer.

Then what made it so special?

That everybody who wanted a car could get one. Before it, a really good car cost as much as a house. And of course when Ford got his business going all his stockholders wanted him to make the most expensive car he could. And he said, No, I want to make the cheapest car I can. He really turned the fundamental principles of monopoly capitalism upside down. If you have cornered the market on something everybody wants, you should raise the price, right? Ford thought exactly the opposite. And he kept bringing the cost down. At the end of its production run, you could buy a new Model T for under three hundred dollars.

Have you ever driven a Model T?

No, I was born a generation too late. Everyone my father's age—he was born in 1905—had driven a T, even if they didn't like the car much. My father hated it, because he remembered as a small boy seeing his older brother cranking one to start it, and the crank kicked back and broke his wrist. The car was full of mean little tricks like that. Anyway, I got as far as getting behind the wheel of one, but I was too scared to actually get it under way. It didn't have an accelerator—that was a lever on the steering wheel—but only these three weird pedals that managed that planetary transmission. Every turn-of-the-century farmer could apparently figure it out in twenty minutes, but I've spent three years reading about that transmission, and I'm still not sure I really understand it. The car was quirky, but it opened the world to the first generation of owners. It broke down the age-old isolation of the farm in about ten years. It looks as quaint as a butter churn to us now, but there never was a more formidable engine of modernism and change.

What was it like getting to know Ford?

I'm not at all sure I ever truly did. But I take some comfort in the fact that his closest associates all said they hadn't either. It is very strange reading about him, because I can't think of another famous man whose life has such a peculiar arc. For the first half of it he was a genuinely great man—generous, friendly, civic-minded, altruistic—and for the second half he was increasingly terrible. And that drastic change seems to have taken place in just a couple of years.

What happened?

Insofar as the causes are knowable at all, I believe the main one was frustration. In 1919 he was selling one of every two cars on the American road, but already a new generation of carmakers was seeing the automobile as more than an object of utility. It had become an object of desire as well. To Ford, this was an awful heresy. He saw his car not just as an amazing wealth generator but as a moral force, and any suggestion that he change it absolutely infuriated him.

Edsel Ford, Henry's only child, understood that times were changing. Edsel was, as the industry's high accolade put it, "a real car man." Henry had received the unlikely blessing of a son who was perfectly suited to lead the company into its second generation. Edsel saw that the Model T was a pioneer, and its days were numbered. Ford hated the very thought of that, and he turned on his son. He made him head of the company, and never allowed him to exercise any authority. When Edsel tried to advance improved models, his father humiliated him in front of the high Ford executives. And when the executives pushed for changes on the Model T, Ford fired them in ugly ways. In the end, he was so cruel to Edsel that his grandson, Henry Ford II, once said that he believed his grandfather had killed him.

And then there was the anti-Semitism.

Oh, yes, the saddest and most frustrating part of his legacy. Someone said that for every really complex problem there is one simple solution—and it's always wrong. Ford had already discovered one titanic solution—his moving assembly line—and he thought he knew about great many things that he didn't. So he lit on the idea that the Jews somehow had their hands on all the levers of world capitalism—Ford was a hugely successful capitalist who hated capitalism—and he went on his terrible crusade. Eventually he shut down his two-year tirade, but he had done immeasurable damage to his company (damage that almost from the moment of his death the Ford Motor Company has worked quietly and with great diligence and intelligence to redress).

What surprised you most when you were writing the book?

Something Ford said about how technology advances. It was quick and short; I almost missed it, but it made me think about something that had never occurred to me before.

In his autobiography, Ford talks about starting out and says in passing, "There was no demand for the automobile. There never is for a new product." This completely reverses the old bromide about necessity being the mother of invention. Ford says exactly the opposite: It is the invention that gives birth to the necessity. And who's to say he's wrong? People never knew they needed an iPhone until they had one in their hands.

How was it spending three years with this man?

Never boring. But not always pleasant: How much did I want to read the book of his collected anti-Semitic broadsides? And yet, every now and then a redeeming courage gleams out at you. For one thing, it was brave of him to stake his future on producing automobiles at a time when the industry was completely fetal. He had to imagine every bolt and gasket in his first car. When he needed a carburetor, he had to invent one; there wasn't even a word for the device.

And it's largely forgotten that he fought alone against an absurd patent that had the whole car industry in shackles. An upstate New York attorney had somehow managed to get a patent on the *idea* of an automobile. His name was George Selden. He'd never built a car, but he had his patent, and every carmaker rolled over and paid him, even General Motors. But not Henry Ford;

he battled the Selden patent for twelve years, and he won, and his victory liberated the entire automotive industry.

Sometimes, too, he can be extremely entertaining. He was often very funny in a quiet, almost reticent way. When he became famous, he attracted the attention of the clergy, and there were a lot of sermons about how God had led him to his success. In one particularly effulgent one the minister said that Mr. Ford kept a copy of the scriptures in every room of his mansion, so they'd always be close to hand when he needed guidance. With this in mind, a reporter asked Ford if he attended church regularly. "Nah," he said. "The last time I went somebody stole my car."

And he liked to tell a story about how one time he was driving around the Upper Peninsula of Michigan, checking how his car was behaving, and he came across another Model T pulled over to the side of the road, with the driver scowling helplessly under the hood. Ford stopped and asked what was wrong. The man said he didn't know, but the car wouldn't go. Ford rooted around in his tool kit—every Model T came with a tool kit—and worked on the engine and in a few minutes he had the car ticking over nicely. The owner was very grateful and pulled two dollar bills out of his pants and tried to give them to his helper. Ford waved them away, but the man kept insisting, and finally Ford thanked him, but said he had all the money he needed. At this the man laughed and said, "The hell you do—you drive a Ford!"

Looking back on Ford's life, how would you assess his impact?

I grew up in the world he made, and I don't think I'd like farm work any more than Ford did. So I'm glad he came along. But of course he handed us a Pandora's box. I think what Will Rogers said seventy years ago still holds true. He dropped his usual friendly folksiness to tell Ford, "It may take a hundred years to tell whether you've helped us or hurt us, but you certainly didn't leave us where you found us."

ABOUT THE AUTHOR

Richard Snow was born in New York City in 1947, graduated with a BA from Columbia College in 1970, and worked at *American Heritage* magazine for nearly four decades, serving as editor in chief for seventeen years. He is the author of several books, among them two novels and a volume of poetry. Snow has been a consultant for historical motion pictures—among them *Glory*—and has written for documentaries, including the Burns brothers' *The Civil War* and Ric Burns's award-winning PBS film *Coney Island*. His most recent book is *A Measureless Peril: America in the Fight for the Atlantic, the Longest Battle of World War II.*